Emile Durkheim

Emile Durkheim

Sociologist and Philosopher

by Dominick LaCapra

The University of Chicago Press
Chicago and London

The University of Chicago Press, Chicago 60637
The University of Chicago Press, Ltd., London

94 93 92 91 90 89 88 87 86 85   5 4 3 2 1

Library of Congress Cataloging in Publication Data

LaCapra, Dominick, 1939–
  Emile Durkheim: sociologist and philosopher.

  Reprint. Originally published: Ithaca, N.Y.:
Cornell University Press, 1972.
  Bibliography: p.
  Includes index.
  1. Durkheim, Emile, 1858–1917.   2. Durkheimian school
of sociology.   I. Title.
HM22.F8D83   1985   301′.092′4   85–1190
ISBN 0–226–46726–0 (pbk.)

To
my mother and father

It is much easier to point out the faults and errors in the work of a great mind than to give a distinct and full exposition of its value.

—Schopenhauer, *Criticism of the Kantian Philosophy*

Contents

Preface, 1985

This, which was my first book, is an extended essay not simply in the history of sociology but in intellectual history more generally. It is informed by a hidden polemic against the orthodox, liberal-conservative uses made of Durkheim by Talcott Parsons and the American sociological establishment. But it is not a book that is shaped by narrowly "presentist" interests. Nor, on the other hand, is it an "historicist" attempt to see Durkheim purely in his own terms and to situate (indeed to bury) him in his own times. Both "presentism" and "historicism" are ways of forgetting the past—the first by reducing it to superficiality through unscholarly abuse and the second by rendering it sterile through abusive scholarship. Nothing could be more intellectually facile and politically suspect than to empty Durkheim out conceptually, for example by applying the techniques of contemporary analytic philosophy, and to fill him in empirically by furnishing massive documentation about life during *la belle époque*. The point of intellectual history should rather be to bring about a "dialogue" with the past in which there is a mutually informative relation between what something meant in its own time and what it may mean for us today. The challenge of the past becomes evident when research is not the alternative to "rhetorical" exchange but its necessary complement.

My approach to intellectual history is thus guided by a Renaissance ideal that is largely out of favor in recent historiography. But it is, I think, an ideal that was shared by Durkheim. Indeed, when one rereads Durkheim today, one is struck by his ability to integrate careful scholarship and an ethicopolitical commitment to democratic and republican values. His is an attempt to revive the tradition of civic humanism, to eliminate its ethnocentric features, and to make it relevant to modern conditions. Here he looks back to the Greeks, and he affirms the principle: nothing in excess. But he also reformulates the principle in a tellingly modern way, for in his hands it becomes: nothing in excess—including excess! Durkheim neither follows a constricted and rigid "structuralist" conception of order, nor does he give way to an unqualified strategy of transgression, chance initiative, and absolute risk. His abiding concern is the nature and possibilities of life in society as a whole, and he inquires into the actual and desirable conditions for the interplay between order and anomie, as well as between groups that embody these forces in significantly different ways. In what may perhaps be interpreted as an attempt to find the place in modern history where the regulative ideals of the city-state may once again come to life, he turns to democratic (but not populist or demagogic) corporatism. While one may criticize the limitations (at times the naïveté) of both his general vision and his particular embodiment of it, one may nonetheless share the concerns that activated him and recognize the generosity and grandeur of his effort.

In rereading Durkheim one is also struck by another virtue—in one significant sense, a civic virtue—to which I would like to pay homage: his magnificent stylistic decorum and poise in addressing difficult if not intractable problems. This style of writing and of thought was, I think, the counterpart of the ethicopolitical vision he had for society—a rhetorical and dialectical way of enacting in his own use of language the ends he advocated for social and cultural life at large. In this respect, too, there may still be much to learn in the *école de* Durkheim.

Acknowledgments

An early version of this work was read by H. Stuart Hughes and Charles Maier, a later version by Edward Tiryakian. I would like to thank them for their criticisms and suggestions. I also wish to thank the staff of Cornell University Press for editorial assistance.

Preparatory work for this book was made possible by a fellowship from the Foreign Area Studies Program. I was aided in the writing by a summer fellowship from the Society for the Humanities at Cornell University.

DOMINICK LACAPRA

Cornell University
Ithaca, New York

1 «

Introduction

> If you wish to mature your thought, attach yourself to the
> scrupulous study of a great master; inquire into a system until
> you reach its most secret workings.
> —Advice of Emile Durkheim to a disciple

The present study attempts to provide a comprehensive interpretation and assessment of the thought of Emile Durkheim.
By and large, it falls within the venerable tradition of the *étude
du système*. Often it treads the dangerous but challenging line
between *haute vulgarisation* and a history of a learned discipline.
Its primary object is to treat Durkheim's thought as an integral
whole comprising sociological analysis, policy, and philosophy.

Some reference is made to the work of other members of the
Année sociologique school which formed around Durkheim as its
acknowledged master. In many basic ways, the thought of
members of this school was a unitary reflection. And the periodical which became the school's workshop was a collective product. Durkheim's thought provided the elementary structure for
a close working relationship and a fairly cohesive theoretical
outlook. But full justice could be rendered to members of the
Année school only in a separate work. Marcel Mauss alone, who
was perhaps inhibited in his scholarly production by a life spent
in the shadow of his more famous uncle, would merit a full-
length study to bring out the magnificent contributions which
he managed to compress into the creative compass of relatively
few published works.

I sketch some pertinent features of Durkheim's biography

1

and situate his experience within the matrix of his own society. While Durkheim's thought was not merely symptomatic of his milieu, his ideas did to a significant extent arise in response to the needs of the Third Republic in France. In fact, he often conceived his own society as a test case of the needs of modern society in general. Concerning Durkheim's life, however, I do not pretend to have discovered vitally new and deep-seated facts. All that remains is the surface. And on the surface Durkheim's life often appears to be of the sort that many people might like to lead but about which few could find much of sustained interest to say. The one source of possibly new and more profound information about Durkheim—which might well have an importance comparable to the Freud-Fliess correspondence—is the set of letters exchanged betweeen Durkheim and his close friend and colleague Georges Davy. These letters (except for quotations in the work of Davy himself) remain closed to the idle curiosity of commentators by the French sense of privacy which identifies publicity with a betrayal of the intimacy of friendship.

Durkheim was the first to attempt the institutionalization in social science of what Auguste Comte had termed the era of specialization. Durkheim advised would-be disciples to choose a circumscribed area of enquiry. His founding of the famed periodical *L'Année sociologique* was intended to further this aim. Hence there is much to be gained from seemingly so superficial a task as the examination of the tables of contents of the twelve volumes of the *Année* published under Durkheim, for they embody a telling conception of the classificatory cadres of sociology in his mind. In the pages of the *Année* and elsewhere, Durkheim's own preferred object of investigation was the relationship between society and morality. His very first published article contained a programmatic announcement which exercised a constraining hold on his entire life's work: "Of all the various branches of sociology, the science of ethics is the one which attracts us by preference and which will command our attention first of all." [1]

But Durkheim retained Comte's over-all ambition of philosophical synthesis. He became increasingly convinced that specialized expertise and the professionalized purge of dilettantism should not be effected at the expense of interdisciplinary coordination and of the speculative imagination restrained, tested, and matured by patient investigation. Like nearly all the members of his school, Durkheim was trained in philosophy, a preparation made necessary by the educational system of the time. And despite his earlier attempts to define sociology as an autonomous discipline, he became convinced that all serious enquiry is founded in philosophy and that philosophy is related both to understanding and to action. It might be said that for Durkheim sociology had not only a scientific field to explore but also an exploratory vision and a civilizing mission. In time sociology culminated for him in a philosophical anthropology which drew the investigator from methodology to epistemological and even metaphysical problems.

Toward the end of his life, Durkheim wrote to Georges Davy: "Having begun with philosophy, I tend to return to it, or rather I have found myself drawn back to it naturally by the nature of the questions which I found in my path." [2] In an important article written at about the same time, Durkheim expressed this need for a return to his philosophical origins in more impersonal terms: "Since our method has been postulated upon the attempt to emancipate sociology from a philosophical tutelage which could only prevent it from being constituted as a positive science, we have at times been suspected of a systematic hostility for philosophy in general or at least of a more or less exclusive sympathy for a narrow empiricism in which one has rightly seen

[1] "Cours de science sociale: Leçon d'ouverture," *Revue internationale de l'enseignement*, XV (1888), 45.

[2] Letter to Georges Davy; quoted in Davy, "Durkheim," *Revue française de sociologie*, I (1960), 10.

only a lesser philosophy." But an antiphilosophical position implied, for Durkheim, "a very unsociological attitude." In his mind, sociology had "to pose as an axiom that questions which have held their place in history can never be out-moded; they can become transformed but cannot perish." Thus he found it inadmissible that "even the most audacious problems which have agitated philosophers" could ever fall into oblivion.[3] He went on to conclude that "sociological reflection is called upon to prolong itself by its natural progress under the form of philosophical reflection; and everything permits the assumption that, considered in this way, the problems which philosophy treats will present more than one unexpected answer."[4]

Thus Durkheim conceived of his project in terms of a rational coordination of social analysis, informed prescriptive recommendation, and philosophical speculation with special relevance for thought and action in modern society. He completed only a fragment of a synthetic philosophical work entitled "La Morale." But, in an important sense, all his thought was oriented toward this magisterial treatise on morality—his last will and testament—which he did not live to complete. For the question running like a red thread through Durkheim's thinking was the role of reason in life and its relation to the sentiment of solidarity among men in society. His ultimate concern with epistemology and metaphysic subsumed a certain conception of the social system and of morality as its inner motivation. In a crucial sense, Durkheim's thought was as much the culmination of classical philosophy as the initiation of modern social science. Indeed, this ambivalent status constitutes its peculiar fascination.

Partial and highly selective readings of Durkheim have often resulted in grievous misinterpretations. But the attempt through

[3] "Sociologie religieuse et théorie de la connaissance," *Revue de métaphysique et de morale,* XVII (1909), 755–756.
[4] *Ibid.,* p. 758.

exegesis to set the record straight by seeing Durkheim whole is admittedly problematic. This is because of the seemingly ambiguous character of his thought itself. Durkheim is one of the best known and one of the least understood major social thinkers. The controversies that surround his thought bear upon essential points, not details.[5] This state of affairs poses a formidable barrier for the uninitiated but genuinely interested reader attempting to acquire some insight into his thought and its relevance. Durkheim was a very vigorous advocate of the idea of a social science. Incongruously, the interpretation of the body of ideas in which he tried to lay the foundations of this science

[5] A superficial review of the major orientations and difficulties of some of the most important interpretations of Durkheim will give the reader a sense of the problem. In his monumental *The Structure of Social Action*, Talcott Parsons presented Durkheim's thought as caught in an unresolved tension between early positivism and latter-day idealism as it tortuously worked its way toward convergence with other voluntaristic theories of social action. (Parsons' ideas formed the basis for the treatment of Durkheim in H. Stuart Hughes's *Consciousness and Society* [New York: Knopf, 1958].) In his *Essais de sociologie*, Georges Gurvitch saw in Durkheimism a denial of social science itself in the attempt to construct a "metamorality." According to Gurvitch, Durkheim transfigured society into a modern contender for the traditional role of logos. In his idea of the relation of sociology to philosophy, Durkheim was like Columbus, who discovered America while sailing for the Indies. Gurvitch denied the validity of the integral bond between methodology and philosophy in Durkheim's idea of social science. With typical virtuosity, Claude Lévi-Strauss has termed himself an "inconstant disciple" of Durkheim and has treated his thought over the years with a combination of wholesale praise and retail criticism. Lévi-Strauss is perhaps the thinker who—despite notable omissions—has been most successful in retaining the valuable elements in Durkheim's thought while casting doubt on many of its most questionable features. Indeed, it is difficult to treat Durkheim without using Lévi-Strauss as the implicit horizon of one's discussion. Yet Raymond Aron, whose interpretive skill is often beyond comparison, gave what seemed to be a counsel of despair. In his *Etapes de la pensée sociologique* (Paris: Gallimard, 1967), he observed, after a *seriatim* commentary on the texts, that he had found himself forced to resort frequently to direct quotation, not to illustrate substantive points of an argument but, on the contrary, because he felt "a certain difficulty in entering into Durkheim's way of thought, no doubt because of a lack of sympathy necessary for understanding" (p. 360).

seems often to circumscribe it with a magic circle whose center is everywhere and whose circumference is nowhere.

Since Durkheim's ideas are the object of highly divergent interpretations, it is important to make clear the basic interpretive schema that informs this study. Unfortunately, to begin a work with even a schematic "showing and telling" brings a loss of dramatic unity. The last act is given away in the first. And aesthetic unity threatens to be replaced by the tedious rigor of a syllogistic treatise. In the case of a thinker like Durkheim, it is perhaps better to incur these risks than to be open to misunderstanding.

Durkheim was a convinced and unrepentant rationalist. To characterize his own perspective, he rejected all current labels, including the Comtean and Spencerian forms of positivism. But he was willing to assert that "the sole appellation which we accept is that of rationalism. Indeed our principle is to extend scientific rationalism to human conduct in showing that, considered in the past, it is reducible to relations of cause and effect which a no less rational operation can transform into rules for the future." [6] Durkheim most opposed romantic irrationalism and renascent mysticism as intuitive responses to the complexities and disorientation of modern society. His *Les Règles de la méthode sociologique* (*The Rules of Sociological Method*) was an attempt to do for the study of society what Descartes had done for the study of nature. His lifelong ambition was to reanimate and renovate classical rationalism until it became a more flexible, complex, and informed medium of both thought and action. Reason for Durkheim had its full traditional sense: it was a mode of analysis, criticism, prescription, and reconstruction in society.

Unintimidated by the application of the sociology of knowledge to sociology itself, Durkheim concluded that sociology was the product of two major historical and cultural forces: the man-

---

[6] *Les Règles de la méthode sociologique* (15th ed.; Paris: Presses Universitaires de France, 1963), p. ix.

ifestation of rationalism in the natural sciences and the concrete experience of crisis in modern societies. The role of reason in the study of nature intimated a promising future for rationalism in social science. But the second and more existential cause was perhaps the more important. For Durkheim, social consciousness arose in response to the doubt and anomic anxiety caused by the breakdown of tradition. The role of rational consciousness was to state as clearly as possible the causes of crisis in society and the way to overcome them. Indeed the primary function of rational consciousness for Durkheim was reparative: to replace what had been destroyed with new forms of life. Unlike certain reactionary conservatives, Durkheim did not present conscious thought as a cause of disintegration in modern society. He defended consciousness, and science which was its highest expression, as the only effective instruments men had to guide them in reconstructing the social order. Durkheim was concerned with healing, not salvation. His fascination with medical metaphors attested to this fact. The sociologist was not the prophet of an abstract, utopian ideal situated beyond human limitations. He was the doctor who lucidly diagnosed the ills of society and prescribed rational remedies. The alliance of Durkheim's rationalism with his conception of the relation of theory to practice and his diagnosis of modern society was well expressed in relation to his own society when he delineated with his habitual combination of analytic rigor and moral fervor the reasons why sociology (in his sense) was born in France. His statement deserves to be quoted at length:

This [the genesis of sociology in France] was due in the first instance to a marked weakening of traditionalism. When religious, political, and juridical traditions have preserved their rigidity and authority, they contain all will toward change and by that token preclude the awakening of reflection. When one is brought up to believe that things must remain as they are, one has no reason to ask what they ought to be and, consequently, what they are. The second factor is what may be called the rationalist spirit. One must have faith in the power of reason in order to dare an attempt to explain in accordance with its laws this sphere of social facts where events, by their complexity, seem to resist the formulas of science. Now France fulfills these two conditions to the highest degree. She is, of all the countries of Europe, the one where the old social organization has been completely uprooted. We have made a *tabula rasa,* and on this land laid bare we must erect an entirely new edifice—an enterprise whose urgency we have felt for a century but which, continually announced and continually delayed, is hardly more advanced today than on the morrow of the French Revolution. Furthermore, we are and we remain the land of Descartes. We have an irresistible urge to see things through defined notions. No doubt, Cartesianism is an archaic and narrow form of rationalism, and we must not rest content with it. But if it is necessary to transcend it, it is even more necessary to conserve its principle. We must fashion for ourselves more complex ways of thought, but we must keep this cult of distinct ideas which is at the very root of the French spirit and at the root of all science.[7]

The truly basic philosophical tension in the thought of Durkheim was related to his rationalism. It involved his partial failure to transcend classical rationalism. Durkheim's thought was caught up in a tension between the narrowly analytical and the dialectical heritages transmitted to him through Charles Renouvier.

With reference to the most important historical influences on Durkheim, one might simplistically label the narrowly analytical tendency of his thought a Cartesianized and socialized neo-Kantianism. The most obvious influence of neo-Kantianism was in his passion for dualistic antinomies. The more profound influence, which fed into his dialectical attempt to reconcile or at least relate antinomies, was his ultimate affirmation of a philosophy of finitude based upon a normative sense of limits. The treatise on morality which Durkheim did not live to complete would have been a reformulation of Kant's *Critique of Practical Reason* fleshed out with the results of sociological reflection.

[7] "La Sociologie en France au XIXe siècle," *Revue bleue,* 4th series, XIII (1900), 651.

The influence of Cartesianism was most obvious in Durkheim's reliance upon the antinomy between mind and matter. This antinomy was expressed in the idea of *homo duplex*—the dual nature of man—which was interpreted by Durkheim in terms of the opposition between the organic and what he called the *sui generis*—or specifically—social. By this interpretation, Durkheim arrived at the idea that mind was made up of a *"sui generis* realm of social facts."* Sociology was defined in the first instance not by its perspective or method but by the supposedly antonomous status of its object, which was identified with the object of idealistic philosophy. But the sociologistic revision of the idea of *homo duplex* was only the most extreme example of Durkheim's tendency to force "clear and distinct ideas" into an analytical dissociation of reality.

The notion of the dialectical is most often associated with the name of Hegel. But before the limits of knowledge which Hegel attempted to transcend were reached, Kant himself sought a mediation of antinomies. Kant, like Durkheim, is perhaps best seen as primarily a moral philosopher. His conception of religion, like that of Durkheim, was related to the needs of practical reason. But in his *Critique of Judgment,* Kant saw the central position of aesthetics in its mediation of oppositions.[8] And Kant's conception of religion itself held out the promise of resolving the tragic antinomies which divided man in a way that was more than aesthetic because it was, from his perspective, more than subjective.

Durkheim did not recognize the importance of Kant's *Critique of Judgment.* His studies of primitive cultures did not open up to him the importance of aesthetics and the ways in which art itself might be more than a subjective phenomenon. Nor did these studies fully reveal to him the limitations of a purely sociological view of religion. His interpretation of religion culminated in a vision of society as a rather disincarnate functional equivalent of

[8] On this problem, see Herbert Marcuse, *Eros and Civilization* (Boston: Beacon Press, 1955), chap. ix.

divinity—somewhat a collective ghost in a "morphological" machine.

The antipathy between positivism and idealism, which Talcott Parsons, in his *Structure of Social Action,* took as the faulted foundation of Durkheim's thought, is best seen as a facet of Durkheim's Cartesianized neo-Kantianism. Indeed, the philosophical assumptions of both these methodological foci were idealistic or, in Durkheim's own term, "hyperspiritualistic." In the context of his idea of *homo duplex* which identified mind and society, positivism and idealism related to aspects of the ideal, autonomous object that society was for Durkheim.

In Durkheim's early thought, positivism was most pronounced. It was epitomized in the assertion in *The Rules of Sociological Method* that social facts were to be treated like things. By this Durkheim did not mean to classify "social facts" among material things. But he did enjoin the sociologist to adopt a methodological attitude of extreme objectivism in the study of society. The primary meaning of "social fact" for Durkheim was the institutional norm. Yet in the study of the genesis, structure, and functioning of institutions, Durkheim carried the analogical value of the natural sciences to a point at which he tended to deny the specificity of a science of persons. Intentions were placed beyond the realm of scientific enquiry. The idea that empathy served as a means of understanding in the social sciences was rejected out of hand.

Durkheim's early positivism presented society primarily as an "action system," and structure as the essence of social facts. Methodologically, it focused upon two sorts of causation (often conceived "mechanistically"): efficient and functional. It attempted to determine how "social facts" were causally generated by antecedent conditions and how they functioned to produce certain consequences in the social system. Sociology, paradoxically, was to be restricted to a mechanistically causal explanation of the most external, reified, and depersonalized aspects of the ideal things constitutive of social facts. The criteria of social facts were asserted to be exteriority and constraint. And Durkheim held to a rather dissociated, if not schizoid, idea of the relation of the inner to the outer, of subjective experience and objectively observable behavior. This was the source of his frequently confusing pronouncements on the relationship of sociology to psychology. Inner, subjective experience was ascribed to the individual and often assumed to be objectively unknowable. Instead, Durkheim in his early thought stressed the importance of "hard" data, "morphological" indices, legal codes, and statistical procedures. His idea of the relation between society and morality emphasized formal obligation and duty.

Durkheim's early positivism at times culminated in an arid formalism. *Homo duplex* was divided further into an "outer" self defined by institutional norms and an "inner," hidden self of ineffable subjectivity. Sociology amounted to an objectivist study of the outer self and the structures which defined its external and constrained relations with other selves and the material environment. Durkheim's early positivism may have stemmed in part from a mystified generalization of the nature of experience in a society characterized by extremely formal and markedly bureaucratic relations. In his own France, the state, the military, the church, and notably his own specific milieu—the state university system—were highly bureaucratized. And the typical personality of members of his republican peer group displayed the dissociated combination of a formal, constrained exterior and a repressed well of inner spontaneity and private feeling.

A historical watershed in the development of Durkheim's thought was the Dreyfus Affair. It represented the break-through of *communitas* and idealistic spontaneity in a structurally hidebound French society. And Durkheim's subsequent thought tended to conceive of the individual in terms of the bodily organism and to stress the "inside" of shared values in the collectivity. Paramount was a concern for *communitas*, "collective representations," and the subjective desirability of internalized values, especially in their relation to symbolic cult and the sacred. But Durkheim often treated *communitas*, ideas, and ideals in abstraction from operative institutions and practical realities. Indeed he at times envisioned ideals—and especially the ideal of *communitas*—as the abstract objects of a vague, contemplative mystique. And methodologically he insisted upon an objectivist study of ideologies and ideals which provided little insight into the relationship of the questioner to the questioned in social research or the relationship of theory to practice in social action.

In his second and more dialectical tendency, Durkheim partially overcame a Cartesianized neo-Kantianism. He attempted to relate the elements and entities which he analytically distinguished. It is in the light of the more dialectical strand of his thought that it is fruitful to understand his conception of the relation of philosophy to methodology and of theory to practice. The notion which provided orientation in this respect was Durkheim's guiding metaphor of a tree of social life. This metaphor served as a logical axis for the classification of forms of human experience and entire social systems. The trunk of the tree corresponded to the invariant conditions of social and cultural life, while the branches represented different types of society. In the light of this model (or some more sophisticated analogue) Durkheim's ideas were developed by his disciples, notably Marcel Mauss and Claude Lévi-Strauss. It was no accident that Mauss was reading Hegel when he wrote his pivotal essay *Le Don* (*The Gift*).

Considered dialectically, social structure constituted one crucial dimension of human experience. But the broader problem was the comprehensive study of forms and levels of symbolically informed experience and their relations to anomie. In his core concept of anomie, Durkheim referred to the social and cultural —perhaps what one might call the existential—position of man possessed of (and frequently by) symbolism but devoid of substantively limiting norms and meaningful paradigms which give a viably coherent order to experience. Anomic disorientation, confusion, and anxiety were basic causes of breakdown and of new creation in society.

The one question Durkheim never asked was whether the extreme tendency to decompose reality analytically was itself symptomatic of the dissociation of sensibility which he correlated with social pathology. Yet the concepts of normality and pathology represented the second elementary axis of Durkheim's thought which intersected the classificatory axis of the tree of sociocultural life. Indeed these concepts are crucial in the attempt to situate Durkheim's thought in relation to a school which has frequently taken him as a founding father: structuro-functionalism. This school has of course many internal variants which at times display significantly different orientations. And the entire perspective has been attacked by proponents of a sociology of conflict as a theoretical excuse for a conservative ideology.[9]

On the questions both of a structuralist methodology and the concepts of normality and pathology, Durkheim did not display the degree of sophistication one might have expected of him. His ideas were rarely "clear and distinct." They were often more nebulous than is expectable in an initial, tentative, and exploratory statement. Allowing for this vagueness, one may nonetheless attempt to discover the basic intention of his thought.

There was indeed an important if insufficiently defined sense in which Durkheim's conception of the relationships among aspects of society was structural and functional in nature. He attempted to see things whole. More specifically, he identified science with the attempt to show how an object of investigation

[9] Robert K. Merton's discussion probably remains the most concise and useful examination of functional analysis in sociology. Merton stresses the importance of the concept of "dysfunction" for the study of social conflict (*Social Theory and Social Structure* [rev. ed.; Glencoe, Ill.: Free Press of Glencoe, 1964], chap. i; repr. as chap. iii of *On Theoretical Sociology* [New York: Free Press, 1967]).

could be made to reveal systematic relationships. Very often, these relationships were hidden and could be made manifest only through scientific investigation. Thus his notion of rationalism, as well as his belief in the existence of important analogies between natural and social science, rested upon a notion of laws which comprised structural models, functional correlations, and tendential regularities. In his own words, things social are "rational: by which one must simply understand that they are linked to one another by definite relations called laws." [10] On this basis, the most pertinent methodological similarity between natural and social science was the status of the comparative method and concomitant variation as the analogues in sociology of experimentation in the natural sciences. Related to the role of the comparative method was the use of statistical procedures in specifying the prevalence of conditions of social life and the direct or indirect consequences of the functioning of social structures and symbolic systems.

The implication of the existence of definite relations among social and cultural phenomena for rational prescription was the requirement that the purposeful intention of man work with a definite, complex, and often little known reality. Ignorance of typical relationships might frustrate human purpose through the generation of unintended consequences. The only specificity of society in this respect was a greater range of what Comte had termed "modifiable fatality." Durkheim believed firmly that sociology, in discovering the laws of social reality, would permit men "to direct with more reflection than in the past the course of historical evolution; for we can only change nature, moral or physical, in abiding by its laws." Auguste Comte, Durkheim himself observed, "even remarked with insistence that of all natural phenomena, social phenomena are the most malleable, the most accessible to changes, because they are the most complex." Thus Durkheim could conclude that "sociology does not in the least impose upon man a passively conservative attitude; on the con-

[10] "La Sociologie en France au XIXe siècle," p. 649.

trary, it extends the field of our action by the very fact that it extends the field of our science." [11]

One cannot understand the sense in which Durkheim was a rationalist or a conservative unless one understands his distinction between social normality and pathology. Yet this distinction, which was essential to all of Durkheim's work, has often been ignored or rejected by commentators and disciples alike. One general problem, of course, was that Durkheim's ideas remained at the level of gross approximation. Here, where careful and rigorous conceptual analysis should have been a foremost concern, Durkheim's ideas were little more than suggestive. Nor did he ever try to apply the concepts of normality and pathology to historical societies in a comprehensive and convincing way, distinguishing, for example, between kinds and degrees of normality and pathology. The chapter devoted to a sustained discussion of the normal and the pathological in *The Rules of Sociological Method*, a chapter which should have been the expression of Durkheim's intellectual powers at their most impressive, failed even to formulate the principles operative in his own works. Instead of drawing together the various strands of his conception of social structure and morality, the chapter relied excessively upon biological analogies, often without indicating their relevance for social life. Except for the concluding section on crime, the discussion of the normal and the pathological in *The Rules* is probably the least successful piece of writing in all of Durkheim's work. Since the distinction between social normality and pathology was one of the fundamental postulates of Durkheimism, we shall try to make more explicit what remained largely implicit in his writings.

The concepts of social normality and pathology referred to paradigms or models of social systems (or more delimited social settings) which had both methodological and normative status. As instruments of investigation, they enabled the formulation of

[11] "Sociologie et sciences sociales," in *De la méthode dans les sciences* (Paris: Alcan, 1909), p. 266.

problems within the overarching paradigm of the tree of socio-cultural life and made possible the discovery of relations which might not be apparent to naïve introspection or unguided empirical observation. Their basis was the core problem of Durkheimian sociology as a whole: the dialectic of order and disorder in society and culture. And they informed Durkheim's idea of the relation of theory to practice. The characterization of a state of society as pathological implied a critique and a call to action.

Roughly speaking, the normal state was characterized by a highly specific sort of functional integration in society. In the normal state, conditions of social life were flexibly controlled by limiting institutional norms. Norms were in turn legitimated by values consensually accepted as valid objects of commitment. This state of affairs functioned to strike a viable balance of differentiated structure and *communitas*—the dual bases of social solidarity—with a dynamic, creative leaven of anomie. Given the universal conditions of social normality, the precise nature of the normal state varied with different types of society. To the extent that it corresponded to the vital necessities of the various branches of the tree of sociocultural life, moral relativism was understandable and justified.

A condition of social pathology characterized states of society beset with varying sorts of internal contradiction. Like the normal phenomena of which they were the counterpart, pathological phenomena differed in content according to social type. Symptoms of pathology on the most general level comprised social conflict in extreme, unregulated forms, but they also included excessively high or low rates of deviance. Symptoms were to be distinguished from causes, which resided in the faulted nature of the social system itself and its bearing on the lives of members of society. The concept of social pathology enabled Durkheim to combine a structuralist methodology with the recognition of chaos, irrationality, and conflict in social life. The most important requirement for analysis and prescription was to be objectively clear about the fundamental causes of pathology in society and the most rational means of effecting a passage from pathology to normality. There was nothing in Durkheim to support the belief that he defended penal sanctions or systematic repression as the appropriate responses to symptoms of social pathology. On the contrary, he consistently invoked the principle that institutional change alone attacked the causes of pathology.

States of both pathology and normality were for Durkheim formally rational in the sense that phenomena in them could be made to reveal intelligible relations. There was method to social madness. It made sense, for example, that certain pathological states of society would be characterized by high rates of crime, suicide, and endemic violence. And means might be suited to ends which were themselves pathogenic. But Durkheim did not argue that anything which functioned in society was justified—if by functioning is meant formal adaptation or efficiency in maintaining a status quo. On the contrary, only the normal state of society and forces adapted to its creation or maintenance were justified or substantively rational. In the normal state, conditions were "everything that they ought to be." In the pathological state, they "ought to be other than they are." [12] The normal state of society would have as the foundation of its structure a culturally relative variant of practical reason which would function as the sole possible basis for the reconciliation of legitimate order and progress. Substantive rationality as the basic principle of social structure was, moreover, the only foundation for commitment and solidarity in society as a whole. In the normal state of society, the *conscience collective* would be the shared psychological ground of practical reason and solidarity in the personalities of members of society: it would be objectively real and subjectively internalized at the same time.

The practical implications of Durkheim's ideas have been the subject of intense controversy. Most often, Durkheim has been seen as a conservative. In one important sense, this conception of

[12] *Les Règles de la méthode sociologique*, p. 47.

Durkheim is correct. But Durkheim's broader rationalist dream was to transcend partisan ideological struggles and to forge a dialectical reconciliation of conservative, radical, and liberal traditions in modern thought. Scientific sociology, in Durkheim's conception of it, had this rationalist dream as its foremost practical goal.

One thing was blindingly clear. Durkheim became increasingly convinced that modern society was significantly pathological. In what sense was he a conservative? He was definitely not a reactionary traditionalist or, for that matter, a protofascist. He did not advocate the restoration of monarchy, feudal relations, aristocratic values, an established church, or medieval versions of corporatism. Nor did he share the cultural despair of conservative revolutionaries who felt an indiscriminate need to destroy all existing realities in order to clear the ground for a conservative utopia.[13] His thought reveals no parallel to the fascist combination of leader principle, elitism, mystical nationalism, scapegoating of an out-group, and totalitarian integration of the ingroup under class privilege and party dictatorship. Despite their idealized aspect, moreover, his studies of archaic societies do not display the obscurantist sort of neolithic nostalgia that might make the individual a dupe of authoritarian political movements ostensibly holding forth the value of community.

In his own France, the viewpoint of Charles Maurras and the Action Française, inspired by a reaction against the Dreyfusard position and the republican form of government which Durkheim supported, was antithetical to his own outlook. Nor did Durkheim share with the authoritarian Comte, whom Maurras followed, a high estimation of what Comte called the "Immortal Retrograde School" of Maistre and Bonald. Comte, according to Durkheim, was his master in sociology. And the "organic" conception of society, which asserted the group to be "prior" to the individual, was shared by a sociological tradition

---

[13] See Fritz Stern, *The Politics of Cultural Despair* (first pub. 1961; Garden City, N.Y.: Doubleday, 1965).

that included Maistre, Bonald, Comte, and Durkheim. But Durkheim departed from Maistre and Bonald, on the one hand, and from Comte, on the other, in his prescriptions for modern society. When Durkheim referred to the reign of moral authority in the normal society, he referred to the impersonal authority of norms compatible with autonomy and reciprocity, not authoritarian hierarchies or the elitist subordination of certain groups to other groups in modern society. His primary sources in this respect were Kant and the Rousseau whom Kant admired. Durkheim's rationalism served to obviate the anxiety-ridden longing for order which had prompted Comte to propose a rigidly authoritarian system amalgamating cultural debris of the ecclesiastical past, prophetically technocratic features, and idiosyncrasies of his own personal biography. For Durkheim, the institutional lessons of the past were relevant to the present only if they were adapted to the conditions and values of the present, including democracy.

Moreover, Durkheim did not believe that any status quo might be presumed to embody the traditional wisdom of the ages which deserved to be transmitted with only minor modification from generation to generation. This assumption applied only to the normal state of society. In a pathological state, this assumption converted conservatism from a living force into a tragicomic attitude detached from social realities and conducive to stereotyped reactions to situations of crisis.

Durkheim was not a simple status-quo conservative. He was what may be called a philosophical conservative. He desired the emergence and maintenance of a predominantly stable state of society which deserved to be the basis of historical continuity. Durkheim was not a pure optimist. For him the perfect society was an impossible dream. But he did affirm the value of a state of society which was relatively harmonious and in which anomie was confined to marginal proportions. In this "normal" state of society, the mind and heart of man would be united, and freedom would be reconciled with a normatively ingrained sense of limits.

In the context of modern societies, Durkheim's conservatism was discriminatingly radical and often future-oriented. He did see elements in modern society which genuinely deserved to be continued and strengthened: constitutionalism, representative government, and a certain type of division of labor. But he also realized that in certain areas of modern life the basic problem was the absence of legitimate traditions which might plausibly claim rational commitment and sacred respect. In these areas, Durkheim—as analyst, prophet, and lawgiver—longed for the creation of institutions which would bridge the gap between reason and sentiment and open the way to a livable, stable social environment in which only the incorrigibly criminal and the extraordinarily creative would not be basically conservative. Unlike many conservatives in modern history, he did not reconcile himself to a position of tragic resignation in the face of rapidly changing realities which contradicted his values. To achieve stabilization, consensus, and flexibly traditionalistic ends in critical areas of society marked by significant, if "transitional," conditions of social pathology, he believed that structural reform was imperative. In a sense, Durkheim was a structural reformer selectively open to radical ideas so that one day men might be authentically conservative in good conscience.

Durkheim is justly remembered as a severe critic of utilitarianism and classical liberalism. But from the liberal tradition he did accept the idea that the highest values of modern society include the rights of the individual and parliamentary control. He also defended a specific sort of pluralism—what might be called a normative pluralism. He did not present the competition of interest groups as the desirable end state of modern society. This would amount to a substitution of sociological utilitarianism for the individualistic utilitarianism of the past—a sociological utilitarianism which was often compatible with individual isolation and self-seeking. Durkheim's concrete goal was the formation of communal groups controlled by norms under the aegis of the democratic state. This was the basis of his idea of a revitalized corporatism respectful of individual liberties. What he radically rejected in classical liberalism was the anticommunal ideology which associated universal human rights and personal dignity with atomistic individualism and self-centered egoism, especially in possessively economic forms. He came to see unlimited growth, profit maximization, and unregulated economic relations as crucial causes of modern social pathology. It might be said that Durkheim identified the "economic rationality" of the economists with a prominent case of social irrationality. For him, the individual referred to by the principles of the French Revolution was not the acquisitive calculator who looked upon life as an exercise in pre-empting things with a sovereign "mine." Ultimately, Durkheim came to argue that the valuable core of individualism was a humanistic, responsible autonomy which complemented the commitment to community and reciprocity rooted in the *conscience collective*.

The most problematic elements in Durkheim's practical ideas stemmed from features of his thought which Karl Mannheim identified as characteristic of liberal humanitarianism.[14] These elements severely compromised Durkheim's structural reformism and his philosophical conservatism. They may be reduced to four tendencies: (1) the tendency, especially in his early thought, to provide an insufficiently concrete penetration into the real conflicts, tensions, and ambiguities of social life; (2) the tendency throughout his thought to neglect the problem of means of realizing the ends he advocated; (3) the tendency, especially in his increasingly pronounced social metaphysic, to indulge in a vague, contemplative vision of ideals standing above social realities; and (4) the tendency to rely on an evolutionary optimism which envisaged a progressive approximation of these ideals in some unspecified future.

· These tendencies might well have been embodied in a revisionist attitude toward Marx, as they were to some extent in the thought of Eduard Bernstein. In Durkheim, however, they were

[14] *Ideology and Utopia* (New York: Harcourt, Brace, 1936), pp. 219–229.

conjoined with what might be called a ritual avoidance of Marx.[15] For very often the absence of Marx or, conversely, the hidden presence of Marx as a silent pariah interlocutor haunted Durkheimism. When he did address himself to Marx's thought, Durkheim attempted to situate Marxism as an ideology while ignoring Marx's theoretical contribution. This attitude toward Marx exacerbated some of the greatest defects of Durkheim, especially his inadequate treatment of the role of the economy,

[15] Durkheim's attitude was in marked contrast to Max Weber's open reckoning with Marx. It is significant that Durkheim and Weber indicated no knowledge of each other's work. See Edward Tiryakian, "A Problem for the Sociology of Knowledge: The Mutual Unawareness of Emile Durkheim and Max Weber," *Archives européennes de sociologie*, VII (1966), 330–336. Tiryakian correctly notes the reason why Durkheim and Weber should have been interested in each other's work, e.g., their conviction concerning the importance of religion in social life. But, in accounting for their "mutual unawareness," he stresses the role of exogenous factors such as opposing national allegiances. He does not investigate the relation of serious intellectual differences to "mutual unawareness" or, perhaps, mutual avoidance. One basic difference was on the issue of the ethical neutrality of social science. One might hazard the generalization that, on subjects extending from epistemology to politics, the differences between Durkheim and Weber were between a thinker who was traditional, philosophically conservative, and often naïve and one who was modern, heroic, and irreducibly tragic. (Tiryakian, in his *Sociologism and Existentialism* [Englewood Cliffs, N.J.: Prentice-Hall, 1962], gives a thoughtful, if brief, analysis of Durkheim's thought, stressing the importance of his conception of the relation between society and morality.) Alvin Gouldner, in his generally insightful introduction to *Socialism* (New York: Collier Books, 1962), makes two exaggerated assertions which are opposed, if not contradictory, to one another. Gouldner sees Durkheim as attempting to build a bridge between the traditions of Comte and Marx in sociology. But he also presents Durkheim as concerned with the "fine-tuning" of modern society. I would maintain that at least some bases for integrating Durkheim and Marx do exist but that Durkheim himself did relatively little to build upon them. This was true, for example, of the problem of relating anomie to class conflict. But to characterize Durkheim's idea of needed reforms as "fine-tuning" is extreme. Durkheim increasingly believed that the problems besetting modern society were severe. One might well argue that his proposed reforms were excessively vague or inadequate for solving the problems he perceived. But they were basic, at least in certain respects. It is true, however, that Durkheim believed modern society would naturally evolve in the direction of "normality," certainly without violent revolution.

of classes, and of group conflict in social life. One problem to which Durkheim never convincingly addressed himself was central: whether a Marxist-type analysis was in significant measure still relevant to the understanding of antagonisms in society under advanced industrialism, and, if it was, how it could be related to the issues which for Durkheim were paramount. This was a problem which remained even if the conception of class conflict and its revolutionary potential in the specific form in which Marx presented it was becoming increasingly irrelevant.

Like Marx, Durkheim tried to integrate a critique of political economy, German speculative philosophy, and the French socialist tradition in a comprehensive theory of the genesis and functioning of modern society. Again, like Marx, he often perceived history—especially modern history—as the story of social pathology. And, in contrast to theorists with a "value-neutral" conception of social science, Durkheim saw a link between theory and practice. But his antipathy toward Marx prevented a balanced estimate of Marx's achievement and of the actual role of factors through which Marx explained the historical process. Durkheim fell far short of the profound feeling for tragedy which dramatically informed Marx's reading of history and which gave a heroic cast to his idea of a dialectical "overcoming" of the burdens of the past. Unlike Marx, moreover, Durkheim rarely displayed a telling sense of the concrete with which to bring to life (and temper with life's nuances) his analytical models and statistical surveys; and he rarely was able to grasp imaginatively the developmental possibilities of a complex set of interacting factors in society as a whole over time. One finds no *Eighteenth Brumaire* among Durkheim's works. Marx had both a sense of history and an almost cannibalistic sense of irony. Durkheim's more abstract and staid approach lacked these cutting edges.

The Marx whom Durkheim especially abhorred was the Marx who advocated class conflict and violent revolution in modern society. In contrast with Marx, Durkheim viewed modern society

—and particularly his own France, which was always his center of reference—as suffering from severe but transitional symptoms of pathology and offering the possibility of social justice without recourse to violent revolution. This primary focus upon the conception of modern society as passing through a pathological state of rapid transition on the way to normality was crucial for the shape of Durkheim's thought as a whole. For Durkheim, modern society was experiencing, not death throes, but prolonged and disruptive birth pangs. Marx had mixed his metaphors and mistaken the nature and direction of modern society.

If Marx was both too pessimistic in his idea of the historical evolution of the industrialized West toward collapse (at least in terms of the precise processes he emphasized) and too optimistic in his messianic faith in cultural regeneration after apocalyptic upheaval, Durkheim combined extreme pessimism about the potential of the individual "left to himself" with extreme optimism concerning the ability of modern society to resolve the severe problems presented to it in the course of history. This false optimism, which vacillated between the mechanistically sober and the euphorically inflated, generated in Durkheim an air of complacency that was alleviated only by genuine concern and a devotion to social action. Durkheim often seemed able to snatch the spirit of normality from the jaws of anomie. Despite his sensitivity to possible abortive miscarriages in the development of modern society, he had an almost religious faith in the evolution of modern society, on the whole and in good time, toward justice and reason. If Durkheim's social idealism at times included elements of political naïveté, he at least recognized problems in the modern status quo that certain of his epigoni preferred to overlook. And the least questionable aspect of his faith in a straining toward normality and social sanity in modern life was the assumption that the reformer with constructive intentions—even when he failed to be moved by the spirit—might be constrained to accept optimism as somewhat a social duty.

A final remark should indicate the general conception of Durkheim's thought which informs this study. The idea of sociology as a life science implied for Durkheim a fidelity to the living. In his last major work, which treated the vanishing religion of Australian aborigines, Durkheim seemed to be very far from his initial inspiration. In one sense, the very opposite was true. In the opening pages of *Les Formes élémentaires de la vie religieuse* (*The Elementary Forms of the Religious Life*), Durkheim asserted:

Sociology raises other problems than history and ethnography. It does not seek to know the bygone forms of civilization with the sole end of knowing and reconstituting them. Instead, like every positive science, it has as its object the explanation of a present reality, near to us and thus able to affect our actions: This reality is man and, more precisely, the man of today, for there is none other whom we are more interested in knowing. Thus we will not study the very archaic religion which is our subject for the sole pleasure of recounting its bizarre and singular features. If we have taken archaic religion as our object of research, it is because it appeared to us more apt than any other in allowing us to understand the religious nature of man, that is to reveal to us an essential and permanent aspect of human nature.[16]

The theoretical goal of *The Elementary Forms* was to arrive at a general notion of culture and society through an intensive analysis of religious symbolism and its relation to solidarity. But the more specific object preoccupying Durkheim was his idea of the "moral mediocrity" of modern society and his desire to learn something of basic value from the savages before their forms of life were uprooted by a civilization whose mode of advance was often symptomatic of its moral mediocrity. At times this intention of the *moraliste* led Durkheim to perceive archaic societies through a superficial type of benign reverse ethnocentrism: he focused upon abstracted features in primitive life which he felt were missing in modern society but vital to all

[16] *Les Formes élémentaires de la vie religieuse* (first pub. 1912; 4th ed.; Paris: Presses Universitaires de France, 1960), pp. 1–2.

normal society. His analysis of religious belief and ritual in archaic societies reduced these phenomena to selected aspects which accorded most with his lifelong moral concern with creating legitimate institutions in modern society and his latter-day sensitivity to the universal need for significant community. *The Elementary Forms* was the *summa* of Durkheim's written works. In a larger context, it was but the preface to his might-have-been chef-d'oeuvre, "La Morale," which Marcel Mauss accurately characterized as the "but de son existence, fond de son esprit" (the goal of his existence, the substance of his mind).[17] A curious abstractness reaching out with elusive feeling for human solidity in values and moral solidarity in men; a Cartesianized, socialized, and somewhat mystified neo-Kantianism of a rabbi *manqué* who had stoically imperturbable good will—these were often the most apparent qualities of Durkheimism.

[17] "In Memoriam: L'Oeuvre inédite de Durkheim et de ses collaborateurs," *Année sociologique*, n.s., I (1923), 9.

2 »

Durkheim's Milieu

> Once one has established the existence of an evil, what it
> consists of and on what it depends, when one knows in con-
> sequence the general characteristics of the remedy, the
> essential thing is not to draw up in advance a plan which fore-
> sees everything; it is to get resolutely to work.
>
> —*Suicide*

To historicize Durkheim's ideas by restricting their range to
his own immediate experience and social context would obviously
be to lose sight of their broader relevance. But it is informative
for reasons of historical perspective to situate Durkheim in his
own social milieu. And the effort is prompted by Durkheim's
tendency to take his own society as a test case of the needs of
modern society in general. The broadly ethical and philosophical
impetus behind Durkheim's thought must be in the forefront of
any approach to his ideas. For him the problem of a just social
order in modern society presented itself very much in the light
of rational specification of the principles of the French Revolution in terms which would enable men to humanize and absorb
the industrial revolution. The moral mission of sociology itself
was to provide, through an analytic and comparative study of
institutions and values, orientation in reaching this goal. By and
large, Durkheim's life was a subdued and intellectualized passion devoted to this task—scientific and moral at the same time.

Durkheim was born in 1858 in the town of Epinal, in the
province of Alsace, and died in 1917. Ceded to the Germans in
1871, Alsace housed both the most traditionalist enclave of French
Jewry and one of the most ardent centers of French patriotism.

Durkheim grew up at a time when the Jewish ghettos of eastern France were rapidly breaking up.[1] The disintegration of these communities posed the problem of assimilation into the larger society and the threat of personal disorientation which Durkheim later was to analyze in terms of anomie. To this problem was added the loss of *patrie* for those suffering the consequences of the Franco-Prussian War.

The early death of his father imposed upon the young Durkheim the responsibilities of a *chef de famille*. According to familial tradition, Durkheim was destined to follow in his father's footsteps by becoming a rabbi. Of course he was not to follow literally the wishes of his family. He was never to make an express commitment to any established religious institution. But those who found an agnostic temperament in Durkheim identified religious sentiment with orthodox belief in a personal deity or with other-worldly transcendentalism—identifications which Durkheim was at pains to dispel in his own definition of the religious phenomenon. The relation between religion and society which Durkheim tried to establish theoretically had an analogue in the personality of this founder of modern sociology. The one theme that recurs in the reminiscences of his friends is the profound religiosity and the sense of mystique running like an undercurrent in his dialectical rigor and rationalism. As his close friend Georges Davy recalled: "This convinced rationalist always kept, on the fringe of the orthodoxy of his milieu, a sort of fundamental religiosity which took on the allure of mysticism when, with the impassioned ardor of a prophet, he expounded his doctrine."[2] And here is the testimony of the founder of the *Revue de métaphysique et de morale*, Durkheim's good friend Xavier Léon: "This face and this body of an ascetic, the glowing light of a look profoundly buried in the orbit of his eye, the timbre and the accent of a

[1] Georges Weill, *Histoire du mouvement social en France, 1852–1910* (Paris: Alcan, 1911), pp. 469–483.

[2] "Emile Durkheim," *Revue française de sociologie*, I (1960), 6.

voice animated by an ardent faith that in this heir of the prophets burned with the desire to forge and temper the conviction of listeners." [3]

One sequence of events in Durkheim's life stood out with special prominence. Durkheim was not known for his sense of humor or taste for irony. In part, the lack was due to the intellectual purity, classical restraint, and moral incentive of his thought. But Durkheim's outlook was also indicative of a strait-laced tendency to identify seriousness of purpose with solemnity. Davy has remarked that Durkheim's austere conception of life "perhaps even went to the point of preventing him from enjoying without scruples any pleasure except the Spinoza-like joy which is brought by enthusiasm for an idea." [4] The sole recorded instance of humor and irony in Durkheim's life was self-directed, and it involved religion. In a rare pun, Durkheim played upon the ambiguity of the French word *chaire* ("academic's chair," "church pulpit"). Passing in front of Notre Dame Cathedral, Durkheim turned to a colleague, Célestin Bouglé, and remarked, "It's from a chair like that, that I ought to be speaking." [5]

Durkheim's life seems dominated by a strong sense of discipline which kept the man together while the academic moved steadily from rung to rung up the professional ladder and ultimately to a professorship at the Sorbonne. As a young man, however, Durkheim experienced a number of crises that revealed how he combined a strong mind with a fragile and anxious spirit. Under the influence of a Catholic instructress, for example, he underwent a passing infatuation with mysticism. [6] In Paris, he prepared for the Ecole Normale Supérieure at the

---

[3] *Revue de métaphysique et de morale,* XXIV (1917), 749. Compare the testimony of René Maublanc, "L'Oeuvre sociologique d'Emile Durkheim," *Europe,* XXII (1930), 298.

[4] "Emile Durkheim," p. 6.

[5] Reported by Bouglé, "L'Oeuvre sociologique d'Emile Durkheim," *Europe,* XXII (1930), 281.

[6] Georges Davy, "Emile Durkheim: L'Homme," *Revue de métaphysique et de morale,* XXVI (1919), 183.

Lycée Louis-le-Grand and lived at the Pension Jauffret, where he formed his lifelong friendship with Jean Jaurès. But his life at the pension was full of anguish and left him with bad memories.[7] He was admitted to the Ecole Normale after having failed two years in succession to place high enough in the entrance examination.

Durkheim entered the Ecole Normale in 1879. "Lanson, S. Reinach and Lévy-Bruhl had just been graduated. Bergson, Jaurès and Belot had entered the year before. Rauh and Maurice Blondel were to be admitted two years later. Pierre Janet and Goblot entered along with Durkheim. It is not an exaggeration, therefore, to say that a veritable philosophical renaissance was germinating at the Ecole Normale."[8] But once he was finally in the Ecole, Durkheim's attitude was highly ambivalent. In his last year a grave illness which may have been psychosomatic in origin compromised his chances for the *agrégation*, in which he was nonetheless received next to last.[9]

In retrospect, Durkheim felt that the Ecole Normale was a "scientific and social milieu of exceptional value," and he sent his son there.[10] He retained a lasting respect for two of his professors: the historian Fustel de Coulanges and the philosopher Emile Boutroux. To Fustel, who preceded Durkheim in the advocacy of the comparative method and the conception of the importance of religion in social life, Durkheim dedicated his Latin thesis on their common intellectual ancestor, Montesquieu. To Boutroux, who impressed Durkheim most by his "penetrating and objective way of reconstituting and rethinking systems,

[7] Davy, in commemorative issue, *Annales de l'Université de Paris*, No. 1 (Jan.–March 1960), 19.

[8] Harry Alpert, *Emile Durkheim and His Sociology* (first pub. 1939; New York: Russell & Russell, 1961), pp. 16–17.

[9] Davy, "Emile Durkheim: L'Homme," *Revue de métaphysique et de morale*, XXVI (1919), 187. The disorder was diagnosed as erysipelas, an acute febrile disease associated with intense local inflammation of the skin and subcutaneous tissue. The *agrégation* is the competitive examination qualifying successful candidates to hold teaching posts in French high schools (lycées).

[10] *Ibid.*, p. 184.

renewing and founding scientifically before his students the history of philosophy," [11] Durkheim dedicated his thesis on "The Division of Labor."

At a deeper psychological level, however, Durkheim did not find the Ecole Normale altogether to his liking. The impressionistic humanism and dilettantism which he had found repulsive in *cagne* (the high school class preparing students for the Ecole Normale examination) were dominant traits of the Ecole itself. More important, he instinctively drew back from the supercilious snobbery and defensive air of *noblesse oblige* in an overly self-conscious intellectual elite.

His intelligence, sober and avid for substantial truth, held in horror the literary persiflage and ironic tone so often to be found in the conversation of the students at the Ecole Normale [*normaliens*]. . . . "I have seen him (M. Holleaux recounts) wish ardently for the end of the school year, for vacation time, the moment when he would be able to live again among 'good simple people' (this was his expression). Absolutely simple, he detested all affectations. Profoundly serious, he hated banter [*le ton léger*]."

If many of Durkheim's character traits recall the austere Kant, others bring to mind Rousseau. One of the happiest times of his school years was when he went into the streets to mingle with the effervescent populace during the July 14 festivities.[12] The sense of communal warmth was a force which was increasingly to break through the Cartesianized neo-Kantian surface of his thought, through its cold veneer of devotion to duty. At the Ecole Normale, moreover, Durkheim formed several lasting and genuine friendships. His friend Maurice Holleaux remarked that "few people really knew him. Few realized that his severity covered almost feminine sensitivity and that his heart, a stranger to facile effusions of sentiment, enclosed a treasury of tender goodness." [13]

[11] *Ibid.*, p. 187.   [12] *Ibid.*, p. 188.
[13] Quoted in Davy, "Emile Durkheim," *Revue française de sociologie*, I (1960), 8.

Lines later written by Durkheim himself about his good friend Octave Hamelin could be applied to the attitudes of Durkheim's friends toward their relationship with Durkheim himself. Hamelin had died prematurely in an absurd attempt to save the lives of unknown drowning people in spite of the fact that he was unable to swim. Durkheim edited and made ready for publication the book on Descartes which Hamelin never completed. In words which evoke the sanctity of intimacy in friendship, Durkheim wrote of Hamelin: "As a man, we think that he belongs entirely to his friends, who piously keep the cult of his memory. We would almost believe that we had defiled his memory if we were to allow the public to penetrate the intimacy of an existence which always fled acclaim and which even hid itself from the looks of others with a sort of jealous care." [14]

After leaving the Ecole Normale, Durkheim was granted a period of relative respite to gather himself and his thoughts together. In accordance with the traditional French practice that is now passing out of existence, he began teaching at the secondary level before moving on to the university. If the primary and secondary levels in France represented not stages in the educational process as much as different systems of education highly stratified according to social class, the secondary and the upper levels were strongly integrated with each other. Indeed, certain intellectual leaders of the time, such as Alain, preferred to remain at the *lycée* level from a conviction that it was the locus of more authentic teaching. From 1882 to 1887, Durkheim taught at the *lycées* of Sens, Saint-Quentin, and Troyes. In 1885–1886, he took a year off from teaching in provincial *lycées* to study in Germany.[15] This trip was undertaken after a conversation with Louis Liard, the Director of Higher Education (Directeur de l'Enseignement Supérieur), a lifelong supporter of Durkheim. But it would be a mistake to think that Liard

[14] Preface to *Le Système de Descartes* (Paris: Alcan, 1911), p. v.
[15] Alpert, p. 32.

showed any special or conspiratorial favoritism toward Durkheim. Rather, he saw in Durkheim a thinker whose convictions and ideas coincided with his own deep commitment to the renovation of the French educational system under the auspices of the Republic. Liard had been struck in his own youth by the decadence of education under the Second Empire, and he shared the belief of many republican leaders that educational inferiority had been a key factor in France's defeat at the hands of the Germans. Thus Liard's furtherance of Durkheimian sociology, while not a unique event in his actively innovative life as an administrator, was related to his idea of the institutional and moral needs of the Republic.

In Germany, Durkheim studied social science and its relation to ethics, primarily under the guidance of Wilhelm Wundt. He was considerably impressed by the efforts of Albert Schaeffle and the "socialists of the chair" to devise reforms of the economy in accordance with the demands of social ethics. Yet he almost cut his visit short in order to return precipitately to France because of an overly scrupulous fear that he would not be able to derive from his stay in Germany all that he expected.[16] Despite his anxiety, publication of two articles based on his period of study in Germany brought Durkheim to the attention of the broader public.[17] The year 1887 marked the institution in France of the first university course in social science. It was to be taught by Durkheim at the University of Bordeaux. The proposal for this course was in all probability initiated by Alfred Espinas, the author of Les Sociétés animales and himself a professor at Bordeaux, and it had the support of Louis Liard.[18] The ministerial decree, dated July 20, 1887, bore the signature of Eugène

[16] Davy, Annales de l'Université de Paris, No. 1 (Jan.–March 1960), 19.
[17] "La Philosophie dans les universités allemandes," Revue internationale de l'enseignement, XIII (1887), 313–338, 423–440; and "La Science positive de la morale en Allemagne," Revue philosophique, XXIV (1887), 33–58, 113–142, 275–284.
[18] René Lacroze, Annales de l'Université de Paris, No. 1 (Jan.–March 1960), 26.

Spuller, who ten years earlier had brought before the Chamber of Deputies the *projet de loi* of Jules Ferry on the reform of higher education.

Just before the appointment at Bordeaux, Durkheim had married. According to his friend Davy, "His choice could not have been happier both for himself and for the atmosphere of his work." [19] His wife's maiden name, portentously, was Dreyfus, but she does not seem to have been related to the famous Dreyfus whose defense Durkheim would later take up. With her Durkheim had two children, a boy and a girl.

In a letter to Marcel Mauss (who once described Durkheim as "the professional conscience personified"), [20] Durkheim wrote that he had "passed his first year of teaching at the Faculty in a trance of unsuccess." [21] But, once again, Durkheim was being excessively uneasy. At about the age of thirty, he started to acquire the security and stability which were probably necessary for him to control his feelings of anxiety and begin a period of enormous productivity and creativity.

The first full professorship and university chair in social science were created for Durkheim at Bordeaux in 1896. In 1902, he received a call to Paris as a replacement for his fellow educator and friend Ferdinand Buisson, who had been elected to the Chamber of Deputies. He was given Buisson's chair in the Science of Education in 1906. As Durkheim's disciple Maurice Halbwachs later phrased it, sociology was not admitted directly to the Sorbonne "but was introduced into it through the narrow gate of pedagogy." [22] Indeed, throughout his career Durkheim devoted from one-third to two-thirds of his teaching time to pedagogy. He did not look upon this as a waste of time, for he

[19] *Annales de l'Université de Paris,* No. 1 (Jan.–March 1960), 19.

[20] Marcel Mauss, "In Memoriam: L'Oeuvre inédite de Durkheim et de ses collaborateurs," *Année sociologique,* n.s., I (1923), 9.

[21] Quoted by Davy, *Annales de l'Université de Paris,* No. 1 (Jan.–March 1960), 19.

[22] Introd., Emile Durkheim, *L'Evolution Pedagogique en France* (Paris: Alcan, 1938), p. 1.

approached education sociologically as an institution having the crucial function of socializing the child into the larger society. By special decree in 1913, the title of his chair at the Sorbonne was changed to the Science of Education and Sociology. Comte's neologism, barbarically combining Greek logos and Latin *societas*, finally gained official recognition in the University of France through the instrumentality of a thinker who questioned the preponderant role of the classics in traditional French education. Durkheim was awarded the *Légion d'honneur* but was denied access to the Institut de France. Davy remarks that he received news of both events with the same detachment.[23] He had achieved the essential; the superfluous was unnecessary.

In Durkheim's works, sociology underwent its "identity crisis." Hence his tendency to assert militantly and even overstate his point of view. In his own France, his attempt to found a discipline was so successful that his sociology emerged in time as somewhat a "collective representation." As a historian sensitive to the importance of social theory observed almost a decade after Durkheim's death:

Such indeed has been the influence of Durkheim in our University that he seems to have monopolized sociology. The latter in our mind is so closely bound up with the work of Durkheim that we have almost become unable to realize that it can have an existence beyond his works and those of his disciples. In our discussions, in our manuals, Durkheimian sociology and sociology *tout court* seem to be more and more synonymous.[24]

[23] "Emile Durkheim: L'Homme," *Revue de métaphysique et de morale,* XXVI (1919), 190.

[24] Roger Lacombe, *La Méthode sociologique de Durkheim: Etude critique* (Paris: Alcan, 1926), p. 1. The continuing presence of Durkheim in French sociology was indicated by the fact that the immediate string of successors to his chair in sociology at the Sorbonne were his disciples P. Fauconnet, M. Halbwachs, and G. Davy. Since World War II, however, the influence of Durkheim in French sociology has waned. The holders of the two chairs in sociology at the Sorbonne, Raymond Aron and, to a lesser extent perhaps, Georges Gurvitch, were more often than not hostile critics of Durkheim. The centenary of Durkheim's birth in 1958 passed al-

Durkheim's intellectual life coincided with the founding
and establishment of the Third Republic, whose initial and more
optimistic phase came to a tragic end, like Durkheim's life itself,
with the traumatic shock of World War I. The events which
heralded the coming of the Republic—the debacle of the Franco-
Prussian War, followed by the agony of the Paris Commune—
were interpreted by many republican leaders as evidence of the
internal instability of the Second Empire rather than as inaus-
picious indices of continuing foreign and domestic problems.[25]
Despite the almost mystical optimism engendered by the mere
durability of the first long-lived democratic republic in French
history, Durkheim himself placed at least the recurrent domestic
upheavals in France in the larger context of the industrial revolution and the turbulent wake of the French Revolution. As he
observed of Saint-Simon's long-range, structural theory of European and especially French history, which presented the Revolution of 1789 as a phenomenon which had destroyed certain

most unnoticed in France, partly because of the Algerian crisis which
brought de Gaulle to power. The celebration at the Sorbonne of Durkheim's
centenary took place almost two years later, long after similar ceremonies
in other countries. Younger social thinkers in France, however, seem to be
reviving interest in Durkheim with an understanding guided by the sym-
pathetic desire to discover and develop what is still alive in his thought.
This attitude may be found, for example, in the perceptive introduction by
Victor Karady to an edition of the very Durkheimian works of the young
Mauss—a publication which is itself a phenomenon of importance (Marcel
Mauss, *Oeuvres, I: Les Fonctions du sacré* [Paris: Les Editions du Minuit,
1968]). The neglect of Durkheim after the war was due in part to the
impact of structuralism on anthropology, general methodology, philosophy,
and even Marxism (as well as to the vogue of phenomenology and existentialism). Re-evaluation of Durkheim might make it possible to retain the
elements of structuralism which clearly constitute a genuine theoretical
advance over Durkheim while phasing out those of its inclinations which
induce sterile formalism and damaging obscurantism.

[25] One even finds an echo of the republican attack on the Second Empire, which frequently lent itself to ideological uses as a basis for a legitimating myth of the Republic and its original purity, in Léon Blum's comment in *A L'Echelle humaine* (Paris: Gallimard, 1945): "The Empire had
been guilty, but the Republic was only unfortunate [*malheureuse*]" (p.
41).

vestiges of the old order but which had miscarried in the creation of the new:

[After the Revolution] royal authority was re-established. But these revivals of the past did not constitute a solution. So the problem is posed on the morrow of the Revolution, at the start of the nineteenth century, in the same terms as on the eve of 1789, only it has become more pressing. The denouement is more urgent if one does not wish to see each crisis produce another, exasperation the chronic state of society, and finally, disintegration more or less the result. Either completely restore the old system or organize the new. It is precisely this that is the social problem.

As we view it, it cannot be posed with greater profundity.[26]

In the excellent judgment of David Thomson, "The Third Republic . . . was at heart an attempt to reconcile the conflicting forces of modern France."[27] The republican ideal of a just modern consensus healing the wounds of history found no more ardent proponent than Durkheim.[28] In his inaugural lecture at Bordeaux, Durkheim stated his intensely moral goal in no ambiguous terms:

Our society must restore the consciousness of its organic unity. . . . No doubt these ideas will become truly efficacious only if they spread out into the depths of society, but for that it is first necessary that we elaborate them scientifically in the university. To contribute to this end to the extent of my powers will be my principal concern, and I shall have no greater happiness than if I succeed in it a little.[29]

The realities of the Third Republic were of course less elevated, and its operational consensus proved to be purely negative. Astute, if cynical, observer-participants like Adolphe Thiers

[26] Emile Durkheim, *Socialism*, trans. Charlotte Sattler, ed. with Introd. by Alvin Gouldner (New York: Collier Books, 1962), p. 160.

[27] David Thomson, *Democracy in France* (London, New York, Toronto: Oxford University Press, 1958), p. 27.

[28] Cf. Alpert, pp. 28ff.

[29] "Cours de science sociale," *Revue internationale de l'enseignement,* XIV (1888), 48–49.

were able to see this from the very beginning. The monarchist Right, which in the 1870's had proved unable to settle upon a compromise formula reconciling the houses of Bourbon and Orléans, accepted the Republic *faute de mieux.* After the Dreyfus Affair, resistance from the Right became increasingly militant. The far Left was equally unable to propose a constructive alternative to existing policies. Between these two extremes, most of those who agreed upon a democratic and republican form of government did so with the tacit assumption that politics would not disturb the basic configuration of vested interests in society. Symbolically, the French legislature held its meetings in a "house without windows." French labor legislation remained the most backward of the advanced industrial societies. And French society continued to be highly stratified, with little equality of opportunity, less equality of reward, and no positive consensus on the legitimate nature of the social structure or political regime. The boundaries of invidious distinction between socially distant and uncooperative classes continued to be defined with the Cartesian rigor so accurately described by Tocqueville in his *Ancien régime.* The youthful promise of the Republic turned increasingly into the senile reality of a detached, deadlocked democracy superimposed upon a stalemated society.[30] In this context, there was little chance of developing social and political institutions which could viably control the disruptive effects of the industrial revolution: memories of the great Revolution created expectations which heightened unrest.

The precise nature of the economy and of its impact upon society in Durkheim's France is a complex subject which still engages experts in debate. In the famous dictum of John Clapham, France underwent industrialization without having a

[30] For a concise account of the social bases of the Third Republic, see Thomson, chap. ii. See also the compact and intricate essay of Stanley Hoffmann, "Paradoxes of the French Political Community," in Stanley Hoffmann *et al., In Search of France* (Cambridge: Harvard University Press, 1963).

full-fledged industrial revolution.[31] The rate of economic change in France until quite recently was not comparable to that of Germany or England, but the degree of disparity has often been exaggerated.

Durkheim tended to see the problem of industrialization within the broad context of modern society as a whole. But, during his own lifetime, the rate of change in France itself, especially in the concentration of industry, was probably more rapid than it had ever been, and its effects were quite perceptible to the sensitive observer. In fact, the unbalanced nature of the economic transformation in France exacerbated problems common to all industrial societies. The one area of modern life in which the family retained extensive social control in France depended on the role of the bourgeois family firm in the economy.[32] In the large sector of the economy dominated by relatively small family firms, production was restricted and prices were kept high to defend the social position and honor of the family unit. Thus workers were deprived even of the gains they might have expected from increases in productivity and the imperatives of mass consumption in a privately owned and operated economy.[33]

[31] See his *Economic Development of France and Germany* (4th ed.; Cambridge: University Press, 1936), especially pp. 232ff.

[32] Jesse Pitts, "Continuity and Change in Bourgeois France," in Stanley Hoffmann *et al.*, *In Search of France*. On the way in which social attitudes of businessmen affected economic activity, see David Landes, "French Entrepreneurship and Industrial Growth in the Nineteenth Century," *Journal of Economic History*, IX (1949), 45–61, and "Business and the Business Man: A Social and Cultural Analysis," in E. M. Earle, ed., *Modern France* (Princeton: Princeton University Press, 1951).

[33] Louis Chevalier, in his *Classes laborieuses et classes dangereuses* (Paris: Plon, 1958), has observed that from 1848 to 1870 small industry not only predominated but was on the increase in Paris (pp. 76ff.). For Chevalier, the prevalence of crime in the Paris region during the nineteenth century was due to the pathological state caused primarily by demographic change. The rapid influx of people into Paris caused a crisis situation which resulted not only in high crime rates but in class conflict of ex-

In a famous critique of the *Année sociologique* school, A. L. Kroeber stressed the repugnance of the Durkheimians for field work.[34] E. E. Evans-Pritchard has taken up this plaint and extended its scope: "One sometimes sighs—if only Tylor, Marett, Durkheim and the rest of them could have spent a few weeks among the people about whom they so freely wrote!"[35] Whatever the justice of this sentiment regarding archaic societies, it overlooked the fact that a sociologist like Durkheim did have a direct "field" experience of one massive phenomenon in world history: the transformation of modern societies through industrialization.[36] The attempt to make sociological sense of the complex events he beheld firsthand was basic to Durkheim's *De La Division du travail social,* and *Le Suicide,* and it remained a fundamental issue in his *Les formes élémentaires de la vie religieuse.*

Within the context of his own society, Durkheim's intent was to eliminate the basic causes of social pathology and propose ways to achieve a positive consensus through the viable realization of values adequate to the conditions of modern social life. Although his own sphere of immediate concern was largely confined to the educational system, Durkheim did not believe

---

treme virulence. Citing an interesting statistic on the issue of class consciousness versus professional consciousness, Chevalier noted that at the end of the Empire and the beginning of the Third Republic the indication of occupation on electoral lists tended increasingly to change from a precise denotation of métier to a designation of social class as "worker" (p. 173).

[34] "History and Science in Anthropology," *American Anthropologist,* XXXVII (1935), 539–569.

[35] *Theories of Primitive Religion* (London: Oxford University Press, 1965), p. 67. See also p. 6, where Evans-Pritchard observes in the manner of Lévi-Strauss: "It is a remarkable fact that none of the anthropologists whose theories about primitive religion have been most influential had ever been near a primitive people. It is as though a chemist had never thought it necessary to enter a laboratory."

[36] Cf. Jean Duvignaud, *Durkheim* (Paris: Presses Universitaires de France, 1965), p. 13.

that reforms restricted to the initiatives of an educational and scientific estate were sufficient. He undoubtedly shared Gambetta's belief that a democratic republic could not endure "without distributing education with both hands." [37] But Durkheim recognized clearly that uncoordinated partial responses to major social problems would in all probability aggravate pathological conditions instead of alleviating them. Changes in education and in the social attitudes of educators could be effective only in conjunction with changes of a basic structural nature in the primary source of social problems in modernity—the economic and occupational spheres. Durkheim's corporatist proposals were addressed to this problem.

A measure of positive consensus stemming from similar social origins and philosophical convictions did characterize the educational leaders who formed Durkheim's immediate reference group. One fact emerges when one examines the backgrounds of key figures in the educational system who, like Durkheim, were genuinely committed to working toward the creation of a social and political order based upon republican ideals. In disproportionately significant numbers, they were self-made men from marginal social groups in traditionally Catholic and status-conscious France. These men were afforded the opportunity to rise to positions of prominence in the nation through the involvement of more traditional elites in the vicissitudes of the Second Empire, the futile maneuverings of promonarchists in the 1870's, and, most important, the allegiance of traditional elites to anti-republican ideologies. With the achievement of established positions, these newer men assumed an attitude of "reasonable" reformism which, especially after the Dreyfus Affair, was increasingly open to the influence of mystique.

Durkheim and certain of his collaborators on the *Année sociologique* were of Jewish ancestry. We have already noted Durk-

[37] Quoted in John Eros, "The Positivist Generation of French Intellectuals," *Sociological Review*, III (1955), 265.

heim's rabbinical heritage, which was shared by his nephew Marcel Mauss. We know, moreover, the primary scientific importance Durkheim attributed to the *Année sociologique:* "Because it embraces the entire domain of science," Durkheim wrote, "the *Année* has been able, better than any special work, to impart the sentiment of what sociology must and can become." [38] But aside from its scientific importance and its role in the Republic, the *Année* school formed "almost a spiritual family united by the bond of a common method and a common admiration for its *maître.*" [39] This "little society *sui generis,* the clan of the *Année sociologique*" [40] seemed to represent in the minds and hearts of its members a prototype of what the professional group could be in modern society—a supplementary kinship, a truly solidary corps combining community and a mutual respect for individuality. As Marcel Mauss recalled: "The *Année* was not simply a publication and the work of a team. Around it we formed a 'group' in all the force of the term." [41] In sharp contrast with the psychoanalytic movement, the *Année* school was not marked by extreme sibling rivalry and revolts against the symbolic father. Indeed, for its members the *Année* seemed almost to be an intemporal *moment parfait.*

Jules Ferry, perhaps the foremost figure in educational reform under the Third Republic, did not quite fit into the pattern of the "marginal man." From the upper-bourgeois Protestant establishment in the Vosges, he married (late in life) a girl from the Protestant patriciate of Mulhouse. But the men with whom he surrounded himself were largely from smaller Protestant families, and they were more impregnated than the rather bureaucratic "cold fish" Ferry with the pietist spirit found in

[38] *Les Règles de la méthode sociologique* (15th ed.; Paris: Presses Universitaires de France, 1963), p. xii.

[39] Davy, "Emile Durkheim: "L'Homme," *Revue de métaphysique et de morale,* XXVI (1919), 194.

[40] *Ibid.,* p. 195.   [41] "In Memoriam," p. 2.

Kant himself. Of the men assisting Ferry, especially significant was the trinity of Ferdinand Buisson, Jules Steeg, and Félix Pécaut.[42]

These three came to France from Switzerland. Steeg and Pécaut had been Protestant ministers, and Buisson a teacher. Ferry appointed Buisson ("my very dear friend, the apple of my eye") Director of Primary Education. His role in the Republic has been described as that of "lay high priest."[43] In 1898 he was elected president of the Ligue pour la Défense des Droits de l'Homme (League for the Defense of the Rights of Man).[44] This voluntary association, of which Durkheim was an active member, had been founded by Clemenceau during the Dreyfus Affair to combat the anti-Dreyfusards. Buisson had been appointed in 1896 to the chair in the Science of Education at the Sorbonne, where he was replaced upon his election to the Chamber of Deputies in 1902 by Durkheim.

Jules Steeg also became a deputy, and finally Inspector General of Public Instruction. Into the task of developing a program of moral and civic instruction in the school system, he poured his immense store of spiritual energy. Like Durkheim, he was the author of works on moral education. Prominent among his contributions to this favorite genre of the period was a *Cours de morale à l'usage des instituteurs*.

Perhaps the most interesting figure in this group was Félix Pécaut. He was the exemplar of neo-Kantian morality, liberal Protestantism, the *culte de la patrie*, and a democratic civic spirit. He was appointed by Ferry to head the *école normale* for *institutrices* at Fontenay-les-Roses, one of the schools designed to free the women of France from the influence of the Church.

[42] See Adrien Dansette, *Religious History of Modern France* (New York: Herder & Herder, 1961), II, 54ff. See also Georges Duveau, *Les Instituteurs* (Paris: Editions du Seuil, 1957), pp. 122ff.

[43] Duveau, p. 122.

[44] John Scott, *Republican Ideas and the Liberal Tradition in France, 1870–1914* (New York: Columbia University Press), pp. 185–186.

Fontenay-les-Roses has been described as "the sweet lay convent where Pécaut was the fisher of souls." [45] Pécaut was the author of a very interesting article on Durkheim, which seized with penetration the contemporary import of Durkheim's theory of religion that was of special interest to men like himself:

The secret finality [of rites] was not to be expressions of faith but the means by which the *moral experience* is created and re-created. . . . In the heart of religion, one always finds the multiform experience of the moral conscience. . . . In our time we have asked ourselves if a morality without religion could justify itself in the eyes of reason and especially if it could take hold of men's hearts. To this troubled question, Durkheim answers that there is only one morality, created by society, but which may be thought either *theologically* or *positively*, that is with reference either to God or to society. . . . The difference is in the form of the representation, not in its object. . . . And how could positive morality fail to act upon men's hearts, since at the basis of religion, there is unknown to it the action upon individual consciences of the collective conscience? [46]

Two men were above all others instrumental in the diffusion of Durkheimian sociology and social philosophy throughout the educational system: Louis Liard and Paul Lapie. In addition to the contexts in which he has already been mentioned, Liard had a hand in the introduction of Durkheimism in secondary schools before World War I. Furthermore, he invited Durkheim to lecture at the Ecole Normale Supérieure to candidates for the *agrégation*. From these lectures came the posthumously published *Evolution pédagogique en France* (1938). Paul Lapie came under Durkheim's influence as a professor at Bordeaux, and he subsequently became an active member of the *Année sociologique* school. He continued Durkheim's work as Director of Primary Education, rector of the Academy of Paris, and editor of the *Revue pédagogique*. After World War I, his great innovation

[45] Duveau, pp. 117–118.
[46] Félix Pécaut, "Emile Durkheim," *Revue pédagogique,* n.s., LXXII (1918), 14–15.

was the introduction of Durkheimian sociology into the curriculum of *instituteurs* in the state normal schools. Thus Durkheim's
ideas could be found at all levels of the educational system. A
critic of the time observed: "The requirement that M. Durkheim's sociology be taught in the two hundred normal schools
of France is among the gravest perils to which our country is
subjected." [47] Even the sharp and witty Thibaudet remarked, in
his *République des professeurs*:

The introduction of the teaching of sociology in our normal schools for
instituteurs by Paul Lapie, upright and militant layman [*laïque*], the
lineal descendent of the Buisson, Pécaut, and Steeg of the Republic,
marked a most important date on the sundial of republican spiritual
power. Through this measure, the state, in its schools, furnished to
instituteurs what the Church in its seminaries furnished to the adversaries of the *instituteurs:* a theology. Lapie believed that the *instituteurs* would react critically to this teaching. Not at all. They reacted
theologically.[48]

To appreciate the element of truth in Thibaudet's characterization of the function of Durkheimism among *instituteurs,* one
need only read the actual statement of a teacher who enunciated
the lesson he derived from Durkheim: " 'Durkheim?' certain people
sneer. 'That no longer catches on. Speak to us of neo-Thomism.'
I'm not disturbed by this attitude. The vain resurrection of old
medieval catechisms will long have disappeared when Durkheimism will still be standing." [49]

The personalities and ideas of the professor-philosopher-admin-
istrators Liard and Lapie show the extent of their affinity with
Durkheim.[50] Louis Liard is often credited with having made

[47] Jean Izoulet; quoted in Célestin Bouglé, *Bilan de la sociologie française contemporaine* (Paris: Alcan, 1935), p. 168n.

[48] Albert Thibaudet, *La République des professeurs* (Paris: Grasset,
1927), pp. 222–223.

[49] Maublanc, "L'Oeuvre sociologique d'Emile Durkheim," p. 303.

[50] On Liard, see Ernest Lavisse, "Louis Liard," *Revue internationale de
l'enseignement,* LXXII (1918), 81–89; see also G. Ribière, *Revue des cours
et des conférences,* XII (1904), 1–13, 49–65, 97–113, 145–161, 193–200,

over the universities in France almost singlehandedly. In his *Souvenirs d'une petite enfance,* Liard described with warmth his adolescence in Falaise, Normandy: his love for churches built in the Middle Ages, the wooden houses dating from the fifteenth century, the ruins of the castle of the dukes of Normandy, and above all the old *collège* built in the shadow of the ancient fortress. His own *instituteurs* instilled in him a taste for study through their selfless devotion to a calling devoid of personal ambition and a concern for getting ahead.[51]

In 1866 (with the same promotion as Buisson), Liard entered the Ecole Normale Supérieure and became a disciple of Jules Lachelier, and, through him, of Renouvier. Liard's thesis, "Geometrical Definitions and Empirical Definitions," was an excellent expression of the Cartesianized neo-Kantianism of the Republic; it was dedicated to Lachelier. Another work, *Positive Science and Metaphysics* (1878), centered on the idea that "to negate the reality of the ideal is to negate our own reality." Liard went on to argue in very Durkheimian fashion that "the social function of metaphysics is to keep up the faith in an ideal and to arrest two contrary but equally deadly errors: the weakening of activity and utilitarian fever." [52]

Under the Second Empire, Liard had been so militantly repub-

which includes an extensive analysis of Liard's published works. On Lapie, see the statements by Célestin Bouglé, Félix Pécaut, André Fontaine, and Xavier Léon in the *Revue pédagogique,* XC–XCI (1927), 115–166.

[51] Many people realized the extent to which the mystique of the *instituteur* was the symbolic recompense for the fact that he was miserably underpaid. In a circular to *instituteurs* in 1833, François Guizot remarked: "The resources which the central power has at its disposal will never succeed in making the simple profession of *instituteur* as attractive as it is useful. Society is unable to give back to those who consecrate themselves to it all that they have done for it. It is necessary that a profound sentiment support and animate the *instituteur,* that the austere pleasure of having served men and contributed to the public good become the worthy salary which his conscience alone gives him. It is his glory to exhaust himself in sacrifices and expect his recompense from God alone" (quoted in Duveau, p. 54).

[52] Quoted in Ribière, pp. 49, 65.

lican that he was dismissed from his first teaching position and kept constantly under the surveillance of the imperial police. When he became, like Durkheim and Lapie after him, a professor at Bordeaux, he was overwhelmed by the parlous state of higher education. In his *Histoire de l'enseignement supérieur* (*History of Higher Education*), he described how courses were opened up to the general public in order to fill seats for which there were not enough students. The audience recruited in this way was a curious medley of *bon bourgeois* with nothing to do and beggars in search of a warm place for a few hours. Liard's taste for organization manifested itself at Bordeaux, where he not only recast the structure of his own courses but drew up plans for the new Faculty of Medicine and Pharmacy. He followed "always the same method: *a priori* determination of the needs of each Faculty in order to deduce the proper installations." In Liard's own words, "The method of my administrative work has always been the Cartesian method." [53] At the request of Ferry, the post of Director of Higher Education which was vacated in 1884 was filled by Liard. " 'You will make the French universities,' Jules Ferry had told him. That was exactly what he wanted to do." [54] Subsequently (1902–1917), Liard was rector of the University of Paris, a position in which Lapie was to succeed him. If the method of his administrative work was Cartesian, its guiding principle was a variant of Durkheim's "organic solidarity." From the lowest to the highest level and throughout all departments and faculties, the University of France was to be characterized by solidaristic cooperation among its differentiated parts in order to ensure "the realization of a superior function—the intellectual and moral life of the nation." [55]

Like Durkheim, Liard had been left fatherless very early in life. His mother, of old Norman stock, was tender and austere, and lived constantly with the idea of death. She had even se-

[53] Lavisse, pp. 86–87.   [54] Lavisse, p. 88.
[55] Quoted in Ribière, p. 9.

lected the wood for her coffin. "She taught her son that one thing was worse than death. Watching a funeral procession pass by in front of them, she said: 'I would rather see you buried than see you fail to do your duty.' " [56] After a life of duty and devotion to a cause, Liard experienced World War I as an unbearable shock which hastened his death. He consented to being confined to bed only when "the categorical imperative commanded him to retire." In 1917, he died of "total exhaustion." [57]

The son of an *instituteur*, Paul Lapie retained throughout his life the mystique of the educator's calling with which his father had imbued him. André Fontaine recalled that when Lapie was first appointed a *lycée* professor, Fontaine had remarked: "I don't know what Lapie's career will be, but I see him very well in the position of Liard. . . . At that time as always I believed Liard to be the greatest university leader we have ever had." [58] As a professor at Bordeaux and as a high administrative official, Lapie continued to seek the society of humble *instituteurs*, and he genuinely shared their *sérieux de la vie*. He combined the typical republican personality traits of an austere exterior and repressed sentiment: for him too the categorical imperative was a sort of symbolic father. Félix Pécaut recalled the impact on republican intellectuals of Lapie's editorial in the *Revue pédagogique* "entitled 'Soyons durs' ['Let's Be Hard']. Hard on ourselves—that goes without saying." [59] On the desk in his office Lapie kept a photograph of Victor Brochard, a blind paralytic teacher who continued to give his courses until his death.

Lapie made trips to The Hague to honor the memory of perhaps his favorite philosopher, Spinoza. His thesis was entitled "The Logic of the Will." In it, he defended the proposition that the will in the service of reason always tends toward justice and self-sacrifice. Needless to say, he rejected the utilitarian corre-

[56] Lavisse, pp. 82–83.   [57] Lavisse, pp. 98–99.
[58] Fontaine, *Revue pédagogique*, XC–XCI (1927), 165.
[59] Pécaut, *ibid.*, pp. 122–123.

lation of reason, will, and self-interest. Under the influence of Durkheim at Bordeaux, Lapie became attached to the idea that logic and social ethics had to be sociologically fed by facts and comparative analyses. He went on to write *Tunisian Civilization, Women and the Family, For Reason* (on the rationalist function of secular education), and, after the Dreyfus Affair, *Justice through the State*. In the last work, Lapie argued that the role of the state was not to increase its own power or to maximize individual economic activity. It was to assure the reign of justice. Judicial authority was the very prototype of legitimate public authority in the struggle against injustice. This doctrine implied the necessity of an economic "magistracy" of the state to further social justice.

A tireless worker, Lapie "was hard to the point of dying from it, and when he finally consented to being confined to bed, it was never to rise again." [60] On his deathbed, Lapie uttered the sentence: "This bed tyrannizes over me." [61] One of the last times Lapie left home in spite of severe illness was to go to the Société Française de Philosophie to hear a report on the teaching of French in Buenos Aires.

A personality type emerges almost of its own accord from these sketches of republican educators and intellectuals who were Durkheim's peers. But a bit more attention must be paid to their attitudes and ideas. Within the relatively stabilized context of the Third Republic, Durkheim and his peers constituted a reform group that sought structural consensus without resort to violent revolution. The *Weltanschauung* of republican leaders was an amalgam of liberal democracy, neo-Kantian spiritualism, and "an immense and grave patriotism, a passionate and somewhat sad attachment to a *patrie* which they wished to make more beautiful, greater, more worthy, and more self-conscious than it is." [62] The Republic was not only the bureaucratic

---

[60] Léon, *ibid.*, p. 160.   [61] Fontaine, *ibid.*, p. 166.

[62] André Canivez, *Jules Lagneau: Essai sur la condition du professeur de philosophie jusqu'à la fin du XIXe siècle,* Association des Publications de la

provider of careers to satisfy all legitimate ambitions; it was to provide "a great and efficacious lesson in moral dignity." [63] The moral philosophy of Kant, which was dominant among republican intellectuals, had received its more Cartesian, readily assimilable, and socially relevant formulation in the works of Charles Renouvier. Indeed, the ideas of Renouvier played for the short-lived democratic republic of 1848 a role similar to the ideas of Durkheim in the Third Republic. For what it was worth, a contemporary *mot* had it that "Durkheimism is still Kantianism but reviewed and completed by Comteanism." [64]

The resultant was a crystallization of the archetypical idea of the republican institution which would assure social consensus and solidarity through a coordination of the educational system, the occupational sphere, and the state under the supreme auspices of a humanistic, universalistic public philosophy. Within this ideological context, one can see clearly emerging an ecumenical spirit in religion and philosophy as well as a reorientation of liberal Protestantism in the direction of civic consciousness, community spirit, and even a socially, morally, and aesthetically grounded interest in ritual. Moral philosophy increasingly became the religion of mass democracy and its conception of the essence of all religion. The Enlightenment nexus of *philosophe* and citizen replaced the medieval union of priest and king and, one might add, the more primitive bond between poet and sorcerer.

The pedagogical effect was the perception of moral education as the common core of all education. And sociology, for Durkheim, had an intimate relation to pedagogy insofar as sociology

---

Faculté de Strasbourg, 1965, p. 275. See also Claude Digeon, *La Crise allemande de la pensée française, 1870–1914* (Paris: Presses Universitaires de France, 1959).

[63] Speech of Paul Armand Challemel-Lacour before the Senate, Dec. 19, 1888; as quoted in Maurice Barrès, *Les Déracinés*, I (first pub. 1897; Paris: Plon, 1959), 64.

[64] Reported by Bouglé, "L'Oeuvre sociologique d'Emile Durkheim," p. 283.

was a groundwork for moral education. Durkheim took as his own special task the attempt to "discover the rational substitutes for these religious notions which for so long have served as the vehicle for the most essential of moral ideas." [65] But a rational conception of morality could not merely cut away religious beliefs. The one Comtean dictum Durkheim always upheld was the idea that one should destroy only what one could replace. Although Durkheim at first conceived his project as an attempt to present moral forces in their "rational nudity . . . without recourse to any mythological intermediary," his idea of rationalism was later expanded to include a type of mythology which, in his eyes, complemented reason instead of contradicting it. Society itself, in his thought, emerged at times as a mythical entity.

Within the republican institution and its rationalist cult, the function of the teacher as a consensus builder became central. As Durkheim saw it, the teacher's mission was to select and disseminate "those principles which in spite of all divergences are from this time on the basis of our civilization, implicitly or explicitly common to all, and which few would dare to deny: respect for reason, for science, for the ideas and sentiments which are the basis of our democratic morality." [66] The aura of mystique which enveloped this conception of the educator's function is difficult to convey. In a magnificent phrase of Canivez, the classroom was "le lieu de discours retenus" (the place for hushed discourse).[67] For Durkheim as for so many other republican intellectuals, the teacher gathered up in his chalk-marked hands the lingering strands of the sacerdotal tradition:

What constitutes the authority which colors so readily the word of the priest is the elevated idea he has of his mission; for he speaks in the name of a god in whom he believes and to whom he feels closer than the crowd of the profane. The lay teacher can and must have some-

[65] Emile Durkheim, *L'Education morale* (first pub. 1925; Paris: Presses Universitaires de France, 1963), pp. 3, 9, 7–8.

[66] Emile Durkheim, *Education et sociologie* (Paris: Alcan, 1922), p. 62.

[67] Canivez, p. 275.

thing of this sentiment. He too is the organ of a great moral person who transcends him: this is society. Just as the priest is the interpreter of his god, so the teacher is the interpreter of the great moral ideas of his time and country.[68]

Thus the unique, symbolically charged contribution of Durkheim to republican ideas was the elaboration of a relatively consistent theory of morality as the institutional and ideological basis of solidarity in society. Not all republican intellectuals who constituted Durkheim's privileged audience agreed with this conception of morality. The *fine fleur* of French neo-Kantian spiritualism subjected Durkheim to a constant barrage of criticism, including face-to-face encounters in the Société Française de Philosophie. This reaction to Durkheim manifested the tenuous basis of consensual public philosophy among educators in a country like France, where despite—or perhaps because of— the extremely centralized and bureaucratized educational system, thinkers have a penchant for dialectical disagreement if only for the sake of marginal differentiation. Durkheim's celebrated "Détermination du fait moral" of 1906 (included in his *Sociologie et philosophie*) provoked an extensive "oui, mais" type of discussion which covered approximately one hundred densely printed pages of the *Bulletin de la Société Française de Philosophie*. The evocation of his own *lycée* education by the last of Durkheim's truly militant disciples in France, Armand Cuvillier, is significant in this respect. Instead of concentrating on the social context of morality in Durkheimian fashion, his philosophy professor, the gadfly Gustave Belot, would direct his "sarcasms against the '*conscience collective*' which he called '*l'inconscience collective*' and against those states of primitive conformism where 'everybody admits what no one has really thought.' " [69]

The criticisms of Durkheim by his contemporaries were often cogent and induced by the ambiguities of Durkheim himself,

[68] *L'Education morale*, pp. 72–73.

[69] Armand Cuvillier, *Où va la sociologie française?* (Paris: Librairie Marcel Rivière, 1953), p. 42.

which at times were great enough to qualify him as whipping boy in introductory philosophy classes. Subsequent criticisms have often unknowingly recapitulated ideas of Durkheim's own peers. Indeed, the charge of sophistry had sufficient staying power to receive an echo in Raymond Aron's 1967 analysis of Durkheim's thought.[70] But something more must have been involved in the reluctance of Durkheim's contemporaries to separate his basic point of view from the terminological husk in which it often was conveyed.

The fundamental reason was that members of the republican elite were often committed to spiritual and moral variants of extreme individualism which at times implied a secularized Protestant metaphysic. The relationship between the individual and the ideal was conceived on the model of an unmediated nexus having little to do with solidarity in society. This tendency was manifested in the influential metaphysic of Bergson's *Two Sources of Religion and Morality* (1932), written partially in reaction to Durkheim's *Elementary Forms of the Religious Life* (1912). And one found the taste for the individualism of an inwardness transcending society even in the doctrine of Alain, with its practical reformulation of the Cartesian mind-body dualism. Alain presented the role of the individual in society as a negative conformism which said "yes" with the body to external constraints, but an eternal, soul-saving "no" with the spirit. Such notions generated resistance to Durkheim's idea that society was a solidary whole greater than the sum of its parts and to the analytic concepts which made theoretical sense of this idea: social structure, *conscience collective* as its psychological ground in the personality, norm, and type. Durkheim, in brief, tended to root Kant's noumenal sphere in the *conscience collective* of society and to situate the transcendental ego as a subject communicating with other subjects in society. The horrified reaction of a thinker who was perhaps the best technical

[70] *Les Etapes de la pensée sociologique* (Paris: Gallimard, 1967), pp. 394ff.

philosopher of his time in France set the tone. In a letter to Durkheim's own philosophy professor Emile Boutroux, Jules Lachelier wrote of an earlier theorist of solidarity:

You must have read in the *Revue philosophique* a very curious article of Marion on the prehistoric family. All that, as I told you the other evening, is frightening, and when it has really come to pass, we must insist that it has not come to pass, that history is an illusion and the past a projection and that there is nothing true except the absolute. There we have perhaps the solution of the problem of the miracle: it is the legend which is true and history which is false.[71]

The intellectual and academic *cause célèbre* of Durkheim's own day, which opposed him to a prominent figure of the Republic, moved on a level less elevated than that of the absolute and often less interesting than that which separated history and legend. This was his notorious debate with Gabriel Tarde, which, like the great debates in the scholastic tradition that it evoked, divided students into two hostile intellectual camps. In contrast with Durkheim's focus upon social structure and impersonal processes in history, Tarde's stress was on the spontaneity and inventiveness of the innovative individual.[72] Yet—as Charles Blondel has shown in detail in his *Introduction à la psychologie collective*—the heat of personality and dialectic frequently prevented Durkheim and Tarde from realizing the extent to which their problems were complementary. In fact, the thought of the early Durkheim and of his opponent Tarde (who died in 1904) represented two halves of a divided entity—the exteriority and constraint of formal institutions and the repressed emotion and inwardness of the individual personality. Only after Tarde's death did Durkheim seem to recognize the "pathogenic" nature of this dichotomy in its extreme forms and propose a model of

[71] Letter of Jan. 1, 1878, "Lettres," Bibliothèque Nationale.

[72] For a brief analysis of Tarde's thought which attempts to show how Tarde was much more than the theorist of the "laws of imitation," see the introduction by Terry N. Clark to *Gabriel Tarde on Communication and Social Influence* (Chicago: University of Chicago Press, 1969).

the "normal" society which combined normative discipline with spontaneous commitment, and the internalization of norms with a margin of anomie that allowed for individual creativity.

The substantive issues involved in the Durkheim-Tarde debate were compromised by a severe personality conflict. Tarde himself was very much the grasshopper to the neo-Kantian ant in Durkheim. His career pattern and style of thought were quite different from those of Durkheim. In contrast with Durkheim, who regularly ascended through the "normal" institutional channels to a professorship at the Sorbonne, Tarde moved laterally from the extra-academic vantage point of a high place in the French magistracy and salon society into the penthouse of the French scholarly world: the Collège de France. His more flamboyant way of life had its counterpart in the carefree, essayistic, and almost impressionistic style of the works in which he developed his idea of the role of the individual in society. As Charles Blondel has aptly put it:

[Tarde] does not have the superstition of order and logic: he writes notes, articles, and, gathering them together, he inserts a few joints and makes of the whole a book. A certain dilettantism gives him the ability to smile and dictates to him the most alert and piquant formulas on the gravest subjects: "Obedience to duty offers two advantages: it absolves you often of the need for prudence [prévoyance] and always of the need for success." [73]

If the controversies opposing Durkheim to republican intellectuals seem in retrospect to have the air of family quarrels, the opposition manifested on the Right was more serious and deeply rooted. The Right in Durkheim's France was a complex phenomenon which an outstanding analytic historian of the period has treated in terms of "anti-revolutionary forces which were negative enough to want to go back to the years before 1789, and the counter-revolutionary forces, which accepted some fruits of the

[73] *Introduction à la psychologie collective* (first pub. 1927; Paris: Armand Colin, 1964), p. 37. This neglected work contains an excellent comparison of Comte, Durkheim, and Tarde.

Revolution but reacted against certain of its historical consequences." [74]

The more intransigent and doctrinaire antirevolutionary forces
found their theoretical forebears in traditionalists like Maistre
and Bonald. These conservatives à outrance, who formed, in
Comte's famous phrase, the "Immortal Retrograde School" of
social theory, became (at times along with Comte himself) the
inspiration for later reactionary movements such as the Action
Française. Charles Maurras, the founder of this movement, was
of course a self-styled disciple of Comte. Born in the opposition
to the Dreyfusard victory, the Action Française not only mobilized forces hostile to Durkheim's Republic ("la gueuse"—"the
slut"—the favorite epithet of Maurras) but eventually became
a mainstay of the Vichy government. The Third Republic of
Durkheim's time was, moreover, the locus not only of the traditional currents of Jacobin and liberal patriotism on the Left and
of anti-Dreyfusard "integral nationalism" on the Right but also
of a newer and more radical nationalism which began to manifest itself about 1905 and reached its prewar climax in 1911.
For a historian of this movement, it was the result of oneup-
manship in patriotic assertions (from which only the Socialist
Party managed to refrain), and it was socially based in the
lower middle classes of Paris before spreading to the provinces
after the Agadir incident.[75] Thus to some extent the protofascist
nationalism which was to feed the "league" movement after
World War I had its origins in the prewar period.

Those who placed Durkheim in the tradition of such conservative thinkers as Maistre and Bonald—not to speak of fascism—
were not only totally insensitive to Durkheim's own historical
context but prone to mistake superficial analogies for profound

[74] Thomson, pp. 27–28. See also the complementary, farther ranging
(if less historically tight) analysis by René Rémond of changing manifestations of traditionalist, conservative-liberal, and nationalist tendencies, La
Droite en France (Paris: Aubier, 1963).

[75] Eugen Weber, The Nationalist Revival in France, 1905–1914 (Berkeley
and Los Angeles: University of California Press, 1959).

historical continuities.[76] Certainly, Durkheim stressed such themes as community, authority, and the desirability of a significant measure of historical continuity. But in his thought they were related to a reformist project. The substantive context into which Durkheim integrated these themes was that of republican democracy and individual autonomy permitting free acceptance of normative structures involving, not rigid hierarchy, but participation and representation. The intellectual feat of Durkheim was to attempt to disengage certain general, if not universal, values such as community and the need for social discipline from reactionary historical longings and to reconcile these values with specifically modern needs, thereby averting such "sociological monstrosities" as later emerged in fascism.

The counterrevolutionary movement in Durkheim's France took the forms of liberalism and Bonapartism in politics and of liberal Catholicism in religion. More pragmatic in tenor than the antirevolutionary movement, it resisted only selected aspects of the Revolution, whose social and economic implications were opposed by liberalism, and democratic and liberal implications by Bonapartism. Liberal Catholics demanded the right of the

[76] For the argument relating Durkheim to conservatives and traditionalists, see Robert Nisbet, "Conservatism and Sociology," *American Journal of Sociology,* LVIII (1952), 165–175. The theme of Durkheim's conservatism was muted in Nisbet's long essay in *Emile Durkheim* (Englewood Cliffs, N.J.: Prentice-Hall, 1965) and his *Sociological Tradition* (New York: Basic Books, 1966). An important idea adumbrated in "Conservatism and Sociology" is not further developed in Nisbet's two later works. (It is discussed in Nisbet's foreword to *The Works of Joseph de Maistre,* trans. and introd. by Jack Lively [first pub. 1965; N.Y.: Schoken Books, 1971], pp. xi–xviii.) This is the idea of philosophical conservatism. Nisbet argues that a thinker may have conservative values although he does not defend the status quo or reaction. It is in this philosophical sense, I think, that Durkheim was conservative. For the assertion of Durkheim's relation to "integral nationalism," see M. M. Mitchell, "Emile Durkheim and the Philosophy of Nationalism," *Political Science Quarterly,* XLVI (1931), 87–106. See also George Catlin's introduction to Durkheim's *Rules of Sociological Method* (first pub. 1938; N.Y.: Free Press, 1964). For the charge of irrationalism and protofascism, see William M. McGovern, *From Luther to Hitler* (London: George G. Harrap, 1946), chap. ix.

disestablished Church to run its own schools. Since any extensive analysis would be beyond the scope of this study, it is sufficient to note that the more liberal demands (manifested in Pope Leo XIII's call for *ralliement* of Catholics to the Republic and Marc Sangnier's social idealism) received little implementation in the Church in Durkheim's time. The alliance of the far Right and the Catholic Church which continued the reactionary alliance of throne and altar confronted the newly formed Republic with extremist obduracy. It was met in kind, with the predictable result that both sides tended to escalate their demands in a bitter syndrome of action and reaction. "Church and State were torn apart, not neatly separated: and political bitterness was fed with new fuel." [77]

The threat from the far Right before the Dreyfus Affair was aggravated by the fact that the military and upper echelons of the state bureaucracy (including the Conseil d'Etat at the highest level) were staffed in significant numbers by men of reactionary leanings. As Alain put it, with some exaggeration, in 1906: "In France, there are a great number of radical voters, a certain number of radical deputies, and a very small number of radical ministers: as for the *chefs de service,* they are all reactionary. The person who understands this well holds the key to our politics." [78] The ultimate clash between the Right (merging the forces of the Church, the Army, the upper bureaucracy, and anti-Semitism) and the Republic (momentarily coalescing the forces of the Left) was of course the Dreyfus Affair. David Thomson has summarized the core issue in this confrontation, which appeared as an apocalyptic moment of truth to all the adversaries:

The fact that Dreyfus was a Jew, and that his condemnation led to a wider drive by the authoritarian militarists and clericals to exclude not merely Jews but Protestants and Republicans from positions of military and administrative power, raised the issue in dramatic form.

[77] Thomson, p. 143.
[78] *Eléments d'une doctrine radicale* (Paris: Gallimard, 1925), p. 25.

It was a clash of rival absolutisms—a challenge of intolerance which bred an equally severe intolerance amongst the Radicals and Free-masons, the anti-clericals and Socialists. Democracy had clearly to be a social and political order based on common citizenship and civilian rights within the Republic: or else it would be replaced by an authoritarian, hierarchic order, dominated by Church and privileged ruling classes in Army and Civil Service. French logic interpreted the conflict in these clear terms, and the battle began.[79]

A crucial long-range problem involved in the ideological confrontation of the Right and the Republic was the control of education. "The separation [of Church and State] was only the negative part of an ideal of which the positive part, or rather the counterpart, implied the reunion of the school and the State." [80] The effort of the Republic to purge the Church from the educational system engendered the related problems of teachers, curriculum, and moral education. The clergy and its spiritual influence had to be replaced. We have noted Durkheim's priestly conception of the lay teacher—the "black Hussar" of the Republic, in Charles Péguy's telling phrase. With respect to the curriculum, it is important to recognize the historical correlation of classical education and conservatism in Durkheim's France. This association led a contemporary observer to quip that the Republic faced two "social questions": the relation of capital and labor and Latin verse.[81] The historical association of the defense of a classical education, of conservative politics, and of a highly stratified social order was the concrete basis for Durkheim's sustained attacks upon dilettantism and Renaissance humanism as antimodern tendencies subservient to the interests of a small elite. Durkheim's conception of reform comprised the democratization of education and a curriculum which would give students, along with a necessary background in general culture, the type of training which would prepare them for special-

[79] Thomson, p. 141.   [80] Thibaudet, p. 196.
[81] Alfred Fouillée, "La Réforme de l'enseignement philosophique et moral en France," Revue des deux mondes, XXXIX (1880), 333–369.

ized functions in modern society. Yet it has not been recognized to how great an extent the spirit of classical philosophy remained the foundation of Durkheim's social philosophy. *Suicide,* with its emphasis on the sense of legitimate limits and its intimation of an institutionally furthered "golden mean" in social life, is Greek in basic conception.

It is synoptically useful though excessively stereotypical to frame the question of the relation of Durkheim's Republic to the Church in terms of contrasts: *instituteur* versus *curé;* social and natural science versus the classics; social and moral philosophy versus old-time religion. In any case, a further point must be made concerning Durkheim's position on the church-state controversy and the battle over education: he never made an express political pronouncement on this issue. He indeed labeled the Catholic Church "a monstrosity from the sociological point of view." [82] But he directed this comment against the extremely bureaucratic, centralized, and hierarchical organizational structure of the Church. In the same vein, he put forth a critique which applied to his own Republic: "A society composed of an infinite dust of unorganized individuals which an hypertrophied state tries to hem in and restrain constitutes a veritable sociological monstrosity." [83] His positive concern in both instances was the creation of small groups in which communal values would be reconciled with institutional organization.

In addition, one did not find in Durkheim the offended, vengeful spirit of the ex-seminarian Emile Combes or the crude positivism embodied in Paul Bert's comparisons of the clergy to the phylloxera blight which destroyed the vines of France, and of the law imposing restrictive state regulation on religious establishments to healing copper sulfate. Nothing was more alien to Durkheim's spirit than penny-ante Voltairianism. The basic in-

---

[82] "Associations de culte," *Libres Entretiens,* 1st series (Paris: Bureau des "Libres Entretiens"), p. 369.

[83] Preface to 2d ed., *De La Division du travail social* (7th ed.; Paris: Presses Universitaires de France, 1960), p. xxxii.

spiration of Durkheim's conception of religion was ecumenical. And he ultimately recognized, however tendentiously, the necessity of special symbolisms of a mythical nature insofar as they complemented rather than contradicted the general rational values basic to consensus in modern society. For different reasons, the social metaphysic which was his own ultimate explanatory approach to religious symbolism was offensive both to students of culture who saw religion analytically "from the outside" and to believers who experienced religion "from the inside." But the practical thrust of his thought within his own historical context was to offer the Church the same sort of living arrangement it had offered to prior religions in occupied territory: tolerance for their symbolic forms if they accepted its basic message. Catholicism, in other words, had to become a nondisruptive part of a larger social consensus.

The classical conservative indictment of the Republic, its philosophy, and its corps of *instituteurs* was *Les Déracinés* (*The Uprooted*) of Maurice Barrès. But the best illustration of Rightest reaction to Durkheim himself and his particular role in the Republic was the report of "Agathon," the pseudonym of Henri Massis and the son of Gabriel Tarde, the more status-conscious Alfred de Tarde. This work [84] was manifestly inspired by conservative politics, traditional religion, activist nationalism, and a romanticized, socially elitist defense of classical education. It claimed to represent the dominant opinion of French university students immediately before World War I.

For the authors of the Agathon Report, Liard had made Durkheim "a sort of prefect of studies, . . . the regent of the Sorbonne, the all-powerful *maître*." Durkheim's position on key committees like the Conseil de l'Université de Paris and the Comité Consultatif enabled him "to survey all appointments in higher education." Under his iron rule, professors of philosophy

---

[84] *L'Esprit de la nouvelle Sorbonne* (Paris: Mercure de France, 1911). See also the same authors' less interesting *Les Jeunes Gens d'aujourd'hui* (Paris: Plon, 1913).

were "reduced to the simple role of functionaries." Pedagogy was Durkheim's "own private domain." But sociology was before all else the "one official doctrine at the Sorbonne." Sociology had taken the place of the old philosophy which had fallen from grace. It had become 'the kingpin of the New Sorbonne." Moving from the conspiratorial indictment to the rhetorical question, the authors of the Agathon Report concluded by asking: "Who is there that does not feel the truly inhuman quality in this debauchery of logic, these cold and deductive reveries, these misty analyses of concepts, and what poor food is offered to the avid heart and intelligence of students?" [85]

Attitudes toward Durkheim constituted one area in which extremes found *ad hoc* consensus in France. The standard Marxist categorization of Durkheim was that of "bourgeois Idealist," and the terms of criticism frequently coincided with those of the Agathon Report. The most sustained, if savagely rhetorical, treatment of Durkheim and his milieu by (at least a *pro tempore*) French Communist close to the controversies of the time was in Paul Nizan's *Chiens de garde* ("The Watchdogs") of 1932.[86] In this youthful book, Nizan rewrote Marx's *German Ideology* to make it apply to intellectual and educational leaders in the Third Republic. One of the most viciously unobtrusive of the "watchdogs" of the Republic was Durkheim, the *"maître* of the Moral Fact."

Durkheim was necessary for the bourgeois university to enter into possession of its own doctrines: this strengthening of the spiritual situation, this passage from the vague to the dogmatic, from the obscure to the distinct, is rather well expressed in Durkheim's declaration to Agathon in November 1906: "Let's get to work and in three years we'll have a morality." They had it all right. This morality exists. . . . Everything really happened as if the founder of French sociology wrote the *Division of Labor in Society* to permit obscure administrators to compose a course of instruction destined for the *instituteurs*. The

[85] *L'Esprit de la nouvelle Sorbonne*, pp. 99, 101–102, 110.
[86] Paris: Maspero.

introduction of sociology into the normal schools consecrated the administrative victory of official morality. . . . In the name of this science *instituteurs* teach children to respect the French *patrie,* to justify class collaboration, to accept everything, to commune in the cult of the flag and bourgeois democracy. . . . The manuals [of the Durkheim school], among other works, manifest the power of diffusion of this doctrine of obedience, of conformism, and of social respect which, with the years, has obtained such credit and such a numerous audience.[87]

To engage in rhetorical overstatement and to dismiss Durkheim *in toto* as yet one more "bourgeois idealist" or airy house ideologue of the status quo was to lose sight of what he actually accomplished. A real problem for an existentially relevant, living Marxism was the selective assimilation of the valid insights of a Durkheim. But it is difficult not to sympathize with critics who found in Durkheim excessive abstractness, naïve social optimism, and tendentious vagueness often combined with dogmatic assertion. Despite his growing concern with modern "social pathology," one problem Durkheim never broached in his pedagogical works was the possibility that a school system in which teachers selected and disseminated consensual ideals might find itself specializing in the transmission of the type of myth that blinded people to social realities and laid inadequate factual bases for social reform. No doubt, Durkheim's own position in the educational establishment contributed to the fact that the treatment of the difficult problem of means to effect the reforms he envisaged was perhaps the weakest chapter in his thought about modern society. He was forever vague about the type of practical activity that was related both to the acquisition of concrete knowledge and to the project of changing society in a desirable direction. An open reckoning with Marx would have deepened Durkheim's penetration into modern institutions and ideologies. At the very least, it would have forced him to treat more adequately the role of economic factors and social con-

[87] *Ibid.,* pp. 109–110.

flict in modern life. Yet in his sole extended discussion of Marxism (in a review of a work by Antonio Labriola), Durkheim took special pains to insist that he had "not in the least undergone the influence of Marx." [88] Indeed the influence of Durkheim in French social thought was one reason why a systematic and detailed confrontation with Marx in France was delayed until the 1930's.

What precisely was Durkheim's position in the spectrum of practical politics? Marcel Mauss has characterized Durkheim's relationship to socialism in the following terms:

Durkheim was quite familiar with socialism at its very sources, through Saint-Simon, Schaeffle, and Karl Marx whom a Finnish friend, Neiglick, had advised him to study during his stay in Leipzig. All his life he was reluctant to adhere to socialism (properly so-called) because of certain features of this movement: its violent nature, its class character —more or less workingmen's—and therefore its political and even politician-like tone. Durkheim was profoundly opposed to all wars of class or nation. He desired change only for the benefit of the whole of society and not of one of its parts—even if the latter had numbers and force. He considered political revolutions and parliamentary evolution as superficial, costly, and more dramatic than serious. He therefore always resisted the idea of submitting himself to a party of political discipline, especially an international one. Even the social and political crisis of the Dreyfus Affair, in which he played a large part, did not change his opinion. He therefore remained uncommitted—he "sympathized" (as it is now called) with the socialists, with Jaurès, with socialism. But he never gave himself to it.[89]

This précis of Durkheim's attitude toward socialism by his nephew and colleague must nonetheless be qualified. For one thing, Durkheim's ideas on the possibilities of corporatism in modern society included certain features of democratic social-

[88] *Revue philosophique*, LXIV (1897), 647. On this problem, see Armand Cuvillier, "Durkheim et Marx," *Cahiers internationaux de sociologie*, IV (1948), 75–97.

[89] Introd., 1st ed., Emile Durkheim, *Le Socialisme*, in *Socialism*, pp. 34–35.

ism. Durkheim definitely did not subscribe to any existing socialist viewpoint, but he did attempt to offer a substitute for existing viewpoints which, he felt, integrated their desirable, and avoided their undesirable, aspects. He apparently did not believe in the necessity or desirability of apocalyptic, violent revolution in his own society or advanced industrial societies in general. But he did see a strong element of value in the French Revolution, although like Tocqueville he was aware of the respects in which traits of the *ancien régime* continued into the present despite the Revolution. The Revolution had failed to realize its ideals in institutions, but these ideals, which depended for their genesis and formulation on social unrest of revolutionary proportions, were of lasting value in modern society. And a democratic republic, which itself was a long-delayed fruit of the Revolution, found a lifelong supporter in Durkheim.

On the whole, it would be accurate to say that Durkheim found parliamentary evolution superficial when politics belied the promise of democracy by remaining within the structural confines that detached it from the real problems of society. To a large extent, politics in his own France did increasingly fall into this category as the years wore on. Toward the end of his life, Durkheim seemed to realize this. He contrasted, we are told, the youthful hopes engendered by the golden age of the Republic with the actual nature of politics circa 1914:

The "political kitchen" was always odious to him and he avoided questions of personality and coterie. Gambetta was to some extent his idol: if he liked him so much, I think it was because of the large and generous spirit he found in him. Chatting with Durkheim in 1914, I heard him complain that politics had become "a very small and mediocre thing." He had always wanted it to be grand: that was the way he saw it in his youth.[90]

In another respect, it did not do to classify socialism as violent and purely working-class in Durkheim's time. Indeed the com-

[90] M. Holleaux, quoted in Davy, "Emile Durkheim: L'Homme," *Revue de métaphysique et de morale*, XXVI (1919), 189.

plexity of socialism and of the problems to which it sought an answer had a great deal to do with Durkheim's hesitancy. In his own France, there was, for example, a measure of cooperation between the relatively small, weak, and internally divided trade-union movement and the parliamentary Socialist Party (composed mainly of bourgeois). But there was no thoroughgoing integration on the model of the British Labour Party. The more violent strand of socialism, with its doctrinaire insistence upon class conflict and *la lutte finale,* was taken up by anarchosyndicalism. Georges Sorel became its ex post facto theorist by borrowing from Marx's theory of classes and Durkheim's ideas on religion in a manner which was faithful to neither Marx nor Durkheim. The upshot was a lyrical eulogy of the "myth of the general strike" and the "poetry of social violence" which were to provide effervescent energy for a working class in movement. Sorel's position came close to a despairing defense of an activist philosophy of violence independent of context and probable consequences—*la politique du pire* in its worst form. As George Lichtheim has argued, Marx himself rejected anarchosyndicalism as an immature reaction and increasingly came to a more reformist conception of effective social action in advanced industrial societies.

France remained important to Marxism [in the period between 1871 and 1918] not merely for the obvious reason, but because of its strategic position—at any rate down to the 1890's—in the propagation of Marxist doctrine. Contrary to a widespread notion it was the first major party where a significant section of the labour movement adopted a Marxist platform. This event took place in 1880, eleven years before the German Social-Democrats followed suit. The platform was a "reformist" one, in that it tacitly repudiated the Anarchist preachment of armed violence and the indigenous Blanquist tradition of Parisian *coups d'état.* Instead emphasis was laid on the need for the working class to build up its organizations as the only basis of the coming collectivist order. This was a return to the classic document of the First International, the *Inaugural Address* [of 1864], and it marked the abandonment by Marx (who helped Guesde to draft the French party programme) of his temporary infatuation with the utopianism of the Paris Commune. It was precisely in this sense that "Marxism" was then understood both by its adherents and by Bakunin's followers all over Europe.[91]

Durkheim himself seems to have continued to identify Marx and Marxism with doctrinaire intransigence about violent class conflict. He undertook his studies in socialism in part because some of his most brilliant students were being converted to Marxist forms of socialism. Mauss was undoubtedly correct in finding Durkheim's closest practical association to be with Jaurès. (One might retrospectively add the name of the Léon Blum of A L'Echelle humaine—For All Mankind.) The main reason for the split between Jaurès and the Marxists in France was the issue of cooperation with the radicals in defense of republican solidarity. Mauss observed that "if it was Lucien Herr who in 1886–1888 converted Jaurès to Socialism, it was Durkheim who in 1889–1896 turned him away from the political formalism and the shallow philosophy of the radicals." [92] But in all probability Durkheim himself would have concurred with Jaurès on the issue of pragmatic alliances to defend the Republic against all threats. In Lichtheim's words: "The fact that Jaurès eventually imposed his outlook on the party had much to do with the evolution of French Socialism from a worker's sect into a mass movement." [93]

Jaurès' position, however, also had much to do with the tendency of the Socialist Party in France to subordinate basic issues to opportunistic considerations, electoral maneuvers, and the "political kitchen." Why was it that Durkheim in this context did not become more politically active in an attempt to use his intellectual powers and influence to defend the basic

[91] Marxism: An Historical & Critical Study (New York: Praeger, 1961), p. 228.
[92] Mauss, Introd., Socialism, p. 34.   [93] Lichtheim, pp. 228–229.

moral and philosophical issues to which he always gave primary emphasis? On this one can only speculate. Unlike many of his disciples, Durkheim did not have an activist temperament. Moreover, he may well have believed that by remaining "above parties" he had a greater chance of influencing contending groups to accept his conception of rational reconstruction. His definition of socialism did in fact influence both Jaurès and Jules Guesde.[94] Summing up in 1904 the lessons he had learned from the Dreyfus Affair, Durkheim observed:

Writers and scholars are citizens; it is thus evident that they have the strict duty to participate in public life. . . .

Men of thought and imagination, it does not appear that they are particularly predestined to specifically political careers; for these demand above all the qualities of men of action. . . .

It is in my opinion above all through the book, the public lecture, and popular education that our efforts must be made. We must above all be counselors and educators. . . .

But whenever a serious question of principle has been raised, we have seen scientists abandon their laboratories and scholars leave their private offices to move closer to the crowd and mingle in its life. Experience has shown that they know how to make themselves heard.

The moral agitation which these events [of the Dreyfus Affair] have provoked has not yet been extinguished, and I am among those who think that it must not be extinguished; for it is necessary. . . . The hour of rest has not yet come for us. There is so much to do that it is indispensable for us to keep our social energies, in a manner of speaking, perpetually mobilized. This is why I believe that the policy followed in these last years [1900–1904] is preferable to the preceding one. It has succeeded in maintaining a continuous current of collective action of a reasonable intensity.[95]

Thus Durkheim's growing sense of crisis led him to believe that the scholar should move from his "normal" activities into a position of more militant concern. Indeed all Durkheim's major works culminated in a call to action. In the final words of

[94] Mauss, Introd., *Socialism*, p. 35.
[95] "L'Elite et la democratie," *Revue bleue* XXIII (1904), pp. 705–06.

Suicide, he perhaps gave clearest expression to his idea of the relation between theory and practice: "Once one has established the existence of an evil, what it consists of and on what it depends, when one knows in consequence the general characteristics of the remedy, the essential thing is not to draw up in advance a plan which foresees everything; it is to get resolutely to work." [96]

These considerations enable us perhaps to gain some insight into the moot question of Durkheim's relation to the solidarist, or solidarity, movement—a question on which we have little objective evidence. After the turn of the century, this movement secured extensive support from governments in power until it became "a sort of official philosophy of the Third Republic." [97] In a sense the concept of "solidarity" came to have in Durkheim's France a status comparable to that of "consensus" in contemporary America, with many of the same obfuscations and ambiguities. Solidarity was a theme—indeed an "idée-force," in the expression of Alfred Fouillée—developed by the politician Léon Bourgeois (who relied on the notion of a quasi contract as the basis of social obligation); a jurist and student of Durkheim at Bordeaux, Léon Duguit; the socially conscious and humane economist Charles Gide; and the pedagogue Henri Marion (whose *De La Solidarité morale* of 1880 predated Durk-

[96] *Le Suicide* (Paris: Presses Universitaires de France, 1960), p. 451.

[97] Célestin Bouglé, *Le Solidarisme* (Paris: Marcel Giard, 1924), p. 7. See also his earlier study *L'Evolution du Solidarisme* (Paris: Bureau de *La Revue politique et parlementaire,* 1903), an extract from *Revue politique et parlementaire,* March 1903. J. E. S. Hayward, in "Solidarity: The Social History of an Idea in Nineteenth Century France," *International Review of Social History,* n.s., IV (1951), 261–284, contends that solidarity as an *idée-force* was associated in the nineteenth century with leftist and reformist movements and that in the Third Republic it increasingly became an ideology justifying the status quo. He places Durkheim in the latter context without attempting to justify this classification. The problem concerning Durkheim is touched upon briefly in Melvin Richter's excellent article, "Durkheim's Politics and Political Theory," in Kurt H. Wolff, ed., *Essays on Sociology and Philosophy* (New York: Harper & Row, 1964), p. 188.

heim's work by almost a generation). Despite all the verbal advocacy of solidarity, few of the concrete welfare measures proposed by advocates of the movement ever passed into law. The parliamentary deadlock stymied all action. For Marxists, solidarism amounted to a rose-colored, ritualistic gesture of academics of good will and bad conscience whose desire for social peace had little relevance to the requirements of social action. Indeed, "the Left had always said that it came to nothing more than a pretentious restatement of the classic slogan, 'Neither reaction nor revolution.' " [98]

What hard facts of a historical nature do we have about Durkheim's relation to the solidarity movement? He was named to the Faculté des Hautes Etudes Sociales, founded in part to propagate solidarism, and an international conference on solidarism (included as part of the Exposition Universelle of 1900) had Durkheim as one of its guest speakers. Beyond these two facts, the historical ground is less firm, and we are forced to rely on opinion and the nature of Durkheim's ideas themselves.

Harry Alpert has flatly rejected any association of Durkheim with the solidarist movement. "It is important not to identify Durkheim with the Solidarity movement. Although he too was immediately concerned with moral questions, and attempted to develop the ethical consequences of social unity, he used the concept of 'solidarité' in its pre-Bourgeois, objective, relational and non-ethical sense." [99] Alpert's argument comprised both the question of historical relationship and the nature of Durkheim's ideas. On the latter point, Alpert, if I understand him correctly, misunderstood Durkheim's usage of the concept of solidarity— a grievous error, since this concept was at the very root of Durkheim's thought and reappeared in different guises in all his works. Certainly, Durkheim insisted upon the objective interdependence or solidarity of social and cultural phenomena in all states of society and hence upon their amenability to formally rational, structural, and functional analysis. But absolutely essential to Durkheim's social philosophy was the notion that so-

[98] Richter, *op. cit.*   [99] Alpert, p. 178.

cial normality is equated with substantive rationality, especially in the latter's moral sense. On the level of human and specifically social relations, Durkheim was not concerned exclusively or even primarily with "objective" solidarity either in the formal, value-neutral sense or in the substantive sense of an interdependence of economic interests. As he stated in the preface to the first edition of *De La Division du travail social* (*The Division of Labor in Society*), his object was "to treat the facts of the moral life according to the method of the positive sciences." [100] Despite certain ambiguities in the argument of the first edition of Durkheim's first major work, the evolution of Durkheim's thought—including prominently the preface to the second edition of the *Division of Labor*—makes it abundantly clear that the social sense of solidarity for Durkheim was preeminently moral and that it included both an "objective" component in institutional and symbolic structures and a "subjective" component in internalization, communal sentiment, and personal commitment.

Alpert did not provide any evidence whatsoever for the contention that Durkheim had no relationship with the solidarist movement. Durkheim's own trusted disciple Célestin Bouglé, who, if anyone, should have known, placed Durkheim within the solidarist movement in a work published (1903) during the latter's lifetime and in a larger work published (1924) after his death. In 1903, Bouglé argued that in contrast with utilitarian individualism, "solidarism helps us to oppose these desiccating, dissolving, and aristocratic forms of individualism with a democratic individualism, a fecund principle of social union and action, whose motto is not 'each man in his own home' [*chacun chez soi*] or 'each man for himself' [*chacun pour soi*] but 'one for all and all for one' [*chacun pour tous et tous pour chacun*]." [101] Indeed Bouglé quoted Durkheim himself as asserting, "One can say that there is not a single sociological prop-

100 *Division du travail social*, p. xxxvii.
101 "L'Evolution du Solidarisme," p. 28. For the explicit reference to Durkheim, see p. 3.

osition which is not a direct or indirect demonstration of solidarity." [102]

The key practical problem (as Bouglé saw) was whether and in what contexts solidarity was proposed as a quality of the status quo or as a goal of action implying the necessity of change. In Durkheimian terms, this amounted to the question of the extent to which the existing social order was normal or pathological, for a primary quality of the normal state of society was the existence of solidarity. The mystifying and ideologically tendentious use of the idea of solidarity to present a pathological status quo as if it were in all essential respects normal and thereby to mask vested interest and legitimate the repression of dissidence was perceived both on the Left and on the Right. The idea of solidarity readily functioned as an ideology passed off as an index of the end of ideology. Paul Bourget in his *L'Etape* observed of one of his protagonists:

Ardent and critical souls are not in the least governed by formulas as vain and as empty as this morality of "human solidarity" which filled the mouth of the anticlerical professor. He believed he could replace by these two words the living tradition of order and love incarnated in the Church! He did not see that this expression of the relative dependence of beings with respect to one another had two significations: the well-meaning one was the only one he wanted to see. But are not all the ferocities of the struggle for life justified by this formula? The lion is in a state of solidarity with his prey, since he cannot live without it; only this solidarity consists in killing and devouring it. [103]

Aside from its reference to the false optimism of republican educators, this evocation of the universe of social Darwinism and the more subtle movement of Hegel's master-slave dialectic pointed to the possible function of the idea of solidarity in justifying exploitation. Despite certain equivocal features of the *Division of Labor*, including its abstract and mechanistic air of false optimism, Durkheim recognized this point. He increasingly

[102] *Ibid.*, p. 7. The quotation is repeated in Bouglé's *Le Solidarisme*, p. 12.

[103] Paris: Librairie Arthème Fayard, 1946 (first pub. 1914), p. 207.

saw the achievement of moral solidarity and social normality as a project of no mean proportions in modern society and one whose realization required basic structural reforms. To this extent, he retained the nineteenth-century usage of the term "solidarity" by the Left, which correlated it with basic social reform rather than with token gestures or the self-serving attempt to bring people together psychologically in a socially pathological status quo.

The importance of the Dreyfus Affair in the context of the battle between the political extremes and the Republic has already been touched upon. What remains is to indicate its importance in Durkheim's intellectual development and to his conception of reform in modern society. The intense *engagement* of Durkheim and his disciples in the Dreyfus Affair indicated the extent of its impact upon them. Durkheim himself was a primary object of attack by the anti-Dreyfusard forces. His classes were disrupted. And his collaborators, in the wake of a series of bombings in cafes surrounding the Sorbonne, were even led to fear for his life.[104]

Durkheim was moved to step into the political arena and write his defense of Dreyfus (in 1898) in opposition to Ferdinand Brunetière, the Catholic apologist and anti-Dreyfusard editor of the *Revue des deux mondes*. Melvin Richter has accurately observed: "It is striking how the theory elaborated in *Les formes élémentaires de la vie religieuse* turns up at the very center of the fervent defense 'L'Individualisme et les intellectuels,' which Durkheim wrote at the height of the Dreyfus Affair." [105] It might be added that in this complex issue, which involved the opposition between justice and the demands of "law and order" in maintaining the status quo, Durkheim came

---

[104] See Terry N. Clark, "Emile Durkheim and the Institutionalization of Sociology," *Archives européennes de sociologie*, IX (1968), 63–64. See also Eugen Weber, *The Nationalist Revival in France;* Charles Andler, *La Vie de Lucien Herr* (Paris: Rieder, 1932), pp. 112–150; Romain Rolland, *Péguy* (Paris: Albin Michel, 1944), I, 306ff.; and Daniel Halévy, *Péguy et "Les Cahiers de la quinzaine"* (Paris: Bernard Grasset, 1941), pp. 68–80

[105] "Durkheim's Politics and Political Theory," p. 175.

out on the side of justice with an argument which was not only more sensitive to the ambiguities involved than the attitudes of many of the Dreyfusards but which revealed much more than his own general discussions of morality an awareness of the complexities involved in any concrete case of choice.

The respect for authority has nothing incompatible with rationalism, provided that authority is founded rationally. . . . It is not sufficient in convincing men to remind them of this commonplace of banal rhetoric that society is not possible without mutual sacrifices and a certain spirit of subordination; one must justify *in the* [specific] *instance* the docility one asks of them. . . . When, on the contrary, one is concerned with a question which, by definition, falls under common judgment, such an abdication is contrary to all reason and consequently to duty. Now, to know whether a tribunal is permitted to condemn an accused person without hearing his defense does not require any special enlightenment. . . . Men have asked themselves whether it is proper to consent to a temporary eclipse of principle in order not to trouble the functioning of a public administration which everybody, by the way, recognizes to be indispensable to the security of the state. We do not know if the antinomy really poses itself in this sharp form; but, in any case, if a choice is really necessary between these two evils, to sacrifice what has been up to the present time our historical *raison d'être* would be to choose the greater evil. An organ of public life, however important it may be, is only an instrument, a means to an end. What good is it to conserve the means if one detaches it from its end? [106]

It was in this defense of Dreyfus, moreover, that Durkheim's humanistic conception of the "normal" role of individualism in modern societies took definite and assertive form. Durkheim observed that the indictment of individualism confounded it with "the narrow utilitarianism and utilitarian egoism of Spencer and the economists." He rejected this facile identification. "One has an easy time in denouncing as an ideal without grandeur this shabby commercialism which reduces society to the status

[106] "L'Individualisme et les intellectuels," *Revue bleue,* 4th series, X (1898), 10, 12.

of a vast apparatus of production and exchange." On the contrary, the individualism which Durkheim defended was "the individualism of Kant and Rousseau, of the spiritualists—that which the Declaration of the Rights of Man tried more or less successfully to translate into formulas, that which we at present teach in our schools and which has become the basis of our moral catechism." According to this sort of individualism, duty consisted in turning away from our personal concerns and "our empirical individuality in order to seek uniquely what our nature as men demands insofar as we share it in common with all other men." This ideal transcended the level of egoistic utilitarian ends to such an extent that it seemed to be "marked with religiosity" and to be "sacred in the ritual sense of the word." The problem was "to complete, extend, and organize individualism, not to restrict and combat it." Reflection alone could aid in "finding a way out of the present difficulties." With a rare ironic flourish, Durkheim concluded: "It is not in meditating upon *La Politique tirée de l'Ecriture sainte* [Bossuet's "Politics Derived from the Very Words of Sacred Scripture"] that we will ever find the means of organizing economic life and introducing more justice into contractual relations." [107]

But what is perhaps most significant is that Durkheim's intense awareness of the crucial role of religion in social life itself became prominent about the time the Dreyfus Affair was breaking. In a 1907 letter to the *Revue néo-scholastique,* Durkheim asserted:

It was only in 1895 that I had a clear understanding of the capital role played by religion in social life. It was in that year that for the first time I found the means of approaching the study of religion sociologically. It was a revelation to me. The course of 1895 marks a line of demarcation in the development of my thought, so much so that all my previous research had to be taken up again with renewed effort in order to be placed in harmony with these new views.[108]

[107] *Ibid.*, pp. 7–8, 13.   [108] XIV (1907), 613.

Durkheim in good scholarly fashion went on to find the scientific basis of his reorientation in the studies of religious history he had undertaken at the time, notably the works of Robertson Smith and his school. But it was no accident that the "revelation" came to him about the time he was deeply involved in the Dreyfus Affair. For the involvement that constituted a peak experience of republican intellectuals had all the markings of Durkheim's idea of an effervescent social movement carried along by the quasi-religious force of a mystique which revived and reanimated great revolutionary ideals of the past. Charles Péguy—the constant critic who, with impassioned partiality, saw in Durkheim only the official representative of petty rationalism and state power—nonetheless expressed a conception of the Dreyfus Affair which Durkheim shared: "Our Dreyfusism was a religion. . . . Justice and truth, which were so loved by us and to which we gave everything, were not at all the truth and justice of the concept, of books; they were organic, they were Christian." [109]

For Durkheim, the *rassemblement* of men of good will in defense of Dreyfus (who at times assumed the status of a totemic emblem symbolic of collective values) enabled modern life to transcend for a moment its ordinary "moral mediocrity." From the time of the Dreyfus Affair—i.e., during the second half of his intellectual life—Durkheim, instead of focusing on the role of formal constraints, stressed the importance of communal sentiment, collective ideals, and religious symbols in social life.

At least until World War I. The war came as a rude awakening to men like Durkheim, shattering many of their intellectual assumptions and the foundations of their personal existence. Brice Parain, in his *La Mort de Jean Madec*, seizes the contrast between the moral atmosphere of *la belle époque*, when things seemed full of hope *quand même*, and the postwar sentiments of intellectuals in France who were faced with an "obstructed path."

[109] Quoted in Romain Rolland, *Péguy*, p. 65.

I grew up among the schoolmasters who organized the Republic after
the Dreyfus Affair. They were good, honest, reliable—but they demanded too much of man and of themselves. . . . Thus they believed
very strongly in the reign of Justice; *their morality fell apart*. It required too much saintliness. One would have preferred the type of
heroism which is more brilliant and which gets along better with a
certain insouciance which is necessary for life. Their principle said:
if you do good, you have only done your duty, but if you do evil, you
must be punished. Well, evil was done all the same, and nobody was
around to punish the wicked. The war put an end to their dream. What
in effect does someone owe when he has received nothing and will
receive nothing? [110]

During the war Durkheim rallied to the *union sacrée* and became intensely involved in administrative work and propa-
ganda.[111] The most that can be said about his propagandistic
pieces is that they are among the most level-headed specimens
of a rather paranoid genre. At times they offered vehicles for the
expression of his thought, e.g., in his attempt, in *L'Allemagne au-
dessus de tout—Germany above All*—to portray the German national character and define imperialism, with special reference
to the works of Heinrich von Treitschke.[112] His confidence in the

[110] Paris: Grasset, 1945, p. 71. For the French intellectual scene between the two wars and after, see H. Stuart Hughes, *The Obstructed Path*
(New York: Harper & Row, 1968).

[111] A list of Durkheim's committees in Davy, "Emile Durkheim:
L'Homme," *Revue de métaphysique et de morale,* XXVI (1919), 193,
includes: Conseil de l'Université, Comité des travaux historiques et scien-
tifiques, Comité consultatif de l'enseignement supérieur, Commission des
étrangers au ministère de l'Intérieur, Comité français d'information et
d'action auprès des juifs en pays neutre, Fraternité franco-américaine,
Pupilles de l'Ecole publique, Comité de publication des études et documents sur la guerre, Comité de publication des lettres à tous les Français,
Ligue républicaine d'Alsace-Lorraine, Société des amis de Jaurès, and Pour
le rapprochement universitaire.

[112] In *L'Allemagne au-dessus de tout* (Paris: Colin, 1915), Durkheim
made an interesting application of his concept of anomie to the problem of
imperialism. For Durkheim, imperialism was a form of anomie fostered by
dominant institutions like the state and military, and a thinker like
Treitschke attempted to legitimate institutionalized anomie in the form of a

justice of his own country's cause was neither diminished by considerations of long-term causation nor mitigated by concern about the postwar settlement. The intensity (but not the mere fact) of his propagandistic efforts, however, must be seen in the light of his anxiety over the fate of his only son. He received definite news of his son's death at the front only after a prolonged period of uncertainty. For the first time, Durkheim seemed to face the temptation of madness. "I need not tell you," he wrote to Georges Davy, "of the anguish in which I live. It is an obsession of every instant which hurts me more than I supposed." Durkheim was haunted "by the image of this exhausted child, alone by the roadside in the middle of the night and the fog. . . . That image held me by the throat." [113] When he finally received definite word of his son's death, the man who had written movingly of the spiritually restorative powers of ritual in moments of crisis withdrew into a terrible silence which prevented him from so much as talking about his feelings with his closest friends: "Don't speak to me about my son until I tell you that it's possible." [114] "Above all, don't speak to me of him." [115] "Don't answer me. All that weakens and exhausts me." [116] Iron self-discipline remained the dominant force in Durkheim's life, and it finally broke him. In 1917 he died of what has been called a "broken heart."

---

national will to power. The limitless expansion of the power of a state at the expense of other states was for Durkheim "a morbid hypotrophy of the will, a kind of will mania" (p. 44). Durkheim realized that anomie might be furthered by dominant institutions, instilled into the personalities of citizens through education, and legitimated by intellectuals.

[113] Davy, *Annales de l'Université de Paris*, 21.   [114] *Ibid.*

[115] Davy, "Emile Durkheim," *Revue française de sociologie*, I (1960), 12.

[116] Quoted by Raymond Lenoir, "L'Oeuvre sociologique d'Emile Durkheim," *Europe*, XXII (1930), 295.

3«

The Division of Social Labor

> We believe that our research would not merit an hour's trouble if it had only a speculative interest. If we separate with care theoretical from practical problems, it is not in order to neglect the latter; it is, on the contrary, to put ourselves in a better position to resolve them.
>
> —*The Division of Labor in Society*

Quo vadis?

The Division of Labor in Society has acquired in modern social thought the dubious status of a sacred text which is almost a dead letter. It is a work which is referred to with the *pro forma* awe which scholars reserve for recognized classics, but to which little real reference is made in the analysis of problems. Indeed Durkheim himself, as well as his disciples, never returned to the massive and cumbrous concepts of organic and mechanical solidarity which were "absolutely fundamental in his first major work." [1] Talcott Parsons, despite his belief that the work has never received the recognition it merits, felt obliged to observe that "it is, however, a book which is far from being complete or clear in many of the most essential points, and is distinctly difficult to interpret." [2]

It is difficult to decide whether *The Division of Labor* merits attention in itself or whether its value derives primarily from its place in the general development of the thought of Durkheim and

[1] Robert Nisbet, ed., *Emile Durkheim* (Englewood Cliffs, N.J.: Prentice-Hall, 1965), p. 30.

[2] *The Structure of Social Action: A Study in Social Theory* (first pub. 1937; Glencoe, Ill.: Free Press, 1949), p. 308.

his school. And it is difficult to understand why certain commentators, even Parsons himself, were tempted to construe this work as indicative of a definitively formulated "first position" in Durkheim's thought which was later subjected to drastic revision. The work ought rather to be seen as an initial, tentative, and somewhat ambivalent exploratory essay putting forth certain problems and themes which in the course of Durkheim's intellectual life were to be—with varying degrees of adequacy—modified, refined, and developed. Durkheim once compared the experience of men in archaic societies to a "primitive nebula" whose laws were in all essentials to be conserved in modern societies.[3] In some measure, this metaphor applies to the relation of The Division of Labor to Durkheim's own later works.

Durkheim, as we know from Marcel Mauss, had at first conceived his thesis in terms of individualism and socialism—a theme which recalled the 1833 essay De L'Individualisme et du socialisme of the Saint-Simonian Pierre Leroux. This popular work had been influential in bringing the term "socialism" into general currency.[4] But the theme of The Division of Labor was later recast in the more scientifically aseptic framework of the relation between the individual and society, or what would today be called personality and social structure. In a turn of phrase reminiscent of Rousseau in the Social Contract, Durkheim posed the question: "How is it possible for the individual in becoming more autonomous to depend more closely upon society? How can he be at the same time more personal and more solidaristic?"[5]

Some of the more ideological reasons why Durkheim recast the theme of his first major work were related to the obvious hesitancies in its line of argument and the timidity in its reflections on reform. Durkheim undoubtedly remembered the harass-

[3] Pragmatisme et sociologie (Paris: Librairie Philosophique J. Vrin), 1955.

[4] George Lichtheim, Origins of Socialism (New York: Praeger, 1968), p. 56.

[5] Preface to 1st ed., De La Division du travail social (7th ed.; Paris: Presses Universitaires de France, 1960), p. xliii.

ment of Alfred Espinas and the furor caused by his thesis, "Animal Societies." Paul Janet, a member of Durkheim's own thesis jury, had tried to convince Espinas to modify a passage on Auguste Comte in his introduction and, because Espinas refused, had had the entire introduction suppressed before publication.[6] During the defense of Durkheim's thesis, Janet lost his composure, rapped on the table, invoked God, and warned Durkheim that sociology led to madness.[7] Emile Boutroux, to whom the thesis was dedicated, could not accept this ambivalent honor "without making a grimace." [8] It was significant that the title of Durkheim's supplementary Latin thesis on Montesquieu referred to his predecessor's contributions to political science rather than to sociology. Durkheim's hesitancy to use the new word "sociology" was one small indication that sociology was suspect, not because of its reliance on orthodox conservative ideas to bolster the status quo, but because it was unsettling. Despite Durkheim's attempt, in his early work, to allay suspicions on this score, his sociological approach to problems involved a new way of seeing things and, consequently, a reordering of modes of interpretation. Politically and socially, it seemed to imply, however obliquely at times, the necessity of basic structural reform for stable order to be possible in modern societies. Mauss reported that Durkheim "clashed with touchy moralists and classic or Christian economists for their objections to collectivism, which they struck at through his *Division of Labor*. Due to conflicts of this kind, he was excluded from professorships in Paris." [9] Bordeaux itself in Durkheim's time became a short-lived intellectual center because of the opposition of established powers in the capital to newer currents in social thought.

Indeed, the fact that *The Division of Labor* could have caused

---

[6] Raymond Lenoir, "L'Oeuvre sociologique d'Emile Durkheim," *Europe*, XXII (1930), 294.

[7] Célestin Bouglé, *ibid.*, p. 281.   [8] Bouglé, *ibid.*

[9] Marcel Mauss, Introd., 1st ed., Emile Durkheim, *Le Socialisme;* in *Socialism*, trans. Charlotte Sattler (New York: Collier Books, 1958), p. 34.

such a stir seems surprising in retrospect, since it is ambiguous both in its theories and in its political implications. Ostensibly, the primary focus of *The Division of Labor* was the structure of modern society, the process of modernization which had brought that structure into existence, and the relation of structure and process to moral solidarity among men in society. In good Gallic fashion, the book was divided into three principal parts: (1) an analysis of organic and mechanical solidarity and their relations to individual personality; (2) an investigation of the process of change which purportedly had led from the mechanical solidarity of primitive and traditional societies to the organic solidarity of modern societies based on the division of labor; (3) a study of pathological forms in which the division of labor did not function to create solidarity in society.

Thus Durkheim approached modernity and the industrial revolution through the study of the division of labor. In this way, he met the classical economists on their own native grounds. But these grounds were to be explored and their sociological features perceived in such a way that the resulting human geography would no longer be familiar to the heirs of Adam Smith. The very title of the work, *De La Division du travail social*—which has been mistranslated *The Division of Labor in Society* instead of "The Division of Social Labor"—was itself highly significant. The division of *social* labor was for Durkheim identical in its broadest sense with social differentiation, and in its narrower and more specifically modern sense with advanced occupational specialization. But in Durkheim the focus shifted away from the economic role of the division of labor, e.g., in increasing productivity. It fell instead on the function of the division of labor in relating men to one another in society. From economic product to social process and the quality of human life—this for Durkheim was the sociological perspective on the division of labor.

In fact, Durkheim's first major work seemed to show a lack of concern with economic problems. Durkheim's methodological goal was to further the idea of a unified social science by stressing the extraeconomic dimensions of economic activity. His increasingly apparent ideological purpose was to subordinate the economy and materialistic motives to the moral and cultural needs of men in society. But his mode of affirmation often approached disciplinary imperialism and disdain for the dismal science with its specific form of abstraction. Indeed, in Durkheim's conception of economics, the mind-body dualism functioned to relegate economic activity to the sphere of the literally material and the individual. By the end of his life, Durkheim considered economic activity to be the profane par excellence. His entire conception of the problem not only failed to offer insight into the nature of economic institutions; it also ignored the moral and religious aspects of modern economic activity which Max Weber treated in *The Protestant Ethic and the Spirit of Capitalism.*

Durkheim's idea of economics was one case in which the normative and critical aspects of his thought submerged the analytic. For he saw the unlimited desire for worldly goods as a prominent instance of modern social pathology. This point of view would become manifest in *Suicide.* But the distinction between social normality and pathology was basic to the general argument of *The Division of Labor.* In that book, Durkheim introduced his basic definition of morality and his idea of the intimate association between social normality and the prevalence of solidarity in society. "We can say in a general manner," he observed, "that the characteristic of moral rules is to enunciate the fundamental conditions of social solidarity." [10] The correlation of social normality, solidarity, and morality revealed the foundation of Durkheim's thought in organizing principles which were methodological and normative at one and the same time.

In his concepts of mechanical and organic solidarity, Durkheim focused upon normal states of society. A consideration of pathological phenomena in modern society was restricted to a concluding section which was disproportionately small in com-

[10] *Division du travail social,* p. 393.

parison with the gravity of the problems treated; it was also
rather dissociated from, or at least inadequately related to, the
preceding discussion of normal states of society. A major ambiguity in Durkheim's argument stemmed from the lack of clarity
about the concepts of the mechanical and the organic. In terms
of his master metaphor of the tree of sociocultural life, it was unclear (1) where given cases, and especially entire societies, fit
into his conception of the mechanical and the organic, and (2)
whether and how these concepts applied to the common trunk
of society and to its typological branches. Furthermore, Durkheim relied on the concepts of the mechanical and the organic
to correlate a series of classifications whose factual basis was far
from certain and whose fruitfulness in research was far from
apparent. The confluence of these problematic features made
The Division of Labor not only the most inertly abstract of Durkheim's works but the least convincing in its ability to handle
theoretical abstractions with logical intelligibility and informative
relevance.

Mechanical and Organic Solidarity

The distinction between mechanical and organic solidarity was
similar to numerous other polar oppositions in the work of early
social thinkers. It was analogous, for example, to Charles Horton
Cooley's distinction between primary and secondary groups. And
it had areas of overlapping with Nietzsche's concepts of the
Dionysian and the Apollonian and with Weber's opposition between charisma and bureaucratization. Durkheim himself, as we
shall see, tried to relate his concepts to Ferdinand Tönnies' influential contrast between *Gemeinschaft* (community) and *Gesellschaft* (society). To some extent, the common root of all these
oppositions was the distinction between *communitas* and differentiated structure.*

* Durkheim himself did not use the term *communitas*. But it best expresses the concept he tried to convey in a term like "mechanical solidarity."
In contrast with differentiated structure, *communitas* constitutes the element

But the terms "mechanical" and "organic" betrayed a peculiar duality in Durkheim's thought. On the one hand, they seemed indicative of the most pretentious sort of positivism. The analogies evoked were physical and biological. On the other hand, the terms were saturated with symbolic value. Romantic thought had made the organic the synonym of the authentic and living, and the mechanical identical with the false and dead.

This duality in connotation belied the fact that Durkheim did not know precisely where he was going in his first major work. Like much modern writing, *The Division of Labor* was a dissertation in search of a thesis. In the most general sense, the term "mechanical" referred to solidarity through "similitudes" (or what might be termed "communal identity"); "organic" referred to solidarity through differentiation with reciprocity and cooperation among differentiated but complementary parts. In referring to the genesis of social solidarity, Durkheim related his sociological principles to the notion in common-sense psychology that people love both what resembles them and what is different from yet complements them.

To refer to community as mechanical was paradoxical. In the works of other social thinkers, the concept of the organic was intimately bound up with the notion of community. In *The Division of Labor*, the fact which overshadowed the concept of organic solidarity was the absence of significant community in modern life. Durkheim recognized this fact but seemed bewildered about how to come to terms with it. The concluding section, on pathological forms of the division of labor, showed that Durkheim was not offering the concept of organic solidarity as a simple legitimation of the modern status quo. But does *The Division of Labor* indicate he believed that solidarity in modern society is even theoretically possible without significant community? The fact that he failed to treat the relation of bureaucracy

---

of communal identity in experience. The term *communitas* has been employed by Victor Turner in *The Ritual Process*, which is discussed later in this chapter.

to organic solidarity does not help to clarify his intent. Nor does the absence of a full discussion of the relations between modern, universalistic humanism and the values adapted to more concrete, face-to-face communities.

At times Durkheim seemed to sense the need for a measure of both organic and mechanical solidarity in any normal society: "It is not necessary to choose once and for all between [organic and mechanical solidarity] and condemn one in the name of the other; what is necessary is to give each at each moment of history the place which is proper to it." [11] But it was only in writings of a later date that Durkheim became more explicit about the possible role of community in modern society. His advocacy of professional groups that would allow for some measure of decentralization had as one of its most essential features the desire to remedy the lack of community in modern life. And his last major work, *The Elementary Forms of the Religious Life,* was postulated on the conviction that a strong measure of continuity was necessary between the bases of legitimate order in archaic and modern societies.

Although Durkheim's ideas about modern society became clearer in time, one feature of *The Division of Labor* which continued to be characteristic of his thought was the tendency to see archaic societies primarily, if not exclusively, in terms of similitudes within a society, homogeneity, and communal identity, to the exclusion of differentiation among roles in the group or among groups in the larger social context. This exaggerated idea of primitive conformism became the basis for the chapter in *The Rules of Sociological Method* on the classification of social types (chapter iv). It was in fact one basic reason why Durkheim's project for a comparative classification of social types remained little more than a pious hope. In *The Rules,* as in *The Division of Labor,* Durkheim gratuitously postulated a hypothetical horde as the basis of group formation in society, and hence the "natural" basis of classification of societies in terms of increasingly complex

[11] *Division du travail social,* p. 393.

combinations of the nonexistent primal horde. Individuals in the horde "do not form in the interior of the total group any special groups which differ from the group as a whole; they are juxtaposed atomically." [12] Durkheim was forced to concede that no historically known societies corresponded to this Darwinian notion of the undifferentiated "protoplasm of the social realm." But the force of this model of primitive homogeneity was so constraining in Durkheim's mind that he concluded, with no appeal to evidence, that the "simplest" types of primitive society were "formed immediately and without any intermediary by a repetition of hordes." [13] The horde which became a "segment" of a larger society by recapitulating the atomistic juxtaposition of its members in its own relations (or nonrelations) with other hordes was for Durkheim the clan. A. R. Radcliffe-Brown detected with acumen how this sociologically false and misleading conception of groups in primitive societies remained basic even in *The Elementary Forms of the Religious Life*: "One of the results of Durkheim's theory is that it over-emphasizes the clan and clan solidarity. Totemism does more than express the unity of the clan; it also expresses the unity of totemic society as a whole in the relations of the clans to one another within the larger society." [14]

The tendency to see phenomena in primitive societies in terms of identity, homogeneity, and confusion was carried to absurd lengths in Lucien Lévy-Bruhl's attempt to make the Platonic principle of mystical "participation" the sole basis of experience among the "primitives." Despite his own criticism of Lévy-Bruhl's tendency to see an unbridgeable gap between forms of experience in archaic and modern societies, a strong element of the tendency remained in Durkheim's attempt to find the source of religious beliefs in undifferentiated concepts like "mana." And Durkheim

[12] *Les Règles de la méthode sociologique* (15th ed.; Paris: Presses Universitaires de France, 1963), p. 82.

[13] *Ibid.*, p. 83.

[14] *Structure and Function in Primitive Societies* (London: Cohen & West, 1961), p. 129.

often continued to see the type of perfect communal identity which is attained within conflict groups in revolutionary effervescence, and within a stable society only periodically, in ritual activities, as the exclusive functional principle of solidarity in ongoing primitive societies. Durkheim's thought, however, was not dominated by the abstract force of concepts alone or by the generally unsympathetic ethnocentrism of a Lévy-Bruhl. What remained from beginning to end in his conception of primitive societies was the idea of savage experience as the total realization of the communal bond that he felt was missing in modern societies. Yet it is no exaggeration to say that a fundamental basis for the advance of social and cultural anthropology beyond Durkheim has been the application of the principle of differentiation to symbolic systems and social structures in archaic societies, with a fuller recognition of both the nature of experience in these societies and the universal role of logical differentiations in all cultural symbolisms. Highly complex occupational specialization was, of course, not typical of archaic societies. Nor were universalistic values (which applied to all men in certain situations, independent of personal status) or functionally specific norms (which were limited to certain spheres of existence differentiated from other spheres). But certain sorts of differentiation were crucial in archaic societies: the problem was their precise nature and relation to *communitas*.

The difficulty of relating the universal and typical conditions of solidarity in modern and archaic societies was compounded in *The Division of Labor* by the inclusion of other concepts and phenomena under the rubrics of mechanical and organic solidarity. Under mechanical solidarity, Durkheim included—along with similitude, or communal identity, in primitive society (indeed "traditional" societies in general)—the notion of *conscience collective,* repressive or penal sanctions as the most objective index of this type of solidarity, and the idea of segmental structure. Under organic solidarity, he included—along with differentiation in modern society—the idea of the weakening, if not the eclipse, of *conscience collective*, restitutive sanction as the most objective index of this type of solidarity, the notion of "organized" structure, and the emergence of universalistic values and individualism. At points in this intricate exercise in opposing modern and traditional societies, Durkheim threatened to fall into the trap of similar dualistic attempts to classify the universe of societies known to cultural history: the basing of "scientific" classification in sociology on the vague and tendentious opposition between "them" and "us."

Perhaps the most logical way to pursue an analysis of this aspect of *The Division of Labor* is to take apart the idea clusters of mechanical and organic solidarity, which were to decompose of their own weight over the years, and to show how Durkheim and his disciples defined and redefined their conceptual components until new and more (or less) relevant classificatory schemes appeared on the horizon of their thought.

Conscience Collective

The core concept of Durkheimian sociology which *The Division of Labor* included under mechanical solidarity was that of *conscience collective*. Durkheim defined the concept thus:

The totality of beliefs and sentiments common to average members of the same society forms a determinate system which has its own life; one can call it the collective or common conscience. . . . It is realized only in individuals [but] it is the psychic type of society, a type which has its properties, its conditions of existence, and its mode of development.[15]

The *conscience collective*, in contrast with the individual and the event, was situated on the level of structure. In one sense, it was the sociopsychological ground of a common culture in the personalities of members of society. In French, the word *conscience* had the ambivalent meanings of "conscience" and "consciousness." Durkheim, however, often stressed that aspects of

---

[15] *Division du travail social*, p. 46.

the *conscience collective* might be unconscious. And the concept, both in its conscious and unconscious aspects, applied above all to norms, constraining symbolic systems, and moral or religious sentiments. Within the French tradition, the concept recalled Comte's notion of consensus and Rousseau's idea of *volonté générale*. It also was similar to Freud's concept of the superego. Durkheim's notion of "collective representation" (somewhat like Freud's "ego ideal") stressed more specifically the conscious component of *conscience collective*. The ideas, values, and symbols expressed in collective representations were sources of legitimation for institutional practices and actual behavior in society. Without going into the complex qualifications that would be required in any extended discussion, one might also note that the concept of *conscience collective*—especially in its unconscious or implicit aspect—resembles later notions, such as Ferdinand de Saussure's *langue* (in contrast to *parole*) and Lévi-Strauss's structure (in contrast to event).

The history of Durkheim's intellectual development was in large part the story of his re-emphasis of factors in social life initially discussed under the rubric of *conscience collective*. Yet, within the confining context of mechanical solidarity, he associated the *conscience collective* with repressive penal sanctions and *communitas*. Repressive sanctions, for Durkheim, were the most objective index or criterion of mechanical solidarity: they imposed expiatory punishment upon the person who offended the *conscience collective*, especially in its religious demands. This punishment was in contrast with restitutive sanctions (correlated with organic solidarity), which simply tried to reinstate the *status quo ante*, e.g., through the payment of damages. The confinement of the *conscience collective* to norms defining crimes leading to repressive sanctions proved in time to be too restrictive a notion for Durkheim, although he never lost interest in the problem of crime and punishment and its relation to the hard core of the *conscience collective*. The correlation of *conscience collective* with communal identity or similitudes in the "internal

milieu" of the group imposed more extreme and at times misleading restrictions on usage (restrictions which, in one sense,
conflicted with the emphasis on repressive sanctions, for, within
limits, society tended to be more communal when it was less
repressive and more repressive when it was less communal). But
the emphasis upon the importance of *communitas* in a normal
state of society was to be retained by Durkheim. And it revealed
the influence of Rousseau on his thought, especially in the belief
that *communitas* was most pronounced in archaic societies.

In time Durkheim's conception of normality in modern society
rescinded the narrow correlation of *conscience collective*, mechanical solidarity, and traditional society. The first edition of *The
Division of Labor* itself presented humanism—the idea of a
common human nature and universal values as the ultimate basis
of personal dignity—as the highest cultural ideal of modern
society. Humanism was the universalistic *conscience collective*
of modern societies, and it enjoined the sentiment of *communitas*
among all men qua men. But its abstract values seemed to evolve
almost as the unintended consequence of a process of elimination
of other, more concrete values, attachments, and face-to-face
relations. Later, Durkheim argued that universalistic humanism
need not be incompatible with more particular (but not narrowly
particularistic) forms of *conscience collective*. Militant nationalism contradicted a universalistic humanism; but liberal patriotism complemented it. In Durkheim's conception of corporatism,
moreover, the insistence upon the necessity of communal intermediary groups was conjoined with the idea that a normal,
solidaristic social system in modernity would require norms and
laws which defined the relational conditions of reciprocity and
cooperation among differentiated elements in the larger social
context. The specialized professional and other particular contents of experience might be restricted to a given group (and
serve as the experiential basis for a particular component of
the *conscience collective* of that group). But, for solidarity to
predominate over particularism, related groups would have to

share a *conscience collective* containing norms which defined the justified modes of interaction, mutual expectation, and exchange with one another. This requirement placed a dimension of organic solidarity within the province of the *conscience collective*. In fact, we find an awareness of this requirement in the discussion of contract law and its social environment in *The Division of Labor* itself.

Crime and Punishment

The Division of Labor stressed the sociological importance of the comparative study of legal systems. It placed special emphasis on the role of organized sanctions in society. This emphasis had both methodological and substantive bases.

Methodologically, the organized sanction was an objective and relatively manifest component of social structure. Thus a focus upon it reduced the possibility of subjective or ideological distortion of facts in the initial orientation of research. As Durkheim remarked in his preface: "To submit an order of facts to science, it is not sufficient to observe them with care, to describe and classify them. But, what is more difficult, one must, in the words of Descartes, find the way in which they are scientific, that is discover in them some objective element which allows exact determination and, if possible, measurement." [16]

Durkheim's later thought was less "positivistic" in that it neither made this degree of methodological objectivity the criterion of all interesting research nor maintained a primary emphasis upon formal constraints and sanctions. But it did retain the substantive basis of the focus on sanctions, which it integrated into a notion of objectivity more adapted to the meaningful demands of socio-cultural enquiry. Sanctions could serve as an index of solidarity in the normal state of society only because they shared in the nature of the social system in general. In the normal state of society, customary or written law was the most organized and stable dimension of social structure.[17] Through its sanctions, a

[16] *Ibid.*, p. xlii.   [17] *Ibid.*, p. 29.

society put its authorized power where its mouthed ideals were.

One apparent defect of *The Division of Labor* was the fact that Durkheim, despite his legalistic focus, did not treat the problem of law and sanctions in a society characterized by significant conflict. What does law express and how does it function in a society riven by conflict? Marx's answer was categorical: law serves the interests of the ruling class.

Durkheim never provided a comprehensive and more nuanced answer to the questions raised by the problematics of law in a conflict-ridden society. His later writing contained only scattered references to the problem. In *Suicide,* he observed in passing: "When the law represses acts which public sentiment judges to be inoffensive, it is the law which makes us indignant, not the act which it punishes." [18] One important problem which the propagandistic World War I pamphlet *Germany above All* emphasized was the crisis generated by a conflict between legal imperatives and the demands of a humanistic ethic. Although the severity of this conflict challenged his optimistic assumptions about the non-authoritarian and democratic course of law and government in modern society, Durkheim's answer was unequivocal. In contrast to the school of juridical positivism in Germany, which had exercised some influence on his early thought, Durkheim without hesitation placed the humanistic *conscience collective* of modern society above legal duties to the state. Had he lived longer, Durkheim would in all probability have extended his theory of value and obligation to include a more inclusive and nonpartisan investigation of civil disobedience.[19]

What was the nature of crime and the criminal from Durkheim's sociological perspective? The criminal was different from others. This difference lay in the criminal's infringement of norms and values in which others found identity through communal allegiance and shared commitment. Crime disrupted the *con-*

[18] *Le Suicide* (first pub. 1897; Paris: Presses Universitaires de France, 1960), p. 426.

[19] Marcel Mauss, "In Memoriam: L'Oeuvre inédite de Durkheim et de ses collaborateurs," *Année sociologique,* n.s., I (1923), 9.

science collective. Punishment was essentially a form of vengeance or retaliation which imposed expiation upon the criminal.
As Durkheim phrased it in a later work:

A violated law must bear witness to the fact that despite appearances
it is always itself, that it has lost nothing of its force and authority in
spite of the act which negates it. In other words, it must affirm itself
in the face of the offense and react in a way that manifests an energy
proportional to the energy of the attack which it has undergone.
Punishment is nothing other than this meaningful manifestation.[20]

From Durkheim's perspective, sanctions in society were essentially different from the conditioning of animals. Durkheim was
never "positivistic" in the behavioristic sense. One of his own
later criticisms of pragmatism (in his *Pragmatism and Sociology*)
was its proximity to purely behavioristic explanations of human
activity. Among people, Durkheim argued elsewhere, "punishment is only a sign of an internal state; it is a notation, a language by which . . . the public conscience of society . . . expresses the sentiment which the blameworthy act inspires in it." [21]
Durkheim did believe that when values were deeply rooted in the
conscience collective, punishment might become an almost in-
stinctive reaction. But the emotion involved in this passionate
response to crime was not pure affectivity. It was sentiment meaningfully, and perhaps unconsciously, structured by norms and
symbols which interposed themselves between stimulus and response. Indeed, punishment served to counter the unsettling
threat of anxiety and anomic affectivity attendant on a challenge
to one's normative structure of experience.

These were the general notions of crime and punishment, first
sketched in *The Division of Labor,* which Durkheim would retain and develop. In *The Rules of Sociological Method,* however,
he pointed to an error in his dominant conception of crime and
the criminal in his first major work: "Contrary to current ideas,

[20] *L'Education morale* (first pub. 1925; Paris: Presses Universitaires de
France, 1963), p. 139.
[21] *Ibid.,* p. 147.

the criminal no longer appears as a radically unsociable or parasitical element, a foreign and unassimilable body within society;
he is a regular agent of social life." [22] *The Division of Labor,* by
Durkheim's own admission, had stressed the negative nature of
the criminal and his relation to society—a viewpoint on the
"deviant" which almost reflected the attitude of the conformist.
In his conception of the possible social normality of crime, Durkheim dialectically perceived the positive element in crime.

A certain rate of crime was an essential and inevitable con-
stituent of the healthy or normal society. Functionally, crime
provided the occasion for a more or less dramatic display of social
solidarity in punishment. Simultaneously, it tested existing institutions and relations, indicating that social structures were flexible enough to allow for a measure of change. Indeed, the criminal and the idealist were related by a hidden functional nexus
which at times portended a certain identity of nature. "For society
to evolve, individual originality must break through; for that of
the idealist, who dreams of going beyond his century, to manifest
itself, that of the criminal, who is below the level of his time,
must be possible. One does not go without the other." [23]

Even in the most "normal" society which came closest to
realizing its values, there would be a necessary gap between ideal
discourse or sacred text and practical reality. Hence the existence
of anomic and indeterminate interstices in which the criminal
would always find his place.

Imagine a society of saints, an exemplary and perfect cloister. Crimes
in the strict sense would be unknown there. But faults which seem
venial to the vulgar would raise the same scandal as ordinary mis-
demeanors in ordinary consciences. Thus if this society found itself
armed with the power to judge and punish, it would qualify these acts
as criminal and treat them as such.[24]

Thus in all states, types, and milieus of society, the nature of
crime said something profound about the nature of society. Crime

---

[22] *Règles de la méthode sociologique,* pp. 71–72.
[23] *Ibid.,* p. 70.   [24] *Ibid.,* p. 68.

and conformity were themselves bound together by a structure of reciprocity. Indeed, especially in periods of rapid transition, it might be impossible to distinguish clearly and distinctly between the idealist and the criminal, for both might ambivalently participate in the destructive and creative potential of anomie. With the collapse of fixed and stable reference points, it would at times be difficult to tell who was above and who below the level of his time. Durkheim's frequent references to the trial of Socrates rested upon an awareness of this dilemma and the problems it presented for moral judgment.

For Durkheim, moreover, the contradictions and equivocations of crime represented like a distorted mirror image the uncertainties of conformity. Revealing his recognition of the tendencies of one form of modern humanism which were antithetical to his own growing desire for communal warmth in modernity, he perceptively observed:

Such are the characteristics of our immorality that they make themselves remarked more by cunning than by violence. These characteristics of our immorality are, moreover, those of our morality. It also becomes more cold, self-conscious, and rational. Sensibility plays an ever more restricted role, and this is what Kant expressed in placing passion beyond morals.[25]

So great was Durkheim's belief in the importance of the intimate relationship between crime and conformity that it led to what was for him a truly significant step: the reorganization of material in the *Année sociologique*. Beginning with Volume IV, Durkheim included a section on the functioning of moral and juridical rules in which he included both statistics and an analysis of conformity and deviance. (This section was paralleled by one on the genesis and structure of norms and institutions.) The explanatory basis of this classificatory reorganization was the realization that disobeying a rule was a way of relating to it. The

[25] *Leçons de sociologie* (Paris: Presses Universitaires de France, 1960), p. 142.

typological variations of conformity were matched by variations of criminality. As Mauss later observed: "In an epoch when few statisticians recognized the fact, he distinguished between violent criminality directed against persons in backward classes and populations and the milder criminality against goods (fraud, abuses of confidence, etc.) in commercial classes and urban, policed populations." [26] Here we have an inkling of what Sutherland was to call "white-collar crime." [27] Whatever the problematics of the manner in which he applied it to specific cases, the general principle which underlay Durkheim's conception of crime was the idea that an institutional order or value system expressed itself in its forms of deviance in a manner fully complementary to its expression in its forms of "respectable" behavior. Thus for Durkheim crime itself was not a social disease. Rather, the crime rate became a symptom of social pathology when it rose above or fell below certain thresholds of collective tolerance: then it pointed to severe causes of pathology in society and attested to the need of social reform.

It would, moreover, be false to conclude, on the grounds that Durkheim assimilated ordinary crime and ideological crime, that Durkheim's theory of crime was convincing evidence of his status quo conservatism. Lucien Goldmann, for example, has written, "It should be pointed out that [Durkheim's definition of crime] includes acts as different as the deed of Jesus driving money-changers from the temple, the activity of Thomas Müntzer, Karl Marx or Lenin, on the one hand, and, on the other, the latest hold-up or murder." [28] This conflation, for Goldmann, is one proof of "the *conservative* perspective in which all of Durkheim's sociology is implicitly elaborated and which allows us to explain a great many other features of both his work and that

[26] Mauss, "In Memoriam," p. 12.

[27] Edwin Hardin Sutherland, *White Collar Crime* (New York: Dryden Press, 1949).

[28] *The Human Sciences and Philosophy*, trans. Hayden V. White and Robert Anchor (first pub. 1966; London: Cape Editions, 1969), p. 38.

of his disciples." Goldmann concludes that "the assimilation of the revolutionary to the criminal naturally turns the reader against the former." [29]

Durkheim's point was that, especially in periods of rapid transition, members of society would themselves experience ambivalence in the judgment of certain phenomena. That the ideological criminal could himself participate in this ambivalence was shown by the case of Socrates. Yet Durkheim did realize that the characteristic of ordinary crime was its parasitical status vis-à-vis existing norms and institutions, whereas ideological crime (or, at times, the ideological aspect of crime) placed in question the existing rules or policies. Durkheim, in an article, tried to take account of a criticism by Tarde that was similar to Goldmann's but that, in contrast, stressed the radical implications of Durkheim's theory of crime. In other words, Tarde felt that the approximation of the revolutionary to the criminal naturally turned the reader in favor of the latter. Durkheim replied:

I said [in *The Rules*] that it was useful and even necessary that in any society the collective type not repeat itself identically in all consciences. . . . When I tried to show how crime could have even direct utility, the only examples I cited were those of Socrates and the philosophical heretics of all times, the precursors of free thought. . . . Then I said that the existence of crime had a *generally indirect* and *sometimes direct* utility: indirect, because crime could end only if the *conscience collective* imposed itself upon individual consciences with such incorrigible authority that all moral transformation was rendered impossible; direct, because sometimes, *but only sometimes,* the criminal was the precursor of a future morality. . . . In all times, the great moral reformers condemned the reigning morality and were condemned by it.[30]

Despite the debatable nature of Durkheim's moral futurism, the essential point was the dialectical relation between crime and conformity. This involved both the destructive and creative

---

[29] *Ibid.*, pp. 38, 40.

[30] "Crime et santé sociale," *Revue philosophique*, XXXIX (1895), 520–521.

aspects of anomie which were pre-eminently marked in ideological crime. Certain questionable features of the argument in *The Division of Labor*, however, would be only partially modified in the course of time.

Durkheim never adequately inquired into the crisis in the modern consciousness of punishment created by the puzzling intersection of an ideology of individual responsibility, the theory of social determinants, and the idea of "mental illness." Nor did Durkheim ever treat the psychological internalization of norms and values with the care that would facilitate the building of bridges to the insights of Freud. In his investigation of crime, Durkheim did not treat self-punishment or the function of the punishment of others in suppressing one's own criminal tendencies or relieving one's own frustrations and anxieties. In Durkheim, there was little feeling for the possibility that men might commit crimes, as they might turn to suicide, in order to find expiatory punishment for a pre-existing sense of guilt stemming from an explicit act, an overwhelming desire, or the general structure of a repressive collective or individual conscience.

In his *Civilization and Its Discontents,* Freud asserted that his intention was "to represent the sense of guilt as the most important problem in the evolution of culture, and to convey that the price of progress in civilization is paid in forfeiting happiness through the heightening of the sense of guilt." [31] Despite his insistence upon the role of expiation in punishment, Durkheim devoted scant attention to the problem of guilt—a critical lacuna in his attempt to relate personality and social structure. Even in his *Education morale,* which contained some of his most acute observations on the social determinants of character formation, he tended on the whole to restrict himself to problems of social structure, solidarity, and blame. Thus crime and punishment did constitute an area in which Durkheim's curiosity was stunted by his positivism and objectivism.

In *The Division of Labor,* moreover, the same problems which

[31] Sigmund Freud, *Civilization and Its Discontents* (Garden City, N.Y.: Doubleday Anchor Books, 1958), p. 90.

plagued his conception of *conscience collective* beset his theory of crime. Associating crime in a one-dimensional manner with social homogeneity and *communitas,* he failed to explore fully the ways in which crime was related to differentiation. The sector of modern life which supported the correlation of differentiation and restitutive sanction was that of the functionally specific division of labor, or specialization, in formally rationalized contexts. But Durkheim's tendency to universalize the correlation of communal identity and penal sanction led him to ignore or underestimate crucial features of social life.

Durkheim's idea that the criminal was different from others was associated with the idea that crime itself was a departure from the communal identity assured by the *conscience collective.* The latter preconception prevented Durkheim from seeing that the criminal might differ from others in deviating from norms stipulating differentiation and that crime itself might consist in bringing together in illicit communal identity "things" which ought to remain separate. Crime as deviation from norms prescribing differentiation was in certain respects singularly significant in the archaic societies that Durkheim interpreted in terms of homogeneity and communal identity. Durkheim's undialectical conception of the role of communal identity in crime accounted for the fact that, while he recognized the importance of ritual interdict in creating the religious nature of crime and the role of the incest taboo in kinship, he was never fully able to account theoretically for these observations. Thus, for example, he never related the incest taboo to differentiation among kinship groups and never saw the way in which incest was (as the Chinese characters which stand for incest express it) a "confusion of relationships."

Durkheim's long article entitled "Deux Lois de l'évolution pénale" ("Two Laws of Penal Evolution") [32] represented an extended footnote to the discussion of crime in *The Division of*

[32] *Année sociologique,* IV (1899–1900), 65–95.

Labor. In this article, he tried to formulate tendential regularities in the development of penal sanctions. His focus shifted from restitutive to repressive sanctions in modern society. He approached the problem through the evolutionary bias of "laws" of qualitative and quantitative development in punishment. His law of qualitative variation asserted that punishments tended to become less religious in nature. In modern society, punishment was increasingly restricted to the deprivation of liberty through incarceration in special houses of detention.

In Durkheim's second law, the element of social optimism which existed as an undercurrent in *The Division of Labor* emerged fully to the surface of his thought. It stated that the intensity or severity of punishment varied directly with the extent to which societies belonged to a simpler or "lower" type and with the extent to which the central government was absolute. This idea was more nuanced than the tendency in *The Division of Labor* to correlate "cruel and unusual punishments" with primitiveness, for it recognized a second variable in the nature of the central government—a factor which was not pertinent to many archaic societies. But Durkheim apparently did not believe that authoritarian government was a real possibility in modern societies. Indeed, the entire problem of the nature of government, which did not readily fit into the simple-complex schema of social organization, was deprived of sociological relevance. "This special form of political organization [i.e., authoritarianism] does not pertain to the congenital constitution of society but to individual, transitory, and contingent conditions." [33] Despite his thesis on Montesquieu, Durkheim at this stage of his thought was far from learning the lessons in political sociology which his great predecessor taught.

The generalized correlation of "simple" or "undifferentiated" society with severe punishment, however, could not withstand the onslaught of evidence. In this respect, Durkheim's *Moral Education* (which began as a lecture course just after the publi-

[33] *Ibid.*, p. 70.

cation of "Two Laws of Penal Evolution") represented a significant advance in his conception of crime and punishment. Com-
menting on the research of the ethnographer Sebald-Rudolf
Steinmetz, Durkheim observed:

A *priori*, one might believe that it is the rudeness of primitive mores,
the barbarism of the first ages which gave birth to this [severe] system
of punishment. But the facts are far from concording with this hypothesis, however natural it may first appear. . . . In the great majority
of cases, discipline is of great mildness [in primitive societies]. The
Indians of Canada love their children tenderly, never beat them, and
do not even reprimand them.[34]

A little later Mauss, writing about an archaic society (that of
the Todas) in the *Année sociologique*, asserted: "Penal law does
not exist to any significant extent. It is probable that the cause of
this absence is the extreme mildness of mores in these populations."[35] Curiously, Durkheim himself observed in an *Année*
review which predated his "Two Laws of Penal Evolution":
"The role of discipline grows with civilization. The notion of
rules, of imperative norms, which holds such a great place in our
morality has nothing primitive about it. It is thus natural that
education becomes impregnated with a certain austerity."[36]

These rather overstated observations on the repressive role of
developing civilization were supplemented in Durkheim's *Moral
Education* with a line of argument that did greater justice to
the function of authoritarian government by placing it in the
broader context of authoritarian and oppressive institutional
structures in general. In early modern history, corporal punishment found a privileged sanctuary in the type of school that was
marked by maximal social distance between teacher and pupil
and a claustration of children that isolated them from their

[34] *Education morale*, p. 154.

[35] Marcel Mauss, review of W. H. Rivers' *The Todas*, in *Année sociologique*, XI (1906–1909), 314.

[36] Review of S.-R. Steinmetz' "Das Verhaeltniss zwischen Eltern und
Kindern bei den Naturvoelken," in *Année sociologique*, III (1898–1899),
446.

families and the rest of society. The educational situation, Durkheim concluded, easily "degenerates into despo_ _m." The means
of avoiding this danger was to prevent the school "from closing
in upon itself . . . and assuming too professional a character."
This could be effected only by multiplying the school's points of
contact with the external world. "In itself, the school, like all
constituted groups, tends toward autonomy. It does not easily
accept control. Yet control is indispensable for it, not only from
an intellectual, but from a moral point of view." [37]

Durkheim went on to elaborate a more inclusive theory of
severe and violent punishments, which he extended beyond the
school to comprise such phenomena as colonialism. Corporal
punishment in the school was "a particular case of a law."

Every time two populations, two groups of individuals, of unequal
culture find themselves in sustained contact, certain sentiments develop
which lead the more cultivated group or the group which believes itself to be more cultivated to do violence to the other. This can be
observed very frequently in colonies and in any country where representatives of a European civilization find themselves at grips with an
inferior civilization. Without violence having any utility, and although
it presents grave dangers to those who indulge in it and who expose
themselves to fearful reprisals, it breaks out inevitably. . . . There is
produced a veritable drunkenness, a shameless exaltation of the ego,
a sort of megalomania which leads to the worst excesses, whose origin
is not difficult to perceive. . . . The individual does not contain himself unless he is faced with moral forces which he respects and upon
which he dares not trample. Otherwise, he knows no limits and asserts
himself without measure or bound.[38]

Thus the truly relevant variable in the severity of punishment
was the degree of authoritarianism in social institutions. Authoritarian structures or relations tended to convert punishment into
a systematic but often anomically unstable form of extreme violence that might be met by the extremely violent reaction of
the oppressed.

[37] *Education morale*, pp. 164–165.   [38] *Ibid.*, p. 161.

Traditional Differentiation

The distinction between segmental and organized structures in *The Division of Labor* paralleled that between the simple and the complex, the mechanical and the organic, the primitive and the modern.[39] The discussion of segmental structures had the merit of bringing out the importance of relatively small, isolated, and self-sufficient populations in archaic societies marked by strong communal ties, inherited status, attachment to traditions (represented sociologically by the prestige of elders), local territory (or vicinage), religious belief and practice, and the importance of kinship. But Durkheim's idea of segmental structures increased the difficulty of relating the various factors which he inventoried, for it reinforced the preconception that archaic societies were based exclusively on homogeneous groups juxtaposed, in Durkheim's simile, "like the rings of a ringworm."[40] Durkheim apparently did not sense the absurdity in the idea of a structure that was not in any sense organized. He could even make the incredible assertion that in archaic societies "kinship itself is not organized."[41]

Given Durkheim's taste for biological metaphors, it is interesting to speculate what might have been the effect on his thought if he had known about the genetic code. *The Division of Labor* relied on the idea that undifferentiated protoplasm was the basis of organisms. In his later years, Durkheim did seem to be on the brink of newer ideas which prefigured the great shift in social and cultural anthropology that was to be effected in France by Marcel Mauss and Claude Lévi-Strauss.

In 1903, Durkheim observed in an article on methodology written in collaboration with Paul Fauconnet:

These elementary forms exist nowhere in a state of even relative isolation which permits direct observation. Indeed, one must not confound them with primitive forms. The most rudimentary societies are still complex, although they have a confused complexity. They contain in

[39] *Division du travail social*, pp. 149ff.   [40] *Ibid.*, p. 150.   [41] *Ibid.*

themselves, lost in one another [*perdues les unes dans les autres*], but still real, all the elements which will be differentiated and developed in the course of evolution.[42]

Durkheim's thought appeared in slightly clearer form in his *Pragmatisme et Sociologie* (reconstituted from a course given just before his death), in which he enunciated the idea of a "primitive nebula."

When Spencer affirms that the universe proceeds from the homogeneous to the heterogeneous, this formula is inexact. What exists at the origin is also heterogeneity, but it is heterogeneity in a state of confusion. The initial state is a multiplicity of seeds, of modalities, of different activities, not only mixed together, but, so to speak, lost in one another so that it is extremely difficult to separate them. They are *indistinct* from one another. It is thus that in the cell of monocellular beings all vital functions are as if gathered up: all are found there; only they are not separated. The functions of nutrition and the functions of relation seem confounded, and it is difficult to distinguish them. In social life, this primitive state of indivision is still more striking. *Religious life*, for example, is rich with a multitude of forms of thought and activity of all sorts. In the order of thought, it comprises: (1) myths and religious beliefs, (2) an incipient science, (3) arts, aesthetic elements, notably song and music. All these elements are gathered up [*ramassés*] in a whole, and it seems difficult to separate them: science and art, myth and poetry, morality, law, and religion— all are confounded [*confondu*] or rather melted [*fondu*] into one another.[43]

This was Durkheim's most complete and perceptive statement of the problem which began to intrigue him in *The Division of Labor*. To find a more adequate conception of the nature and role of differentiation in archaic societies, one must turn from Durkheim himself to a work which perhaps marked the beginning of truly modern social and cultural anthropology in France:

[42] "Sociologie et sciences sociales," *Revue philosophique*, LV (1903), 477–478.

[43] *Pragmatisme et sociologie*, pp. 191–192.

The Gift, by Marcel Mauss. Claude Lévi-Strauss has compared the experience of the anthropologist in reading this essay to that of Malebranche in first reading Descartes. For, despite its suggestively unfinished quality and the honeycomb of erudition with which it is laced, this little essay seems to bring together imaginative conceptualization and massive evidence in a manner indicating a life spent in intimate contact with basic problems and an awareness of the way things fall into place without losing their local color.

Mauss fully realized that the fact that one never finds one homogeneous group in isolation but finds always at least two associated groups is indeed a crucial fact for sociological theory. The idea of an isolated, undifferentiated horde as the basis of social life was untenable. Through an analysis of gift exchange, Mauss sought "a set of more or less archeological conclusions on the nature of human transactions" which amounted to little less than a general theory of the role and nature of differentiation and exchange in human societies.[44] The fundamental status of the exchange of gifts in archaic societies revealed the universality of social differentiation which in the archaic context served to "bind clans together and keep them separate, divide their labor and constrain them to exchange." [45] In his study of the gift, moreover, Mauss sought "the answer to the question posed by Durkheim about the religious origin of economic value." [46]

What underlay and informed the exchange of gifts in archaic societies was a structure of reciprocity which led men in groups to relate to other groups through the obligation to give gifts, accept them, and render gifts in return. Members of indigenous societies conceptualized this structural principle—which normatively combined spontaneity and constraint, interest and obligation, freedom and necessity—in the idea that immanent in the gift was a religious and magical force binding men to return what

[44] Marcel Mauss, *The Gift,* trans. Ian Cunnison (first pub. 1925; New York: Norton, 1967).
[45] *Ibid.,* p. 71.   [46] *Ibid.,* p. 70.

they received. Thus receiving a gift was a dangerous as well as a gratifying experience, for it obliged the receiver to reciprocate, at times with increased largesse, often under the pain of magical sanction.

Differentiation always implied a measure of conflict among differentiated entities. But in certain cases (e.g., in North America and Melanesia) "amiable rivalry" compatible with mutual respect gave way to bouts of arrogant gift-giving whose purpose was to establish political and moral superiority. The circle of reciprocity was broken by the domineering gesture and the unilateral disdain which crushed one's rival with largesse. Gift exchange, in a sense, inverted the principle of capitalistic accumulation by institutionally requiring men to give more than they took rather than to profit by taking more than they gave. In the potlatch—the "monster child of the gift system"—the "agonistic" component in largesse attained the tragic level of *hybris* in ostentatious display: enormous quantities of gifts were not given but contemptuously destroyed or thrown into the sea. The potlatch revealed why men might be feared and suspected of treachery, especially when bearing gifts. The fear of the gift one could not repay was expressed in the ambivalence of the German *Gift*, meaning both "present" and "poison." In a supplementary article on the suicide of a Gallic chief, Mauss developed further the extreme complexity of the moral psychology of gift exchange by recounting the tale of a leader who, unable to reciprocate in kind, gave the only thing comparable in value to what he had received: his life.

But the gift in primitive societies was never an isolated phenomenon. In his concept of the *fait social total*, Mauss extracted the element of truth in Durkheim's idea of a "primitive nebula." It was not that ideas were uniquely confused or differentiations lacking in archaic societies, but that differentiations tended to be *cumulative* in nature and to engage experience on a multiplicity of levels simultaneously: "In these 'early' societies, social phenomena are not discrete; each phenomenon contains all the threads

of which the social fabric is composed. In these *total* social phenomena [*faits sociaux totaux*], as we propose to call them, all
kinds of institutions find simultaneous expression: religious, legal,
moral, and economic. In addition, the phenomena have their
aesthetic aspect and they reveal morphological types." [47]

The difference between primitive and modern societies which
Durkheim sought could, in the light of Mauss's ideas, be formulated, I think, as follows. Archaic societies accumulated relations
among roles, groups, persons, values, and ideas in a way which set
limits to economic growth and technological control of nature,
but which also implicated men in an intricate, inclusive network
of spiritual and symbolic relations with one another and the
cosmos. Modern societies distinguished sharply between nature
and culture, dissociated institutional spheres from one another
(family, job, politics, religion, and so on), defined often depersonalized roles in functionally specific ways, and furthered technological mastery and the accumulation of economic goods. The
saying "Business is business" was a meaningfully tautological
expression of this orientation. In modern society differentiations
tended to be detached from one another in relatively clear and
distinct, Cartesian compartments of activity and boxes of expe-

[47] *Ibid.*, p. 1. Mauss related the study of total social phenomena to a
"holistic" methodology conceived in terms reminiscent of Hegel: "We are
dealing then with something more than a set of themes, more than institutional elements, more than institutions, more even than systems of
institutions divisible into legal, economic, religious and other parts. We
are concerned with 'wholes,' with systems in their entirety. . . . It is only
by considering them as wholes that we have been able to see their essence,
their operation and their living aspect, and to catch the fleeting moment
when the society and its members take emotional stock of themselves and
their situation as regards others. . . . Historians believe and justly resent
the fact that sociologists make too many abstractions and separate un-
duly the various elements of society. . . . Whereas formerly sociologists
were obliged to analyse and abstract rather too much, they should now
force themselves to reconstitute the whole. . . . The study of the concrete,
which is the study of the whole, is made more readily, is more interesting
and furnishes more explanations in the sphere of sociology than the study
of the abstract" (pp. 77–78).

rience. Advanced specialization, in the modern division of labor, was one prominent form of this phenomenon.

What were the implications of this contrast between archaic and modern societies for the problem of "personality and social structure"? In archaic societies, the relation of individual personality to group experience was more total, like the relation of men to nature, because individual and group gave more of themselves in each relationship and in more many-sided ways. Individuality was subordinated to personality in a sense which might deny any existential distance between the individual and his roles. In ultimate forms, the individual found meaning for his own life in the cosmic archetype which negated the reality of chronological, irreversible time and obviated the anxiety-ridden confrontation of the individual with death.

In modern society, each role or group involved only a delimited investment of the personality and called for only a limited commitment, at times largely restricted to external conformity or the stipulations of a contract motivated by self-interest. Individuality became a keynote of sociocultural life. The group was less a milieu of existence, the development of personality less a community project, the "personal" more markedly distinguished from the "official" capacity, the "private" from the "public," occupation more a technically, professionally, and economically rationalized enterprise, and the search for identity an individual quest which often produced more weak books than strong personalities. The way in which a person experienced things or related to other people tended to be "one-dimensional."

In *The Gift*, Mauss drew moral and political conclusions with specific reference to forms of modern society. Analytically, he contrasted the institutions of a capitalistic economy with those related to gift exchange.

Let us now test the notion to which we have opposed the idea of gift and disinterestedness: that of interest and the individual pursuit of utility. . . . If similar motives animate Trobriand and American chiefs and Andaman clans and once animated generous Hindu or

Germanic noblemen in their giving and spending, they are not to be found in the cold reasoning of the businessman, banker or capitalist. In those earlier civilizations one had interests but they differed from those of our time. There, if one hoards, it is only to spend later on, to put people under obligations and to win followers. Exchanges are made as well, but only of luxury objects like clothing and ornaments, or feasts and other things that are consumed at once. . . . It is only our Western societies that quite recently turned man into an economic animal. . . . For a long time, man was something quite different; and it is not so long ago now since he became a machine—a calculating machine.[48]

Mauss went on to consider reform in a train of thought revealing that the only genuine sense in which Durkheim and his school were conservative was in the desire to return to bedrock fundamentals of human existence which were depreciated in modern life. These elementary forms of sociocultural life provided a daily bread of solidarity and led men to experience the necessary contradictions, liminal invitations, and anomic break-throughs of existence in all their tragic profundity. For Mauss as for Durkheim, basic institutional change adapted to modern conditions might enable men to find a path back to the wisdom of primitive societies that was expressed in noble reciprocal gift-giving.

We should return to the old and elemental. Once again we shall discover those motives of action still remembered by many societies and classes: the joy of giving in public, the delight in generous artistic expenditure, the pleasure of hospitality in the public or private feast. Social insurance, solicitude in mutuality or cooperation in the professional group and all those moral persons called Friendly Societies, are better than the mere personal security guaranteed by the nobleman to his tenant, better than the mean life afforded by the daily wage handed out by managements, and better even than the uncertainty of capitalist savings. . . . For honor, disinterestedness, and corporate solidarity are not vain words, nor do they deny the necessity for work. We should humanize the other liberal professions and make all of them more perfect. That would be a great deed, and one Durkheim already

[48] *Ibid.*, pp. 73–74.

had in view. In doing this we should, we believe, return to the ever-present bases of law, to its real fundamentals and to the very heart of normal social life.[49]

The probe into the problems which held the attention of the Durkheim school has been continued by a thinker who has acknowledged the indirect influence of Durkheim and the more direct, informal, and seminally personal influence of Marcel Mauss: Claude Lévi-Strauss. *La Pensée sauvage* (*The Savage Mind*) constituted a nodal point in the development of Lévi-Strauss. (We say more about its relation to Durkheim's thought when we discuss the relation of the human sciences to epistemology.) In this extremely difficult and professedly provisional pause in his work, Lévi-Strauss broached problems which had been relegated to tame oblivion in the thought of Durkheim. These problems included man's perceptual and metaphoric relations with nature, the mediation between sensation and the intellect, the nature of time, cosmic structures of experience, and the dialectic between the real and the imaginary. Indeed, it would not be going too far to argue that *La Pensée sauvage* is basically a study in the epistemology of perception which employs material drawn from archaic societies in a "crucial experiment" in the elaboration of a general theory. In his own conception of the relation of sociology to philosophy, Durkheim was fully aware of the symbolic and structural bases of culture and society, but he was bound by a highly specific metaphysic in his interpretation of this idea. The work of Lévi-Strauss goes beyond Durkheim's social metaphysic in its contention that the notion of mutual respect as the complement of self-respect must be extended to the more generous idea that one cannot respect oneself or others without respecting the whole of nature. This gift of broader solidarity is entailed in Lévi-Strauss's conviction that true humanism must begin beyond man—that it "does not begin with oneself, but places the world above life, life above man, respect

[49] *Ibid.*, p. 67.

for others above egotism." A more intimate knowledge of archaic societies enabled Lévi-Strauss to reassert the primacy of Rousseau in modern cultural thought (and of the Kant who was greatly influenced by Rousseau), whereas Durkheim placed ultimate faith in a Cartesianized neo-Kantianism which culminated in a dualistic conception of mind and body and left little epistemological room for Kant's faculty of aesthetic judgment.

On the more circumscribed problem of the contrast between archaic and modern societies with respect to the existence of differentiation, Lévi-Strauss observed:

We know the taboo on parents-in-law or at least its approximate equivalent. Through it we are forbidden to address the great of this world and obliged to keep out of their way. . . . Now, in most societies the position of wife giver is accompanied by social (and sometimes also economic) superiority, that of wife taker by inferiority and dependence. This inequality between affines may be expressed objectively in institutions as a fluid or stable hierarchy, or it may be expressed subjectively in the system of interpersonal relations by means of privileges and prohibitions.

Thus nothing mysterious is attached to these usages which our own experience unveils to us from the inside. We are disconcerted only by their constitutive conditions, different in each case. Among ourselves, they are clearly detached from other usages and linked together in a nonequivocal context. In contrast, in exotic societies the same usages and the same context are, as it were, ensnared [englués] in other usages and a different context: that of family ties, with which they seem to us incompatible. We find it hard to imagine that in private the son-in-law of the President of the French Republic should see in him the chief of state rather than the father-in-law. And although the Queen of England's husband may behave as the first of her subjects in public, there are good reasons for supposing that he is just a husband when they are alone together. It is either one or the other. The superficial strangeness of the taboo on parents-in-law arises from its being both at the same time.

Consequently, as we have found already in the case of operations of understanding, the system of ideas and attitudes appears here only as incarnated. . . . What appears to us [in modern relationships] as greater social ease and greater intellectual mobility is thus due to the fact that we prefer to operate with detached pieces [*pièces détachées*], if not indeed with small change [*la monnaie de la pièce*], while the native is a hoarder: he is forever tying the threads, tirelessly turning over on themselves all aspects of reality, whether physical, social, or mental. We traffic in our ideas; he makes of them a treasure. Savage thought [*la pensée sauvage*] puts in practice a philosophy of finitude.[50]

The first great theoretical work of Lévi-Strauss, *Les Structures élémentaires de la parenté* (*The Elementary Structure of Kinship*), was tacitly posited on the extension of Durkheim's category of organic solidarity (in the sense of differentiation and reciprocity) to the study of kinship structures in archaic societies. In a summary which Lévi-Strauss gave of his general conclusions, he observed:

Now, in exactly the same way that the principle of sexual division of labor establishes a mutual dependency between the sexes, compelling them thereby to perpetuate themselves and to found a family, the prohibition of incest establishes a mutual dependency between families, compelling them, in order to perpetuate themselves, to give rise to new families. It is through a strange oversight that the similarity of the two processes is generally overlooked on account of the use of terms as dissimilar as *division*, on the one hand, and *prohibition* on the other. We could easily have emphasized only the negative aspect of the division of labor by calling it a prohibition of tasks; and conversely, outlined the positive aspect of incest-prohibition by calling it the principle of the division of labor of marriageable rights between families. For incest-prohibition simply states that families (however they should be defined) can only marry between each other and that they cannot marry inside themselves.[51]

The role of differentiation in archaic societies was also investigated by Lévi-Strauss in a study of totemism which preceded

[50] *La Pensée sauvage* (Paris: Plon, 1962), pp. 352–353.

[51] Claude Lévi-Strauss, "The Family," in H. Shapiro, ed., *Man, Culture, and Society* (first pub. 1956; New York: Oxford University Press, 1960), p. 277.

La Pensée sauvage. In *Le Totémisme aujourd'hui* (*Totemism*), he interpreted totemism on the most general theoretical level as the assertion of a homology between a binary opposition of natural species and a binary opposition between social groups. Lévi-Strauss found the only specificity of totemism as a cultural phenomenon to be the privileged role of natural species as logical operators. The logical "similitude," moreover, was postulated neither within society as a homogeneous whole nor between the group and a natural species. The "similitude" referred to comparable differences between natural species and social groups. Durkheim's later theory of religion comprised a conception of a global totemic institution combining religion, kinship, and alimentary taboos. In *The Elementary Forms of the Religious Life,* Durkheim would center his interpretation on the idea of an identification between a solidary social group (the clan) and an essential principle of religious meaning asserted to be the "hidden" referent in the figurative and emblematic representation of a natural species. Durkheim argued that this "hidden" referent was society itself, and religion for Durkheim had an essentially social meaning. For Lévi-Strauss, religion had a social aspect, but it included this aspect in a broader network of relations, including prominently man's relation to nature. Totemism did not have an invariably religious function. The logical identity affirmed by totemism, moreover, referred to the relation between internally differentiated series of natural and social groups. And the entire notion of an original social and cultural complex gravitating around the totem formed an untenable "totemic illusion."

Through the usage of an animal and plant nomenclature (its unique distinctive characteristic), the alleged totemism does no more than express in its own way—by means of a code, as we would say today—correlations and oppositions which can be formalized in other ways, e.g., among certain tribes of North and South America by oppositions of the type sky/earth, war/peace, upstream/downstream, red/white, etc. The most general model and the most systematic application of this is perhaps to be found in China, in the opposition of the two principles Yang and Yin, as male and female, day and night, summer and winter, the union of which results in an organized totality (*tao*) such as the conjugal pair, the day, or the year. Totemism is thus reduced to a particular fashion of posing a general problem: how to make opposition, instead of being an obstacle to integration, serve rather to produce it.[52]

Thus totemism for Lévi-Strauss amounted to a subcase of the general problem of making differentiation the ground of integration—the very problem which Durkheim had earlier conceptualized in terms of organic solidarity. The highly complex role of cumulative differentiations in symbolic systems and social structure (conceived analytically as one type of symbolic system rather than as an invariably autonomous, "*sui generis* realm of social facts") has been further extended by Lévi-Strauss into the study of mythology, a problem area which Durkheim largely passed over in silence. Since this aspect of Lévi-Strauss's thought is both the most intricate and the least accessible to the nonspecialist, we shall have to be content with its mere mention. It is, however, safe to say that the thought of Lévi-Strauss has thoroughly exploded Durkheim's idea of simplicity, homogeneity, and diffuseness as the essence of archaic societies. In its place, there have arisen problems of such magnitude that modern social scientists often feel compelled to call upon other specialists, e.g., mathematicians, and thereby invoke the modern division of labor in order to track archaic societies' "primitive" complexity and possibly universal implications.

But the transcendence of Durkheim's ethnocentrism has in practice often led to the loss of Durkheim's profound interest in the nature and course of modern societies. Judging from Lévi-Strauss's own work, the major problem of the ethnologist is no longer objectivity in relation to experience in other societies because of his commitments in modern society but detachment from the problems of modern society because of his commitment to the ways of other societies. This attitude easily shades into elegiac remembrance, a form of aestheticism which in its social implica-

[52] *Le Totémisme aujourd'hui* (Paris: Presses Universitaires de France, 1962), pp. 127–128.

tions has little to distinguish it from less elevated forms of escapism and *divertissement*. Yet it was Lévi-Strauss who in his "Inaugural Address" formulated, in spite of his apparent reluctance, the pregnant possibility sensed by Mauss and vaguely felt by Durkheim himself.

If it were—and thank God it is not—expected of the anthropologist that he presage the future of humanity, no doubt he would conceive it, not as a prolongation or a transcendence of present forms, but rather on the model of an integration, progressively unifying the characteristics proper to cold societies [i.e., the type of order, approximated in archaic societies, which rests on the primacy of reversible, cyclical time] and hot societies [i.e., historically turbulent change and "progress," approximated in modern societies]. His reflection would take up the thread of the old Cartesian dream of placing machines, like automata, in the service of man. He would follow the traces of this dream in the social philosophy of the eighteenth century up until Saint-Simon. For, in announcing the passage "from the government of men to the administration of things," the latter anticipated the distinction between [material] culture and society and the conversion, which information theory and electronics enable us at least to perceive as possible, from a type of civilization which historical becoming inaugurated in the past—but at the price of a transformation of men into machines—to an ideal civilization which could succeed in transforming machines into men. Then, culture having received the burden of manufacturing progress, society would be liberated from the millennial curse which forced it to enslave men in order to progress. Thenceforth, history could make itself. And society—placed above, or below, history—could once again assume that regular and almost crystalline structure which the best preserved of primitive societies teach us is not contradictory to human nature. In this perspective, even if utopian, social anthropology would find its highest justification, for the forms of life and thought which it studies would no longer have only historical and comparative interest. They would correspond to a permanent choice for man which social antropology, especially in our most somber hours, would have the mission of safeguarding.[53]

[53] Claude Lévi-Strauss, "Leçon inaugurale," Jan. 5, 1960, Collège de France, No. 31, pp. 43–44.

This notion of reconciling progress with legitimate order in modern society, which Durkheim expressed in his own way in terms of the dialectic of anomie and a structurally informed *conscience collective,* brought Durkheim's school beyond the retrogressive memories of Comte. It showed the way to an idea of the authentically conservative possibilities of modern society. Given the nature of status quo institutions and conditions in modern society, however, this vision increasingly led to what might be called a selectively radical conservatism requiring basic structural change. For only structural change would permit the use of modern material culture in ways compatible with a humanistic return to fundamentals in social life through the planned avoidance of unwanted change.

Yet one crucial problem left by Durkheim has not been adequately resolved by French thinkers influenced by him. Durkheim perceived in an exaggerated fashion the importance of community in archaic societies. Lucien Lévy-Bruhl's stress on this idea was even more one-sided. Durkheim, moreover, increasingly saw the need for significant community in all healthy societies. The problem he left was that of the precise relationship between community and differentiated structure at various levels of the "tree" of social life. A danger in the methodological revisionism of Claude Lévi-Strauss is the radical de-emphasis of the problem of community.

For further insight into this problem, one may turn to Victor Turner, probably the most important English-speaking anthropologist now alive who has been significantly influenced by the thought of Durkheim. Turner deserves more adequate coverage than he receives here, for in his treatment of Durkheim's thought as a living tradition, he has shown himself a thinker of a stature comparable to Lévi-Strauss's. We confine ourselves to a few brief indications of the line of argument in the three concluding chapters of Turner's most synthetic work, *The Ritual Process.*[54]

[54] Victor Turner, *The Ritual Process* (Chicago: Aldine, 1969).

The Ritual Process in a sense revives the problem posed in *The Division of Labor*. For Turner focuses on the roles of structural differentiation and *communitas* as complementary and dialectically related aspects of the social system. *Communitas* is more difficult to grasp than structure. But a study of it is vital and is related to the understanding of structure itself.

Communitas is made evident or accessible, so to speak, only through its juxtaposition to, or hybridization with, aspects of social structure. Just as in *Gestalt* psychology, figure and ground are mutually determinative, or, as some rare elements are never found in nature in their purity but only as components of chemical compounds, so communitas can be grasped only in some relation to structure. Just because the communitas component is elusive, hard to pin down, it is not unimportant. Here the story of Lao-Tse's chariot wheel may be apposite. The spokes of the wheel and the nave . . . to which they are attached would be useless, he said, but for the hole, the gap, the emptiness at the center . . . which is nevertheless indispensable to the functioning of the wheel.[55]

In any society, *communitas* may existentially erupt in the extreme experience of individuals, e.g., in mystical states. In a relatively stable, ongoing social system, however, *communitas* is normatively integrated with structure, for example in rituals such as rites of passage which meaningfully relate the liminal or transitional stages of a person's development to his life cycle as a whole. In a society excessively bound by formal structures, *communitas* may be ideologically affirmed by restive segments of the population. Revolution itself represents a liminal state of society as a whole. Turner concludes that "communitas breaks in through the interstices of structure, in liminality; at the edges of structure, in marginality; and from beneath structure, in inferiority. It is almost everywhere held to be sacred or 'holy,' possibly because it transgresses or dissolves the norms that govern structured and institutionalized relationships and is accomplished by experiences of unprecedented potency."[56]

[55] *Ibid.*, p. 127.   [56] *Ibid.*, p. 128.

Through the concept of *communitas*, Turner is able to relate intelligibly such seemingly diverse phenomena as "neophytes in the liminal phase of ritual, subjugated autochthones, small nations, court jesters, holy mendicants, good Samaritans, millenarian movements, 'dharma bums,' matrilaterality in patrilineal systems, patrilaterality in matrilineal systems, and monastic orders." [57] The mere indication of the problems Turner treats shows the continuing relevance of the questions raised in Durkheim's *Division of Labor*. Turner's ideas, moreover, inform much of my later discussion of developments in Durkheim's thought.

Theory of Change

After his discussion of mechanical and organic solidarity in normal states of society, Durkheim's focus in *The Division of Labor* shifts to the process of change which purportedly has led from one type of solidarity to the preponderance of the other. In view of stereotyped notions of Durkheim's "static" bias, it is significant that the question of change is at the center of his first major work. Increasingly, his reformist goal was the type of institutional structure which would limit uncontrolled historical change and establish legitimate order. In this sense, stabilization was indeed his aim. But, analytically and empirically, Durkheim was not oblivious to the problem of change. The questionable feature of *The Division of Labor* and of Durkheim's thought as a whole is not the neglect of historical change but the idea of it Durkheim at times entertained. Durkheim often assumed that an essential similarity of structure in two societies or social types, one of which was (or was believed to be) in some sense logically "simpler" than the other, permitted the inference that the second society had evolved historically from the first by a process of increasing complexity of structural development. This preconception enabled the theorist to play havoc with the relationship between logic and time.

In fact, Durkheim's entire evolutionary framework in his

[57] *Ibid.*, p. 125.

first major work often amounted to an uncritical reliance on Spencer's idea of evolution as a movement from homogeneity to differentiation. In his *First Principles,* Spencer had formulated his general idea of evolution thus: "Evolution is an integration of matter and concomitant dissipation of motion; during which the matter passes from a relatively indefinite, incoherent homogeneity to a relatively definite, coherent heterogeneity; and during which the retained motion undergoes a parallel transformation." [58] In his parody of Spencer, William James brings out the confusion under the verbiage of this "grand theory" of change from homogeneity to differentiation: "Evolution is a change from a no-howish, untalkaboutable, all-alikeness to a somehowish and in general talkaboutable not-all-alikeness by continuous sticktogetherations and somethingelsifications." [59]

Durkheim's dependence on diffuse ideas of evolution for his model of change accounted, no doubt, for the fact that *The Division of Labor* has no genuine historical dimension. The known process of change—or "modernization," a term which is at times a bare-faced euphemism—in archaic societies took the form of colonialism, imperialism, and "culture contact" with societies which had already attained economic, military, and technological superiority. Yet Durkheim had nothing to say about this process, a process which could be documented historically. Indeed, the uprooting of "primitive" societies by "higher" types of civilization made the "primitive" man in modern history prone, among other things, to anomic suicide—a fact which Durkheim did not discuss, even in *Suicide.* Moreover, the modern industrial societies which most concerned Durkheim had developed, not from a general type of primitive or traditional society, but, with a great deal of turmoil, from a feudal past. As Tocqueville had understood, as experience in France made evident, and as Durkheim himself

[58] Herbert Spencer, *First Principles* (New York: Appleton, 1864), p. 407.

[59] Quoted in Gilbert Highet, *The Art of Teaching* (New York: Knopf, 1954), p. 207.

seemed to realize in his less grandly theoretical moments, the precise nature of the historical development from a feudal past was intimately related to the specific problems faced by various Western countries in the modern period. In the United States, which lacked a pronounced feudal past, a heritage of slavery and racism created severe difficulties for the achievement of consensus in ways which differed according to region. Of these matters, Durkheim said nothing. And one of the most blatant omissions in his discussion of modern society in the West was the absence of any extended treatment of the specific nature of social structure in Germany and its relation to Germany's domestic situation and international position. Durkheim touched upon the "German problem" only in propagandistic pamphlets toward the end of his life. And if he had wanted to investigate an internal process of change from primitive cultures to Western practices and beliefs, the logical historical place to start would have been pre-Socratic Greece. *The Division of Labor,* in brief, often subordinates real problems and real historical processes to models at least as abstract as those of the classical economists whom Durkheim never tired of criticizing.

Although Durkheim's discussion in *The Division of Labor* gives little real historical insight into significant cases of change, it is nonetheless interesting for his general conception of social process and for what it reveals concerning his uncertainties about modern society. The abstract quality of his argument derived largely from the fact that he was addressing himself, not positively to empirical evidence and problems in the analysis of society, but predominantly to the models of other theorists. Durkheim presented massive change in society as a process in which integrated social structures are subjected to conditions beyond their control and which results in a transitional phase of pathological disorder before society can reorganize on new structural bases.

With the frequently false and superficial rigor of monocausal theories of the time, Durkheim selected *population pressure* as the cause of the upset in the functional balance of society. Demography, of course, is to some extent a biological factor rather than a specifically social fact. But this criticism applies to virtually all of Durkheim's explanations, and it bears upon his metaphysical and epistemological tendency to magnify an observation about a crucial social dimension of things into an exhaustive account of them. Durkheim's valid point was that demographic conditions are always socially relevant and that a well-ordered society requires a normatively controlled population policy. In fact, shifts in population did have special importance in causing unwanted change in archaic societies where norms and beliefs generally functioned to keep population down to manageable proportions. The crucial role of demography in "developing" and modern societies has, of course, become increasingly obvious. But a methodologically pertinent criticism is that Durkheim's extreme monocausalism prevented him from devoting sufficient attention to other factors—e.g., technology—in processes of major social change.

Theoretically and ideologically, this model of change, which envisioned a passage from normal structure through a period of pathological transition to a new form of normal structure, had great importance. For Durkheim as for earlier thinkers such as Saint-Simon, Comte, and J. S. Mill, modern society was passing through a transitional phase in which pathogenic causes had not yet been fully transcended. Durkheim's conception of utilitarianism was derived from the thought of Bentham and Spencer, and it was influenced by Social Darwinism. Had he studied the evolution of the thought of Mill, for example, he might have discovered ideas which corroborated his own theories. But, given his conception of utilitarianism, his model of change enabled Durkheim to situate it (as well as Social Darwinism) as a theory relating to a period of rapid transition and social pathology. Durkheim argued in Social Darwinian fashion that population pressure caused an increased struggle for existence which resulted in time in the survival of the fittest. But he did not iden-

tify the fittest with those individuals or social units that maximized their own self-interest or survived rabid competition and
struggle. This entire state of affairs for him was an aspect of
transition and pathology. Rather, he envisioned a process of
evolution which would eventuate in the survival of the *fittest
form of social structure,* i.e., the normal state which would co-
operatively employ the social contributions of all members of
society for the common good.

The most obvious interpretation of Durkheim's assertion that
"everything happens mechanistically" (*tout se passe mécanique-
ment*) is in terms of a comprehensive positivistic theory of
causation which excludes the possible intervention of human will
and conscious effort or control in the historical process. Here,
however, one must distinguish between the passage from the
normal to the pathological and the passage from the pathological
to the normal. In *The Division of Labor,* the assertion that "everything happens mechanistically" appeared in Durkheim's treatment of change from one integrated social system to the transitional state of pathology. Apparently Durkheim did believe that
a major and disorienting departure from a viably integrated
social order was caused initially by impersonal, mechanistic processes which in their socially relevant form were not intended.
Men did not choose to abandon a traditional mode of cultural
integration: they were forced out of it by external conditions
such as population pressure. Here Durkheim's ideas were similar
to those of both Rousseau and Darwin.

But Durkheim was much less clear about the relation of mechanistic process to other factors in the passage from pathology to
normality. He seemed to rely on a Darwinian notion of "natural
selection." And he argued that one could not attribute the functions of social institutions to the manifest intentions of social
agents. But Durkheim never fully sorted out the interaction in
the historical process of such factors as intention, unintended
consequence, unconscious motivation, anomie, and the structure
and functioning of institutions. Significant ideas he developed

are that social consciousness arises in response to social disorder and that sociology, as the most advanced consciousness of modern society, has the task of informing meaningful social action. How these ideas are related to the over-all understanding of the historical process or to the more limited question of the intentional action of social and political agents remains a blank chapter in Durkheim's thought.

Residual Doubts

One feature of *The Division of Labor* which has puzzled many commentators is Durkheim's extensive treatment of the relation of the division of labor to happiness. Yet this question was important for Durkheim in terms both of the theories he opposed and the theories he defended. The idea that the division of labor as the handmaid of economic growth brings happiness and is indeed the result of a conscious pursuit of happiness constituted a favorite theme of utilitarians and classical economists. Durkheim did not investigate the possibility that the pursuit of happiness might function ideologically as a form of false consciousness. His rejection of the correlation between happiness and the division of labor relied upon a statistical means of testing the proposed relationship. Durkheim argued that there was no positive index of happiness which carried methodological conviction. But, he observed, there was an objective index of collective unhappiness: *the suicide rate.* If economic progress brought happiness, the suicide rate should drop. But "on the contrary, true suicide, i.e., sad suicide, is in an endemic state among civilized peoples." [60] Thus economic growth, at least under the extremely unstable conditions which have accompanied it in modern history, does not bring happiness. This point would be more fully elaborated in *Suicide,* which had its origin in the correlation of unhappiness and suicide in *The Division of Labor.* Durkheim related all disruptive change to anomie and saw the degree of happiness pos-

[60] *Division du travail social,* p. 226.

sible in life to be dependent on overcoming anomie and creating solidarity.

Quite apparent in the first edition of *The Division of Labor* was Durkheim's attempt to find a middle way between the complacency of utilitarians and the moral nihilism of prophets of doom. If Durkheim at times in the first edition seemed to share more of the complacency of the utilitarians and classical economists, it was not because he agreed with their idea of legitimate order but because he believed in an evolutionary movement of modern society toward his own ideal of legitimate order, however uncertain he may have been about its precise nature or mode of attainment. Clearly, Durkheim rejected Comte's belief that the division of labor necessarily entails social disorder. But he was tempted, as he so often was, to affirm the opposite of another theorist's view: at times he seemed to argue that the division of labor per se created social solidarity.

Durkheim also wanted to distinguish his position from that of Ferdinand Tönnies, in whom he saw a theorist with an excessively negative view of modern society. In fact, Durkheim's tendentious ideas on archaic societies were due less to ethnocentric *noblesse oblige* than to a desire to avoid the dire conclusions of modern prophets of doom. Durkheim tended to invert Tönnies' equations by finding in modern organic solidarity the virtues Tönnies placed in primitive *Gemeinschaft* (community) and to ascribe to primitive mechanical solidarity the defects Tönnies found in modern *Gesellschaft* (society). Durkheim at points saw primitive societies as miniature mass societies without any "organic" structure, characterized by herd conformity and repressive punishments, and held together by bonds which were weaker and less stable than those in modern society.[61] Tönnies, in *Gemeinschaft und Gesellschaft*, had stated his position in these terms:

The theory of *Gesellschaft* deals with the artificial construction of an aggregate of human beings which superficially resembles the *Gemein-*

[61] *Ibid.*, p. 120.

schaft insofar as the individuals live and dwell together peacefully. However, in *Gemeinschaft* they remain essentially united in spite of all separating factors, whereas in *Gesellschaft* they are essentially separated in spite of all uniting factors. In the *Gesellschaft*, as contrasted with the *Gemeinschaft*, we find no actions that can be derived from an *a priori* and necessarily existing unity; no actions, therefore, which manifest the will and spirit of the unity even if performed by the individual; no actions which, insofar as they are performed by the individual, take place on behalf of those united with him. In the *Gesellschaft* such actions do not exist. On the contrary, here everybody is by himself and isolated, and there exists a condition of tension against all others.[62]

Tönnies asserted that Durkheim's ideas of mechanical and organic solidarity were "altogether different" (*ganz und gar verschieden*) from his own.[63] In an 1889 article on Tönnies' book, Durkheim, with comparable intransigence, made an apparent effort to accentuate the positive in modern society.

The point where I separate myself from him is in his theory of *Gesellschaft*. If I have understood him, *Gesellschaft* is characterized by a progressive development of individualism, whose dispersive effects the state's action could for a while prevent. It would be essentially a mechanical aggregate; everything that remained of truly collective life would result not from spontaneity but from the entirely external impulsion of the state. In a word, this is society as conceived by Bentham. Now I believe that the life in great social agglomerations is just as natural as that in little aggregates. It is not less organic or less internal. Beyond purely individual movements, there is in our contemporary societies a properly collective activity which is as natural as that of smaller societies of the past. It is assuredly different; it constitutes a different type, but between these two species of the same genus, however diverse they may be, there is no difference of nature. To prove it would take a book.[64]

[62] Ferdinand Tönnies, *Community and Society*, Charles Loomis, trans. and ed. (New York: Harper Torchbooks, 1963), p. 64.

[63] Quoted in Harry Alpert, *Emile Durkheim and His Sociology* (first pub. 1939; New York: Russell & Russell, 1961), p. 185.

[64] Review of Tönnies, *Gemeinschaft und Gesellschaft*, *Revue philosophique*, XXVII (1889), 421.

The book was *The Division of Labor*. But the book remained ambiguous about whether and how existing forms of the division of labor or their developmental tendencies created social and moral solidarity. The argument concealed a "missing link" in the evolutionary chain.

Uncertainty also characterized Durkheim's treatment of modern individualism and its relation to solidarity. In addition to other aspects of the problem, Durkheim later tried to distinguish between forms of individualism compatible with solidarity and excessive, atomizing individualism or egoism. *The Division of Labor* attempted to correlate increasing social differentiation, universalistic values, and individualism. But its idea of the relation of individualism to solidarity was veiled in darkness. At times, Durkheim stressed the importance of personal dignity and the individual choice of a function in keeping with humane values and one's capacities. At other times, he seemed to argue that all institutionalized or ideologically shared individualism is the egoistic expression of a self-effacing *conscience collective*—despite his own attempt to base solidarity on phenomena bound up with modern individualism.

If [modern individualism and the cult of the person] are common insofar as they are beliefs shared by the community, they are individual in their object. If all wills are turned toward the same end, this end is not social. Thus individualism is in an entirely exceptional situation in the *conscience collective*. It is from society that it draws its force, but it is not to society that it attaches us: it is to ourselves. Consequently, it does not constitute a truly social bond. This is why theorists who make this sentiment the exclusive basis of their moral doctrine may with justice be met with the reproach that they dissolve society.[65]

Another matter left in doubt in *The Division of Labor* was the relationship of differentiation to stratification, class formation, and structures of domination in society—and their relation, in turn, to reciprocity and solidarity. This was a notable omission in a purportedly general sociology of a world in which the his-

[65] *Division du travail social*, p. 147.

torical price of abundance and "high" culture for the few had typically been the exploitation of the many. Here Durkheim's failure to come to terms with Marx and become aware of Weber lessened drastically the relevance of his sociology to both the understanding of historical societies and the elaboration of his own concepts of normality and pathology. And here more than anywhere else is a basis for the charge that Durkheim was a "bourgeois idealist" whose thought diverted attention from the realities of historical society. Apparently, Durkheim did not believe that functional differentiation necessarily involves stratification or that the nature of a function somehow entails a differential evaluation of roles or groups in terms of higher and lower. But he apparently did believe that all differentiated social orders were correlated with some type and measure of stratification.[66]

[66] See Durkheim's review of Célestin Bouglé's Essais sur le régime des castes (Paris: Alcan, 1908), in Année sociologique, XI (1906–1909), 384–387. One of Durkheim's basic points in this review is that hierarchy is not due to the division of labor itself but, in castes, to a specific sort of ritual principle. Bouglé had analyzed castes in terms of a combination of hereditary division of labor, hierarchical organization, ritual repulsion, and endogamy. For a more extensive structural analysis of hierarchy, see Louis Dumont, Homo hierarchicus (Paris: Gallimard, 1966). See also the course given by Roger Bastide, "Formes élementaires de la stratification sociale," Centre de Documentation Universitaire, Paris. Bastide observes that even in primitive societies where there is no significant stratification among groups, there is always stratification among individuals on the basis of performance. Interestingly enough, Bastide retains the general neo-Kantian frame of reference of the Durkheim school, but he argues that "the fault of Kant was to base his thought upon a particular culture, i.e., that of bourgeois and puritan German society, in order to disengage the a priori form of the moral law" (p. 83). Bastide, in my opinion, makes too much of intimations of stratification in The Division of Labor. True, Durkheim spoke of the central state in organic solidarity, but he always conceived of it in a democratic form which involved a highly specialized type of stratification. And Durkheim had little to say about socioprofessional hierarchy. Bastide, moreover, observes that Lévi-Strauss "is in the process of rewriting the Critique of Pure Reason" (p. 82), but he fails to notice that Lévi-Strauss is often much closer to the Critique of Judgment in his emphasis upon the centrality of aesthetics and perception. But Bastide is to the point in calling for a continuation of Durkheim's work of rewriting the Critique of Practical Reason in a way which would be less ethnocentric

What the causes, mechanisms, consequences, or principles of this correlation might be, either typologically or universally, was never fully examined by Durkheim. Even in his proposed model of a normal, solidaristic form of modern society, he did not offer a sustained, searching, and detailed enquiry into the problem of power, prestige, and economic reward in various institutional spheres and in the total social order. Only certain elementary ideas emerged from his discussions, and they were hardly adequate to the problems raised. These ideas are discussed in the next two chapters.

Contract and Solidarity

Durkheim's tacit acceptance of Spencer's conception of evolution was not indicative of his estimation, in *The Division of Labor*, of the thought of the English theorist. His generally critical reaction to Spencer is most apparent in Book I, chapter vii, in which he contrasts Spencer's idea of contractual solidarity with his own idea of organic solidarity. This pivotal chapter immediately precedes Durkheim's discussion of change from mechanical to organic solidarity, but it introduces the concluding section on pathological forms of the division of labor by bringing out ways in which development in modern society has not reached a stage adequate to serve as a functional basis of solidarity.

For Spencer, industrial society was based upon a vast cash nexus of private contracts sanctioned by a laissez-faire police state. "The typical form of social relation would be the economic relation stripped of all regulation." [67] If this relationship characterized society, Durkheim reasoned, there would be little if any solidarity.

In the fact of economic exchange, the different agents remain outside one another, and with the termination of the operation each one finds

---

and genuinely comparative, focus upon values and the process of evaluating which distinguish men from animals, and concentrate upon whole societies instead of analytically abstracted structures detached from history.

[67] *Division du travail social*, p. 180.

himself alone again. Consciences are only superficially in contact; they neither penetrate nor adhere strongly to one another. If one gets to the bottom of things, one will see that all harmony of interests conceals a conflict which is latent or simply adjourned. For where interest reigns alone, there is nothing to restrain egoism, and each ego finds itself on a warlike footing with all others. Any truce to this eternal antagonism cannot be long-range. Indeed, interest is the least constant of all things in the world. Today it is in my interest to unite with you. Tomorrow the same reason will make me your enemy.[68]

Thus Tönnies' critique, excluded by the front door, seemed to gain entry by the back. Durkheim's own position was summed up in the assertion that "everything is not contractual in the contract." [69] Durkheim meant that the contract could not be reduced to *ad hoc* acts of will among private parties, but that it presupposed a framework of norms and laws upheld and sanctioned by social agencies. As examples, he cited the requirements of the French Code, which forbade the making of contracts by an incompetent and contracts concerning things which could not be sold or involving illicit dealings. There were also positive obligations in contract law, for instance those enabling a judge to grant a delay to a debtor under certain conditions.

The crucial substantive question, however, was whether and to what extent the intervention of the state or other social agencies was restricted to police functions and the enforcement of the rules of the game in a profit-oriented market economy. Were the conditions of organic solidarity fulfilled by the pursuit of self-interest in market relationships as long as one did not break the law (through theft, fraud, and so on)? In other words, was Durkheim at best scoring a debater's points against Spencer by presenting an academic reinterpretation of the same facts, or was he arguing that solidarity in society required structural bases very different from those envisaged by Spencer and the economists?

At this juncture of the argument, Durkheim began to make

[68] *Ibid.*, p. 181.   [69] *Ibid.*, p. 189.

critical comments and to lay down general principles which took him far beyond legal procedures or the "formal" freedom of contracting parties and into substantive considerations of social justice. This prerequisite of solidarity in society cannot be conceived as the automatic resultant of market forces or even as a possible achievement of a Keynesian welfare state. Durkheim's remarks imply that basic structural reform is required to provide the groundwork of solidarity in society.

No doubt, when men unite by contract, it is because simple or complex division of labor has made them need one another. But for them to cooperate harmoniously, it is not sufficient for them to enter into relations nor even to feel the state of mutual dependence in which they find themselves. It is further necessary that the conditions of this cooperation be fixed for the entire duration of their relationship. It is necessary that the duties and rights of each be defined, not only in view of the situation as it presents itself at the moment of contract, but in prevision of circumstances which may develop and modify it. Indeed, it is necessary not to forget that if the division of labor makes interests interdependent, it does not confound them; it leaves them distinct and rival. . . . Each contracting party, while in need of the other, seeks to obtain what he needs at the lowest price, that is, to acquire the most rights possible in return for the fewest obligations possible.[70]

For solidarity to be created in this context, the *conscience collective* relating differentiated functions would have to stipulate institutional norms which would establish and sanction relational conditions of reciprocity. Only the consensually accepted norm could locate the "middle term between the rivalry of interests and their solidarity." Hence Durkheim concluded that "there is only a difference of degree between the law which regulates contractual obligations and [the laws] which fix other social duties of citizens." And he asked whether the absence of effective social control of key sectors of the economy "was not the effect of a morbid state" of society.[71]

[70] *Ibid.*, pp. 190–191.   [71] *Ibid.*, pp. 191, 193.

Significantly, however, Durkheim realized that regulative norms would not eliminate all conflict in society. Although he did not devote adequate attention to the problem of conflict in its various forms and functions, he did see that conflict in itself was not pathological and that, within limits, it might be conducive to "normal" integration. "Normal" social order, he believed, was not static equilibrium. Conflict was one component of social dynamics. The pathological began only when conflict was unregulated. To what extent conflict should be regulated in order to arrive at a "middle term"—a golden mean—was a difficult question Durkheim never fully answered. But, in general, Mauss's term "amiable rivalry" well expressed Durkheim's idea.

Durkheim went on to reject the myth of freedom of contract and to pose the problem of the relation between bargaining positions in society and the social regulation of contract. For Spencer, the object of contract was to ensure that the worker received the equivalent of the outlay his work cost him. Durkheim believed that contract could never fill such a role without contracts "being much more closely regulated than they are today." Classical economists replied that the law of supply and demand would automatically re-establish economic equilibrium. Durkheim countered that this view neglected the social fact that workers living in poverty could not move on to higher paying jobs. Even for classes with greater mobility, changes of occupation took time. "In the meanwhile, unjust contracts which are antisocial by definition have been executed with the complicity of society, and, when equilibrium has been established at one point, there is no reason for its not breaking up at another." [72]

In one of his very first articles, Durkheim was even more explicit about the myth of equating formal legal freedom with real contractual freedom in society:

What can the poor worker reduced to his own resources do against the rich and powerful boss, and is there not a palpable and cruel irony in assimilating these two forces which are so manifestly unequal? If

[72] *Ibid.*, pp. 194–195.

they enter into combat, is it not clear that the second will always and without difficulty crush the first? What does such a liberty amount to, and does not the economist who contents himself with it become guilty of taking the word for the thing? [73]

In the discussion of contract and organic solidarity in *The Division of Labor,* Durkheim went on to draw a very radical conclusion from the idea of social justice:

If a contract is not just, it is destitute of all authority. In any case, the role of society cannot be to reduce itself to the passive execution of contracts. It must also determine under what conditions they are executable and, if necessary, restore them to their normal form. The agreement of parties cannot render just a clause which in itself is unjust, and there are rules of justice whose violation social justice must prevent, even if it has been consented to by the interested parties.[74]

Thus even when society depended most fully on the division of labor, it could not resolve itself into "a dust of juxtaposed atoms" having only "exterior and passing contacts" with one another. According to Durkheim, men cannot live together "without mutual understanding and, consequently, without becoming bound to one another in a strong and durable manner. All society is a moral society. . . . The individual is not sufficient unto himself." [75]

Modern Pathology

Durkheim's reflections on contract were continued in his concluding section on pathological forms of the division of labor. In the pathological state, the division of labor did not function to create solidarity but, on the contrary, was related to social crisis and disease. Biology, for Durkheim, was the science with the greatest interest for sociology, although he always made clear that this interest was limited to the metaphors and analogies that biology might provide. The two sets of concepts with biological

[73] *Revue philosophique*, XXII (1886), 73.
[74] *Division du travail social*, p. 194.   [75] *Ibid.*, p. 207.

analogues which had greatest importance for sociology were, of course, the notions of structure and function and the distinction between the normal and the pathological. Aside from his general methodological belief that in sociology as in biology the study of the pathological was complementary to the study of the normal, Durkheim turned to the study of pathology for the specific reason that historically the division of labor "would not have been the object of such grave accusations if it really did not deviate more or less from the normal state." [76] Thus, despite the apparent conviction in his first major work that society in time would "mechanistically" tend to assume a normal or integrated form, Durkheim did recognize that this condition had not yet been reached.

The pathological forms Durkheim treated were the anomic, the forced, and what might be termed the alienated, division of labor. It is significant that his core concept of anomie made its first appearance in his earliest work and in a context intimately related to illegitimate constraint or exploitative structures. In fact, the concept of anomie, which was to receive its full theoretical development in *Suicide,* already took on in *The Division of Labor* features of what Marx had conceived as structural contradictions in society.

Durkheim began his discussion of the anomic division of labor by giving specific cases, some of which he also included in *Suicide:* "The first case of this genus is furnished by industrial or commercial crises, by bankruptcies, which are so many partial ruptures of organic solidarity; they bear witness to the fact that at certain points of the organism, certain social functions are not adjusted to one another." Instead of decreasing with the division of labor, industrial and commercial crises had increased with its advance. Durkheim recognized, however, that crises could not be unequivocally correlated with economic growth in general, for enterprises had become concentrated to a greater degree than they had multiplied. Indeed, he went on to observe

[76] *Ibid.,* p. 8.

that "small industry, where labor is less divided, offers the spectacle of a relative harmony between worker and boss; it is only in big industry that conflicts are in a bitter state."[77] Anomie in big industry, according to Durkheim, was due to an absence of functional coordination. Unfortunately, he did not consider the possibility that impersonal bureaucratic organizations which minutely coordinated functions and roles on an instrumental and formally rational level might produce anomie on the level of substantive irrationality by denying face-to-face community and fostering meaningless human relationships.

Durkheim found a "more striking" case of anomie in the conflict of labor and capital. "To the extent that industrial functions become more specialized, so far from solidarity increasing, the struggle becomes more lively."[78] Relying on Emile Levasseur's *Les Classes ouvrières en France jusqu'à la Révolution* ("The Working Classes in France up to the Revolution," 1859), Durkheim observed that before the fifteenth century conflicts had been infrequent, largely because master and apprentice were almost equals. In many métiers, the apprentice could look forward to becoming a master in his turn. Beginning with the fifteenth century, conditions began to change, but conflicts remained restricted to matters bearing on specific grievances. With the coming of big industry in the seventeenth century, the third stage in the process of growing class conflict brought the separation of worker and boss, the genesis of two alien "races" in the factories, and the birth of revolutionary ideologies.

After this brief but illuminating slice of history, Durkheim enunciated his own idea of the close relationship between anomie and exploitation. In a sense, social disorder derived both from the absence of the right kind of regulation and the presence of the wrong kind of regulation. More specifically, exploitation could be seen as an element in a broader field of anomie, for it involved an irrational contradiction between the condition or institutional position of a group and its values and needs, if not the values and

[77] *Ibid.*, pp. 344, 346.   [78] *Ibid.*, p. 345.

needs of society as a whole. At this point in the argument, Durkheim's faith in a "mechanistic" trend over time toward integration began to falter; at most, he believed that integration would be achieved only in a postrevolutionary phase of social pathology. In a prerevolutionary social context, "mechanistic" and impersonal processes would not be forces for integration and solidarity.

There is, however, one case where anomie can be produced even though contiguity [among functions] is sufficient. It is when the necessary regulation can be established only at the price of transformations of which the social structure is no longer capable: because the plasticity of societies is not indefinite. When it is at its end, it may make impossible even necessary changes.[79]

Thus, according to Durkheim, society might find itself in a structural bind in which a historical conjunction of anomie and exploitative institutions would require revolution for possible structural transformation. Durkheim never believed that in the modern context violent apocalypse was necessary for structural reform— he never considered it sufficient in any context—but he did increasingly see the need of basic structural change effected through arduous, if ill-defined, effort.

By this point in the argument, the full range of Durkheim's concept of anomie, which has not been adequately grasped by commentators despite his fuller exposition in *Suicide*, becomes more evident. In the first edition of *The Division of Labor*, Durkheim did provide sufficient grounds for rejecting any attempt to identify anomie with a total absence of institutions, norms, or values—a situation which in Durkheim's usage of the term "anomie" constituted only an extreme case. The Durkheimian definition of "anomie" was "the absence of consensually accepted *limiting* norms." Thus contradictions in the social system, including normative contradictions, were, in Durkheim's sense, anomic because there was no norm of a higher order to resolve the structural problems which they caused. And institutions or

[79] *Ibid.*, p. 361n.

ideologies might be anomic in the sense that they imposed *limit-less* assertion or expansion, which for Durkheim was invariably bound up with substantive irrationality in the larger society. One cannot begin to understand the full extent to which Durkheim was a rationalist and the ways in which his concept of social pathology has often been distorted if one does not understand the scope and implications of his concept of anomie.

In *The Division of Labor*, as in *Suicide*, Durkheim treated as anomic an institutional system which structurally imposed limit-less, maximizing activity upon members of society: a profit-oriented market economy. His ideas on the anomic "anarchy of the market" coincided with those of both Comte and Marx, who in this circumscribed respect were in agreement. Durkheim wrote: "Today there are no longer rules which fix the number of economic enterprises and, in each branch of industry, produc-tion is not regulated in a way that makes it remain at the level of consumption. . . . This lack of regulation does not permit a regular harmony of functions." [80]

Although he prudently refrained from making prescriptive recommendations on the necessity of social control for integra-tion and solidarity, Durkheim did go on to assert that the econo-mists' idea of the re-establishment of economic equilibrium through the free play of market forces ignored the social havoc wrought by the market. "The economists demonstrate, it is true, that this harmony becomes re-established by itself when it is necessary, thanks to the rise or fall of prices which, according to needs, stimulates or slows down production. But in any case it re-establishes itself in this way only after ruptures of equilibrium and more or less prolonged troubles." [81]

Durkheim found another case of anomie in modern society in the lack of coordination among specialized disciplines: "Science, which is fragmented into a multitude of detailed studies which do not fit together, no longer forms a solidary whole. What manifests best this absence of concert and unity is the widespread theory

[80] *Ibid.*, p. 358.   [81] *Ibid.*, pp. 358–359.

that each particular science has an absolute value." [82] The integration of science and of society were companion goals of Durkheim's endeavor. And his line of thought implies that structural change and cultural reorientation are the prerequisites for making any interdisciplinary study of modern society more than a large-scale investigation of fragmentation, partial truths, and internal inconsistencies.

Next Durkheim turned to the "constrained" (in the sense of "forced") division of labor; the discussion both resumed his enquiry into contract and overlapped with his treatment of anomie. He began with a pregnant observation which reveals his full awareness that certain types of institutional norms might abet conflict, disorder, and malaise in society.

It is not sufficient that there be rules, however, because sometimes the rules themselves are the causes of evil. This is what occurs in class wars. The institution of classes [apparently intended here to signify orders or estates] or of castes constitutes an organization of the division of labor, and it is a strictly regulated organization; it is, nevertheless, a frequent cause of dissensions. The lower classes, not satisfied, or no longer satisfied, with the role which custom or law has devolved upon them, aspire to dispossess those who are exercising these functions. From this there arise civil wars, which result from the manner in which labor is distributed.[83]

Thus the problem of social conflict was not entirely ignored in Durkheim's first major work. In a direct criticism of Tarde's theory of imitation, Durkheim recognized that rising expectations might be involved in the genesis of social conflict, perhaps as one component of a more comprehensive process of structural change and social uprooting. His ideas on this subject were similar to Vilfredo Pareto's theory of the "circulation of elites." Imitation of one class by another takes place only if there are "predisposing grounds." "For needs to spread from one class to another, it is necessary that differences which originally separated the classes should have disappeared or diminished. It is necessary, through

[82] *Ibid.*, p. 347.   [83] *Ibid.*, p. 367.

changes produced in society, that some become competent in functions which formerly were beyond them, while others lose their original superiority." [84] Once a lower class perceived that opportunities for its growing ability to exercise certain functions were closed off, it was motivated to assert its prerogatives, if need be through revolutionary action.

Durkheim distinguished sharply between constraint, in the sense of obligation rooted in commitment to norms, and pathological constraint based upon the reality or threat of force and violence. "If the commitment which I have torn from someone by threatening him with death is morally and legally null, how could it be valid if, in order to obtain it, I have profited from a situation of which I was not the cause, it is true, but which puts someone else under the necessity of yielding to me or dying?" [85] Durkheim believed that in modern society the creation of solidarity depended upon the abolition of illegitimate constraint both in job opportunities and the interrelations of functions. On the level of job opportunity, the democratic values of modern society enjoined a more complete passage from inherited status to the recognition of equality of opportunity and achievement. In an article on Albert Schaeffle written eight years before the publication of *The Division of Labor*, Durkheim was quite clear about the need for one basic type of individual liberty in modern society:

If by these words ["individual liberty"] one means the faculty of violating the principle of causality, of withdrawing from all social milieus in order to pose oneself as an absolute, there is no merit in sacrificing it. It is a sterile independence; it is the plague of all morality. The one thing which must be upheld is the right to choose among all functions the one which we judge to be the most in accord with our nature.[86]

In *The Division of Labor*, the idea of equality of opportunity as a functional prerequisite of integration in modern society led

[84] *Ibid.*, pp. 368–369.   [85] *Ibid.*, p. 376.
[86] "Albert Schaeffle," *Revue philosophique*, I (1885), 88.

Durkheim to a very radical conclusion which he would later expand and modify.

If one class in society is obliged, in order to live, to have its services accepted at any price, while another class can do without them, thanks to the resources it controls—not necessarily because of some social superiority—the second unjustly imposes its law upon the first. In other words, there cannot be rich and poor from birth without there being unjust contracts.[87]

True equality of opportunity, unjustly inhibited by existing forms of familial inheritance of wealth, was for Durkheim made all the more necessary by the collapse of religious legitimation of the social order. The humanistic conception of social structure as a purely human creation laid it open to the claims of men. As an entirely human work, "it could no longer oppose itself to human demands." This circumstance made the reconciliation of the division of labor with an "ideal of spontaneity" all the more imperative.[88] Equality of opportunity was the first functional prerequisite of just contract and solidarity in modern society. But it was also necessary "to relate functions to one another."[89] This was possible only if functional contributions were limited and adjusted to one another by shared norms.

Durkheim's concept of achievement cannot be identified with a generalized performance principle in society. Limitless competitive achieving was for him a conspicuous case of anomie. Achievement in Durkheim's normal society had the very classical meaning of fulfilling one's nature in ways complementary to the self-fulfillment of others. Limitless striving would be restricted to a marginal aspect of the average personality and to marginal groups of exceptional individuals. This line of argument again brought Durkheim face to face with the need for a *conscience collective* in modern society.

The last pathological form of the division of labor was left unnamed by Durkheim. But the concept of alienation expresses

[87] *Division du travail social,* p. 378.
[88] *Ibid.,* p. 347.   [89] *Ibid.,* p. 374.

his basic idea. This pathological form was exemplified in the extreme division of labor in which functions "were distributed in such a way that they did not offer sufficient matter for the activity of individuals." Here Durkheim took yet another step away from the economists and what has become known as Taylorism. In so doing, he did not content himself with the discovery of a "human factor" among the resources mobilized by the process of production. His conception of the normal state of the division of labor was directly oriented to the human worker rather than the economic process. The division of labor imposed duties if, and only if, it provided the means for an in-depth development of the personality compatible with reciprocity with others. "However one may represent the moral ideal," Durkheim remarks, "one cannot remain indifferent to a degradation of human nature. If morality has as its goal the perfection of the individual, it cannot permit the individual to be ruined to such a degree; if it has society as its end, it cannot let the very source of moral life stagnate: for the evil does not menace economic functions alone, but all social functions, however elevated they may be." [90] Thus Durkheim's indictment of the dilettantism of Renaissance man, which he correlated with undemocratic forms of elitism, was complemented by an equally severe indictment of extreme specialization. Moreover, he fully recognized that improving leisure-time activities and the level of general culture did not resolve the problem of making jobs meaningful. "The division of labor does not change its nature because it is preceded by general culture. No doubt it is good for the worker to be able to interest himself in art, literature, etc. But it is no less bad for him to be treated all day long like a machine." [91]

By this point, it should be obvious where the "missing link" between the division of labor and solidarity was to be found: in the specifically sociological issues of the *institutional organization* of the division of labor, its relation to substantive values, and the historical processes which might lead to its genesis. It was not the division of labor per se which created either solidarity

[90] *Ibid.*, pp. 383, 363.   [91] *Ibid.*, p. 364.

or disorder, but the nature of the division of labor and the way in which it was institutionally organized.

Durkheim's greatest failing in his first major work was his inability to analyze closely existing social realities and the ways in which they might be transformed to make society more livable. He did not systematically investigate the state, bureaucracy as an institutional form, the army, the economy, education, the family, religion, existing occupations, and their interrelations in society as a whole. His treatment of the economy was confined to the specific features which concerned him most from a moral point of view. He did not, for example, treat capitalism as an institutional system and attempt to trace its stages of development or project its probable course. Nor did he try to apply his concepts of normality and pathology in a consistent appreciation and critique of existing realities. It was, to some extent, annoyance at Durkheim's failure to investigate more intensively existing institutional forces and their concrete effects on the lives of human beings which prompted his own disciple Célestin Bouglé to observe in a 1901 article, "Theories of the Division of Labor," in the *Année sociologique* itself:

One can indeed fear that the division of labor, as it becomes perfected, tends in certain respects to isolate individuals and make illusory the interrelations formerly believed to be effective in creating consensus among people. When relations between producers and consumers, or entrepreneurs and workers, remain direct and man-to-man, then one might believe that specialization brings with it certain associations of ideas and sentiments which naturally incline those whom it brings in contact to respect one another. But when these relations become abstract, when some work for others without being in contact with or seeing one another, can the moral effect be the same? Is not one of the consequences of the role of money in our societies the replacement almost everywhere of concrete, living, and human relationships by impersonal and abstract relations? . . . To the extent that the division of labor is responsible for the development of our entire commercial system, one can say that it makes habitual the tendency to see no longer men above things, [but] to treat men as things.[92]

[92] IV (1901–1902), 106–107.

Durkheim's own discussion of anomic, forced, and alienated forms of the division of labor—despite its extreme generality and hypothetical air—did imply the necessity of basic structural reforms before solidarity could be created in modern society. Like all of Durkheim's major works, *The Division of Labor* ended with a call to action:

We feel only too much how laborious a task it is to build this society where each individual will have the place he merits, will be rewarded as he deserves, and where everybody, consequently, will spontaneously work for the good of each and all. . . . It has been said with justice that morality—and by this must be understood not only moral doctrines but customs—is going through a real crisis. What precedes can help us to understand the nature and causes of this sick condition. Profound changes have been produced in the structure of our societies in a very short time. . . . The functions which have been disrupted in the course of the upheaval have not had time to adjust themselves to one another; the new life which has emerged so suddenly has not been able to become completely organized, and above all, it has not been organized in a way that satisfies the need for justice which has grown more ardent in our hearts. If this is so, the remedy for the evil is not to seek the revival of traditions and practices which, no longer corresponding to present conditions of society, can live only an artificial, false life. What we must do is bring this anomie to an end and find the means for making the organs which are still wasting themselves in discordant movements concur harmoniously. . . . In a word, our first duty is to create a morality. . . . What reflection can and must do is mark the goal that must be attained. That is what we have tried to do.[93]

What social and political agents might respond to this call was a question not raised, much less answered, by Durkheim. But Durkheim seemed to conclude, however haltingly, that *communitas* and differentiated structure were complementary elements of society and culture which all normal types of society would have to integrate in their own specific ways.

[93] *Division du travail social*, pp. 404–406.

4 «

Suicide and Solidarity

There is only one truly serious philosophical problem: suicide.
To judge that life is or is not worth living is to answer the
fundamental question of philosophy.
>—Albert Camus, *Le Mythe de Sisyphe*

In a coherent and animated society, there is from all to each
and from each to all a continual exchange of ideas and sentiments—something like a mutual moral support—which makes
the individual, instead of being reduced to his own forces
alone, participate in the collective energy and find in it sus-
tenance for his own life when he is spiritually exhausted.
>—*Suicide*

The Object and Limitations of Suicide

An obvious difference separated *Suicide* from *The Division
of Labor*. *The Division of Labor* began with concepts. *Suicide*
began with a concrete problem which was conceived as an
avenue of approach to the understanding of society and culture
as a whole. This shift in focus did much to dissipate the air
of detached abstraction that hung like a pall over Durkheim's
first major work.

Another significant difference was the direct emphasis on social
pathology in modern society and the clearer conception of the
necessity and direction of structural change to achieve legitimate
social order. Suicide was of primary interest to Durkheim, not
as an isolated tragedy in the lives of discrete individuals, but as
an index of a more widespread state of pathology in society as
a whole. Along with other symptoms of modern social pathology,
suicide, when interpreted sociologically, pointed to basic causes

of disorder and disorientation which revealed the relation of personal crisis to collective malaise.

And more clearly than in *The Division of Labor,* Durkheim showed awareness of the value and limitations of individualism in society. Excessive individualism was symptomatic of social disintegration. But in the normal state of modern society, individual rights would be protected in a manner which would not entail self-defeating, atomizing extremes.

Underlying the differences between the two works, however, were continuities and indications of less significant developments in Durkheim's ideas. The focus of Durkheim's analysis remained the relation of personality to the social system. And the root principle of organization—methodological and normative at the same time—was the distinction between normality and pathology in society. The attack upon utilitarianism continued. And it was more obviously conjoined with the rejection of violently apocalyptic socialism. The selection of the problem of suicide itself seems to indicate that for Durkheim the greatest internal threat to the stability of modern societies was disintegration, not with a bang but a whimper. The higher suicide rate among the socially privileged (managers, members of the liberal professions) indicated for him that all segments of modern society had a real existential interest in fundamental change. Indeed, the anomic absence of meaning in experience had special relevance for privileged groups that were liberated from economic need and from the incentive to carry on provided by the desire for affluence. With the penchant for indiscriminate overstatement often characteristic of the *Année* school, Gaston Richard partially recognized this point in his review of *Suicide* in the first volume of the *Année sociologique*:

This book is one of those works which justify all the hopes which enlightened observers of the great modern crisis place in social science. Parties (and at times individuals as well) use social science, but it can be put to the uses of none of them. Durkheim proves it. Socialists and economists are dismissed back to back with a proof of their incompetence. What can remain of the thesis of class conflict considered as a fundamental law of social structure if it is proved that the regime of unlimited competition destroys the happiness and the existence of the capitalist class even more than that of the proletariat? Now, is not the thesis of class conflict more than ever the foundation of so-called scientific socialism? On the other hand, how can one celebrate with the old faithfuls of the Manchester school the emancipation of economic forces if one sees how these unchained forces can be homicidal—how the quest for wealth engenders disgust for existence? [1]

The main lines of Durkheim's argument were as clear-cut as they were compelling. After dealing with initial problems of definition, Durkheim began by distinguishing between the suicide rate and the individual case of suicide. The rate which displayed a constancy or tendential regularity over time was the specifically sociological phenomenon. It could not be explained by a random distribution of purely idiosyncratic motives or inter-individual imitation. When the suicide rate rose above or fell below a certain threshold, it became an index of social pathology. While Durkheim left this threshold undefined, his analysis implied that its determination bore upon the relation of the suicide rate to the disintegration of substantively rational structures in society. The explanation of the rate depended initially upon its correlation with social conditions, institutional structures, cultural values, and symbolic systems. The meaningfulness of this correlation depended upon its interpretation with reference to the intervening variable of solidarity or integration in society.

Thus the subject of social solidarity and its relation to substantive rationality retained in *Suicide* the central importance it had assumed in *The Division of Labor*. The higher-order typology in terms of which Durkheim classified various social and

[1] I (1896–1897), 404–405. The evolution of Richard's ideas indicated that the *Année* school had its internal conflicts. Richard in time became one of the most hostile critics of Durkheim and a source of the idea that his thought was riddled with unresolved contradictions. The key issue that antagonized Richard (himself a Protestant) was the increasingly critical edge in Durkheim's sociology of religion which came down most negatively upon Protestantism.

cultural phenomena in *Suicide* had as its focal point the nature and degree of solidarity in society: the polar opposites of egoism and altruism, anomie and fatalism, were relevant to the suicide rate through the functional relationship between social solidarity and the phenomena which they characterized.

On the basis of these considerations, Durkheim arrived at his famous suicide "law." This is perhaps the only significant lawlike statement in sociology, but in the works of sociologists it has received divergent formulations. Although Durkheim himself never provided a proposition which formulated his "law," it may be stated thus: the suicide rate varies inversely with the increasing degree of solidarity in society, until the degree of solidarity reaches a certain threshold, at which point the covariation becomes direct.

The elementary ambiguities apparent in *The Division of Labor* continued to plague *Suicide*. Indeed, Durkheim's social metaphysic became increasingly manifest. The metaphysical component of his thought was never concerned with the substantial existence of some sort of "group mind" detached from individual members of society. Rather it dealt with the more subtle problem of the conception of society and social solidarity as providing the essential meaning and ultimate reality behind all forms of cultural symbolism. Durkheim never fully saw how social solidarity itself might be enriched when it became one aspect of a more comprehensive universe of meaning. His ultimate explanatory gesture was invariably reductionistic. In the terms of his social metaphysic, all cultural phenomena became external signs of social reality—icing on the cake of social custom or social action.

If, as it is often said, man has a dual nature, it is because there is superimposed upon physical man a social man. Now the latter presupposes necessarily a society which he expresses and serves. When society disintegrates, when we no longer feel it acting and living around and about us, all that there is of the social in us finds itself devoid of objective foundation. There is only an artificial combination of illusory images, a phantasmagoria which a little reflection suffices to whisk away. Consequently, there is nothing to serve as an end for our actions. Yet this social man is the whole of civilized man; it is he who represents the value of existence.[2]

In his metaphysical moments, Durkheim was almost led to lose a good cause through bad arguments by conceiving a necessary condition and a vital necessity as exclusive, self-contained realities. The social matrix of cultural and symbolic experience became *mater et magistra*. In fact, *Suicide* already contained the interpretation of religion which would be more fully developed in *The Elementary Forms*: "The power which has imposed itself upon man's respect and which has become the object of his adoration is society, of which the gods were only the hypostatized form. Religion is in a word the system of symbols through which society becomes conscious of itself; it is the manner of thinking appropriate to the collective being." [3]

In certain ways *Suicide* was an advance over *The Division of Labor* because in the former the ambiguities of a socialized and Cartesianized neo-Kantianism became so transparent that they were almost inconsequential. Durkheim's confusion was especially apparent in his idea of the relation of psychology to sociology. By "psychology" Durkheim meant a number of things which were not altogether identical. He meant the study of (1) the psychophysical self considered in isolation from society and capable only of sensation; (2) the most general, ill-defined psychic traits of man, e.g., sexual desire or paternal affection; (3) the inner, private, and unobservable aspects of the self; (4) the individualized aspects of the self; and (5) the single individual in his concrete particularity. Sociology was directly concerned with none of these meanings of the psychology of the individual. In contrast, sociology was directly concerned with social psychology and the way in which collective features were internalized by the person. The confusion in Durkheim's thought

[2] *Le Suicide* (first pub. 1897; Paris: Presses Universitaires de France, 1960), p. 228.
[3] *Ibid.*, p. 352.

appeared in two ways. First, the language he used in making the above points was at times ambiguous. Second, he at times seemed to conceive of the person as a mere composite of his social self and his psychophysical self. It was this second source of confusion that stemmed from his Cartesianized neo-Kantian reformulation of the dualism between mind and body. Thus Durkheim at times seemed to argue in *Suicide* that the individual had no role in taking his own life. His psychophysical constitution predisposed him to a greater or lesser degree to the causal action of specifically social forces. Individuals were felled by "suicidogenetic" social forces acting like some fantastic death ray.

One instance of Durkheim's confusion was in the dichotomy he seemed to pose between cognition and intention in acts of suicide. He began by defining suicide as "every case of death which results directly or indirectly from a positive or negative act of the victim himself which he knows will produce this result." [4] Unless investigation (e.g., through the use of depth psychology) reveals otherwise, an act which is performed by a person who knows the consequence of his act is *prima facie* considered intentional. Yet—because of his suspicion of psychology—Durkheim, immediately before offering his definition, impugned an interest in intentions with an argument whose generality seemed to exclude even the cognitive element in his own definition. "Intention is too intimate a thing to be studied from the outside by more than gross approximations. It even escapes self-observation." [5]

Durkheim has at times been mistakenly criticized for including a cognitive element in his definition of suicide. But the value of his definition in this respect is in its recognition that suicide is a relatively complex act which requires initiative and the coordination of thought and activity. A more relevant objection is that Durkheim was not clear about the relation of his conception of the role of cognition to his criticism of the focus on manifest intentions and to the problem of a more general theory of

[4] *Ibid.*, p. 5.   [5] *Ibid.*, p. 4.

motivation. Yet a crucial chapter of *Suicide* itself (Book II, chapter vi) attempted to relate sociological categories to psychological expressions and personality types. Thus, any idea that Durkheim simply ignored psychological factors obviously misses the mark. The basic point is that he was often confused, in part because of the Cartesianized, neo-Kantian strand of his thought, which led him at times to postulate a dualistic division between the "outer" and the "inner" in experience.

At times the main target of Durkheim's attack was the use of naïve introspection and the psychological categories of official gatherers of statistics to provide adequate accounts of motivation. But Jack C. Douglas has observed:

Unfortunately for Durkheim's own arguments, the official categorizations of a death as caused by "suicide" were generally most dependent on their imputations of an *intention to die* by one's own action: since one of the critical dimensions of meanings involved in the statutory definitions of "suicide" as a cause of death and in the general common-sense meaning of "suicide" in the Western world is precisely that of "intention to die," the official categorization of "suicide" can in general be only as valid as official categorizations of "intention." Since Durkheim thought official categories of intentions or motives to be completely invalid and unreliable, he should have concluded the same thing about official statistics on suicide.[6]

Douglas' conclusion becomes more forceful when it is realized that shared attitudes toward suicide influence the reporting of suicides, so that the more solidary groups also tend to be more reluctant about revealing suicides to the outside world. Furthermore, the importance of concealment assumes major proportions given the small fraction of the population committing suicide (between one hundred and three hundred per million). Indeed, some statisticians have argued that, even aside from problems of concealment, the numbers involved are too small for statistically significant variations and, in any event, for inferring

[6] "The Sociological Analysis of Social Meanings of Suicide," *Archives européennes de sociologie*, VII (1966), 259–260.

far-reaching social and cultural propositions about milieus or contexts.[7]

Ambiguity in the conception of the relation of psychology to sociology also appeared in Durkheim's discussion of psychopathology and suicide. Although he recognized a "social factor" in psychopathology, he restricted his discussion to making inverse or inconclusive correlations between rates of suicide and rates of "insanity" in terms of age, sex, religion, and nationality. He did not address himself to the problems of the functional and cultural definition of psychopathology and the relation of rates of psychopathology to cultural variables. But only by considering these problems could he have arrived at a more pertinent conception of psychopathology, its significance in different types of civilization, and its possible relation to suicide and sociopathic states. Curiously, however, his own discussion of personality types stressed the special importance in modern suicides of what would today be called manic-depressive syndromes (which he correlated with anomic-egoistic suicide).[8]

Ambiguity arose as well in Durkheim's conception of case histories. In general, he recognized the fully complementary relationship of the use of case histories and an analytic approach centering on institutional and cultural conditions. At times he accurately saw the specificity of case history in its focus on the concrete individual in whom general factors assumed a particular configuration: "We cannot deduce all the particularities which an individual case may present, because there are some which depend upon the specific nature of the subject. Each suicide gives to his act a personal mark which expresses his temperament [and] the special conditions in which he is placed, and which consequently cannot be explained by the social and general causes of the phenomenon."[9] At other times, however, the

[7] Cf. F. Achille-Delmas, *Psychologie pathologique du suicide* (Paris: Alcan, 1933).

[8] For the discussion of psychopathology, see *Le Suicide,* Book I, chap. i.

[9] *Ibid.,* p. 312.

sociologistic reformulation of the mind-body dualism led Durkheim to conceive the individual personality as a mechanical combination of psychophysical and social factors: "Everything depends upon the intensity with which the suicidogenetic causes
have acted upon the individual." [10] Whether because of methodological and metaphysical inhibitions or because of the unavail-
ability of useful documents, the fact remains that Durkheim does
not use case histories and other empirical evidence to illustrate
his argument. Here again there is a continuation of the institutional and legal formalism of *The Division of Labor* in the
failure to substantiate an analysis with concrete evidence and to
consider the way in which social factors are experienced by people. And like the earlier work, *Suicide* often rested on a (much
more successful) coordination of the models of earlier theorists.
Historians like Roger Lacombe and Albert Bayet were especially sensitive to the absence of documentation which might
reveal whether and how the institutional contexts and analytic
variables discussed by Durkheim manifest themselves operatively
in actual events and real experience. As Bayet puts it in his
Le Suicide et la morale:

What is really a grave difficulty is that one must take the author's
word for things. Where are the usages which prove that Protestants
"punish suicide"? How is the "drawing away" from those who touch
the suicide expressed? What facts permit one to say that common
morality blames suicide? Durkheim does not tell us. No doubt he
believes that the morality of his time is his own and he knows it. . . .
But the testimony of the greatest philosopher cannot from the scientific
point of view, replace observations subjected to control and criticism.[11]

On a conceptual level, certain ambiguities evident in the typology of *The Division of Labor* also persisted in *Suicide*. In keep-

[10] *Ibid.*, p. 337.
[11] Paris: Alcan, 1922, p. 3. Roger Lacombe's strictures are to be found
in his *La Méthode sociologique de Durkheim* (Paris: Alcan, 1926), where
he dwells upon the point that correlations and statistics are relatively un-
interesting if interpretations are not fleshed out and substantiated.

ing with the emphasis on modern social pathology, the category of egoism replaced that of organic solidarity, and anomie became a central problem. But the analytical dissociation of reality was at times carried over from Durkheim's first major work. Thus Durkheim seems at points to have believed that a concept like egoism applied to a discrete set of historical phenomena (e.g., Protestantism) and that the concept of anomie applied to other phenomena (e.g., capitalism). Durkheim did not ask whether his analytic variables applied simultaneously to a number of institutional contexts (e.g., whether Protestantism or capitalism was characterized by both egoism and anomie) or whether institutional contexts or symbolic systems were historically related to one another in ways which could be illuminated by the application of models (*vide* Weber in *The Protestant Ethic*).

But just as the typology in *The Division of Labor* was based implicitly upon a notion of the universal conditions of social normality, the *Suicide* typology was based implicitly upon a notion of the universal causes of social pathology. In fact, the idea of a *coincidentia oppositorum* seems to surface in the notion that any extremely pathological social state would in some way display a particular combination of the general causes of social pathology. One virtue of the concept of anomie was its ability to mediate the mind-body dualism; it showed how organically rooted desire and aggressiveness existed in dialectical relation to binding norms and symbols, erupting chaotically in cases of normative and symbolic breakdown. And Durkheim concluded that anomie and egoism were "generally only two different aspects of the same state of society." [12] Thus, in *Suicide* the second and more Hegelian strand of Durkheim's thought strongly asserted itself and tended to overlay his Cartesianized neo-Kantianism with a more dialectical notion of experience and analysis.

In one crucial respect, however, this was not the case. Although Durkheim intended his study of suicide to serve as a means of approach to the analysis of society as a whole, he did

[12] *Le Suicide*, p. 325.

not adequately investigate the relation of his variables to social phenomena in the global social context. The only area in which he extended his analysis was in a discussion of homicide. Durkheim failed in *Suicide* to relate his sociological and cultural variables not only to their individual and interindividual manifestations (suicide and homicide) but to more specifically social forms of action and reaction. Yet one typical response to anomie and the anxiety it provoked was the attempt to "reintegrate" experience through collective action and group mobilization. Indeed, it would seem that anomie led to suicide only in association with egoism. In cases where atomistic individualism was not present or could be overcome, anomie might give way to the formation of groups which responded to severe disintegration by seeking new and perhaps more demanding forms of solidarity. The precise manner in which this could take place depended, of course, upon specific historical circumstances.

Here there was a basis for convergence with the ideas of Marx—a basis upon which Durkheim himself failed to build. Durkheim was to make at least an oblique reference to capitalism in his discussion of anomie. But he did not provide an intensive and direct investigation of the structural contradictions in a capitalist economy. Nor did he see class consciousness as an integrating force which counteracted the effects of anomie in the "internal milieu" of a group. The very focus upon suicide as the key problem for an analysis of modern society may be seen as diverting attention from this possibility and from the revolutionary potential Marx believed it held.

At the other end of the ideological spectrum, the relation of anomie to the rise of totalitarianism was another possibility Durkheim ignored. This matter has received extensive coverage in subsequent literature. Karl Mannheim, for example, observed:

The secret of taboo and the collective formation of symbols in primitive societies is mainly that the free expression of impulses is held in check by the various mechanisms of social control and directed towards certain objects and actions which benefit the group. Only the impul-

sive energies which have been set free by the disintegration of society
and are seeking integration about a new object have those eruptive
destructive qualities which are customarily and vaguely regarded as
characteristic of every type of mass behavior. What the dictatorships
in certain contemporary mass-societies are striving to do is to coordinate through organizations the impulses which the revolutionary
period unchained and to direct them towards prescribed objects. The
consciously guided fixation of mass impulses upon new objectives
takes the place of earlier forms of wish fixation which found their
objectives organically, that is to say, through a slow selective process.
So, for instance, the attempt is made to create a new religion, the
function of which is first to destroy the old emotional setting, and then
to make these disintegrated impulses more subservient to one's own
aim through the use of new symbols.[13]

In a certain context or group, anomie might foster suicide. In
a complementary aspect of the group's life, in another context,
or in the same context over time, anomie might lead to various
types of group mobilization and ideological assertion. Problems
of this sort, however, could be investigated only by analysis
within the context of society as a whole over time in a manner
which went beyond one-dimensional correlations of variables
such as anomie with phenomena such as suicide rates.

On the basis of the foregoing considerations, one might conclude that Durkheim's *Suicide* has limited value as an attempt
to use a particular problem as a means of approach to an analysis
of society as a whole. It may be argued that Durkheim was
basing highly significant interpretations and practical conclusions
upon statistically insignificant information. In this respect, two
things may be said in defense of Durkheim. A crucial aspect of
his argument was that social and cultural forces which account
for suicide rates are operative, consciously or unconsciously, in
men who are not moved to take their own lives. To put it
crudely, the few people who commit suicide in modern society
are symbols of a much larger number of miserable people who

[13] *Man and Society in an Age of Reconstruction* (New York: Harcourt,
Brace & World, 1940), p. 62.

are handling their malaise in more or less authentic ways. One of the apparent implications of Durkheim's discussion is that, as a rule, men in primitive societies, when left to their traditional forms of existence, tended to sacrifice their lives in defense of their values, while men in modern societies are driven to the extreme act as a sign of personal negation and a vote of no confidence in society, either in spite of shared values or because of an absence of values. Durkheim clearly perceived the crisis of meaning and legitimacy in modern societies. The second defense is that, from the perspective of humanistic values, even a small number of suicides represent a morally and spiritually scandalous sacrifice of life, especially when the sacrifice is meaningless.

Anomie and Egoism

Durkheim's typology in *Suicide* attempted to provide a conceptual framework for the systematic classification of social and cultural causes of extremely high or extremely low suicide rates, which served as one objective index (among others) of states of social pathology. The typology may be represented diagrammatically thus:

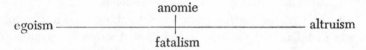

Anomie and fatalism were conceptually polar opposites, as were egoism and altruism. Anomie signified the absence of an institutionally grounded and ideologically legitimated sense of substantive limits in society and the personality. The absence of an ingrained sense of limits was for Durkheim the sociocultural cause of disorientation and aggression in society. In the normal society, a normative sense of limits became in time a person's second nature, indeed his mode of being; it was, moreover, the only possible basis of individual self-fulfillment and cooperative reciprocity in society. Fatalism, in contrast, was caused by the setting of limits which were excessively authoritarian in repressive or oppressive ways and which, by that token, resulted in rules which were themselves obstacles to self-fulfillment and reciprocity. "Egoism" referred, in its most general sense, to a state in which the principle of individuation was carried to the extreme of particularistic and self-centered atomistic individualism. Conversely, "altruism" denoted a state of excessive community which in its figuratively incestuous intimacy submerged the individual in the group and inhibited solidarity in society as a whole.

The *Suicide* typology had the merit of transcending certain limitations of the "organic" and "mechanical" schema of *The Division of Labor*. It also clarified Durkheim's idea of the relation of sociology to morality. On the level of society as a whole, the argument in *Suicide* implies that any normal or healthy social system would be based upon some optimal combination of community, a reciprocal relationship among different parts (individuals, roles, groups), and an autonomously accepted, disciplined sense of substantive limits to personal or collective assertion. In this light, the fundamental moral function of institutions and values in society was seen as the provision of the objectively given and subjectively internalized foundation for these qualities in a *conscience collective* which furthered viable solidarity in society as a whole. Integration in the normal or good (but not perfect) society thus involved simultaneously the relatively (but not totally) coherent nature of institutional norms and symbolic systems, the autonomous and spontaneous acceptance of norms and symbols by the individual, and the creation of meaningful moral solidarity in society as a whole.

In *Suicide* it also becomes clear that Durkheim did not conceive of the normal or healthy society as a crystal palace. Even the normal society—and the healthy personality—would contain a marginal leaven of anomie, egoism, and extreme altruism. Some types of society would normally develop certain of these characteristics more than other types. Community was developed in archaic societies to an extent impossible and undesirable in large and functionally differentiated modern societies, while ego-ism in modern societies was an excessive development of the cardinal emphasis on individual rights and personal responsibil-ity. Moreover, certain milieus within a society would normally have certain extreme tendencies which, within limits, were neces-sary and positive forces in the development of society as a whole. A measure of anomie corresponded to an element of "free play" in society and the personality: anomic indeterminacy and daring risk were conditions of progress and prerequisites of an ability to respond creatively to changes in relevant conditions of exis-tence. And anomie would be especially typical of artistic and innovative milieus. Egoism was to some extent a concomitant of intellectual originality. To this extent, Durkheim recognized the importance of the considerations which preoccupied a theorist like Gabriel Tarde or were included in Weber's notion of per-sonal election as an element of charisma.

But Durkheim considered pathological the distorted, unbal-anced, or runaway development and universalization of these qualities in society. The sociopathic began at the point at which the conceivably valuable exception in society tended to become a harmful rule. Thus, for Durkheim as for Aristotle, a vice was in the last analysis an excessive development of a virtue. In fact, the concept of anomie in its primary meaning of an absence of a sense of legitimate limits recalls the notion of *hybris*. And im-plicit in *Suicide* and its typology was an optimal point of inter-section of Durkheim's variables which corresponded to the Greek idea of a golden mean. Nowhere else was Durkheim's indebted-ness to the classical tradition of Western philosophy more telling. And nowhere else was the vision of his own France—with its insistence on *mesure*—as the guardian of what was valid in this tradition more apposite. In the normal society, the golden mean —incarnated in the *conscience collective*—would restrict *hybris* to the exceptional individual or the extraordinary feat whose shocking singularity ambivalently fascinated and repelled society as a whole.

Durkheim's concept of anomie as the absence of a normative sense of legitimate limits at times covered a great deal of territory rather indiscriminately. The meaning of anomie as an operational concept, its relation to egoism, and its connection with such "structural" problems as stratification, exploitation, scarcity, and group conflict have been sources of confusion.

The basic cause of generalized anomie was rapid and uncontrolled change in the conditions, institutions, or values constitutive of the social system in the largest sense. The relevant effect of runaway change was the unsettling displacement, uprooting, and disorientation of the groups or categories affected by historical change. Rapid transformation might have positive value for social development only at certain euphoric phases of transition (e.g., a classical revolution). An after-birth of banalized and misdirected *hybris* plagued modern society. Prometheus had been taken down from his predestined rock and made over into a face in the crowd. And tragedy had become trivialized. Modern society needed structural reform that would bring legitimate stabilization and put a stop to irrational, runaway change imposed by the status quo and its historical tendencies. For in modern society the pathological functioning of the status quo frequently exacerbated anomie and helped determine the irrational components of sociologically and philosophically uninformed, merely self-indulgent protests against it. In a pathological status quo, one of the legitimate functions of sociology (in Durkheim's sense) was the diffusion of a consciousness of problems within the society and of the ways in which they could be transcended in an attempt to achieve substantive rationality and social justice. High suicide rates constituted a problem of this sort. And Durkheim's classical study of their causes and concomitants concluded with a recommendation of structural reform and a call to action.

A limited meaning of "anomie," as its etymology suggested, was "a state of complete normlessness and meaninglessness of experience attendant upon institutional and moral breakdown."

The psychological expression of anomie in the individual personality was the feeling of anxiety and frustration. In the absence of meaningful symbolic systems and norms which controlled anxiety and provided a connective tissue in society, the individual became prey to limitless desires and morbid fears. In one important sense, Durkheim's concept of anomie situated Hobbes's defiantly defensive and power-hungry man as a personality type within a specific, pathological state of society. Hobbesian man did not represent "human nature" but only one pathological possibility of human nature which emerged in an anomic state of society. Distrust and an obsessive fear of others became a prevalent mode of social interaction only when normative structures failed to create an institutional foundation for solidarity.

The term "anomie" also referred to the presence of extreme distortions and imbalances in the social system which might lead to the nightmarish state of normlessness. In this sense, "anomie" recalls Marx's notion of structural contradictions. Durkheim formulated this notion in terms of a contradiction between felt needs and expectations on the one hand, and values and institutionalized means of satisfaction on the other. Structural contradictions were the basic cause of passing ruptures in the social system which might have more or less durable effects for the overall shape of social life. Moreover, the general theory of anomie revealed that the effect of either a depression or an economic boom might be similar in the uprooting, social displacement, and moral disorientation of men. In a depression, the economic means at one's disposal dropped below one's customary level of expected satisfactions. In a windfall situation, one's means soared above one's accustomed needs and might further unsettle one's level of expectation. Both imbalances distorted the traditional structure of experience and generated anxiety. Rapid change in economic position, which might come to the individual in the appearance of good or bad luck, thus had similar sociological and sociopsychological effects. Implicit in this entire line of argument was a return to the theme of the social, moral, and psychological costs of economic growth which preoccupied Durkheim in his first major work.[14]

As has already been observed, from Durkheim's viewpoint exploitation could be seen as a variant of anomie, insofar as it involved a contradiction between institutional practices or social conditions and the felt needs or values of an oppressed group, if not of society as a whole. Thus, in his discussion of anomie, Durkheim wrote:

Discipline can be useful only if it is considered just by the peoples subjected to it. If it maintains itself only through habit and force,

[14] Durkheim's assertion that prosperity fostered high suicide rates was challenged by his disciple Maurice Halbwachs in his *Les Causes du suicide* (Paris: Alcan, 1930). Halbwachs also stressed the need for a clearer conception of the relation of sociology and psychology and criticized Durkheim's tendency to focus upon one-dimensional correlations of suicide rates with factors abstracted from society as a whole. He noted the importance of urbanism, which overlapped with membership in Protestant sects, and proposed the notion that types of civilization were more inclusive and historically useful units of analysis. The assertion that the suicide rate tends to drop with prosperity was further supported by the statistical evidence and its interpretation in Andrew F. Henry and James F. Short, *Suicide and Homicide* (Glencoe, Illinois: Free Press, 1954). The key question was of course whether prosperity was related to uprootedness and frustration. If there was no positive correlation between suicide rates and peaks of a business cycle, there might still be one between suicide and long-term upward changes in a group's position related to basic processes of economic transformation. Neither Halbwachs nor Henry and Short addressed themselves to this broader historical question. The analysis of Henry and Short, however, had the merit of bringing to the center of analytic attention the role of stratification, the concept of relative deprivation, and the relation of the choice of an object of aggression (self or other) to the situation of the relevant group. Suicide was generally found to be a response to frustration among high-status groups, for whom a depression had greater impact in terms of relative loss. Moreover, a low-status group might become increasingly frustrated in the face of prosperity which it did not share. Aggression bred by frustration in low-status groups, however, found an outlet in homicide rather than suicide, because the more integrated nature of these groups provided "love objects" upon whom anxiety and frustration might be projected. In Durkheim's terms, anomie led to suicide only when it was conjoined with egoism.

peace and harmony exist only in appearance. The spirit of unrest and
discontent is latent. And superficially restrained appetites waste little
time in becoming unleashed. This is what happened in Rome and
Greece when the beliefs on which the old organization of the patri-
cians and plebeians rested were shaken, and in our modern societies
when aristocratic prejudices began to lose their sway.[15]

In the context of the classical idea of exploitation, one clearly
defined group benefited from the injustices imposed upon
another clearly defined group. Alienation, however, might result
from a contradiction between needs or values and institutional
patterns or social conditions which created a feeling of frustration, meaninglessness, and hostility to the "system" even when a
group had not been directly subjected to invidious exploitation.
Indeed, alienation might be experienced by groups which mate-
rially benefited from exploitation. The frustrations of the privileged in an anomic situation generated a type of restlessness
which, in the absence of constructive alternatives, might feed the
suicide rate or find other negative outlets.

In this respect, a little-noticed aspect of Durkheim's argument
was crucial. He went beyond the ideas of structural contradictions and gaps to a notion of institutionalized or ideological
anomie. Where institutional and ideological anomie existed,
limitless assertion was actually prescribed or lauded, with what
Durkheim considered invariably damaging consequences for
society as a whole. He saw this form of *le mal de l'infini* (infinity sickness)[16] in numerous aspects of modern culture, e.g., in
romanticism. But it was especially in his conception of the economy that he advanced beyond the analysis of *The Division of
Labor* to a perspective which anticipated the similarities between
liberal capitalism and a certain sort of socialism.

[15] *Le Suicide,* p. 279.
[16] *Ibid.,* p. 324. In his *Education morale* (first pub. 1925; Paris: Presses
Universitaires de France, 1963), Durkheim continued his attack upon
"this dissolving sensation of the infinite" (p. 35). Nowhere more than
in his correlation of anomie and the quest for infinity was Durkheim
closer to the Greeks.

Governmental power, instead of being the regulator of economic life, has become its instrument and servant. The most opposite schools— orthodox economists and extreme socialists—agree that it should be reduced to the role of a more or less passive intermediary between different social functions. One side wishes it to be simply the guardian of individual contracts. The other side delegates to it the task of collective bookkeeping, i.e., to chalk up the demands of consumers, to transmit them to producers, to inventory aggregate income, and to distribute it according to a set formula. But both sides refuse government the right to subordinate other social organs and have them converge toward a higher goal. On all sides, men declare that nations ought to have as their sole or principal objective the achievement of industrial prosperity. Thus the dogma of economic materialism serves as the basis of these seemingly opposed systems. And since these theories merely express the state of opinion, industry, instead of being viewed as a means to an end which transcends it, has become the supreme end of individuals and societies.[17]

Durkheim's conception of this state of affairs and the ideologies which legitimated it was unequivocal: it was a paradigm case of institutionalized and ideological anomie.

Thus the appetites which industry activates have been freed from all limiting authority. The apotheosis of well-being has, in sanctifying these appetites, placed them above all human law. To check them seems to be a sort of sacrilege. . . . Here is the origin of the effervescence which reigns in this part of society [the economy] and from it has spread to all the rest. It is because the state of crisis and anomie is constant and, so to speak, normal. From the top to the bottom of the ladder, desires are stimulated without the possibility of satisfaction. Nothing can calm them, because the goal toward which they aspire is infinitely beyond anything that can be attained. . . . Henceforth the least setback leaves one unable to recover. . . . One may ask whether it is not especially this moral state which today makes economic catastrophes so productive of suicides. For in a society with a healthy moral discipline, men are better able to cope with the blows of fortune. . . . And yet these dispositions have become so inbred that society has grown to regard them as normal. It is continually repeated that it is man's nature to be eternally dissatisfied, to advance constantly without rest or respite toward an indefinite goal. The passion for infinity is daily presented as a mark of moral distinction, whereas it can appear only within unregulated consciences which elevate to the status of a rule the lack of regulation from which they suffer. The doctrine of the most rapid progress at any price has become an article of faith.[18]

Such statements indicate a frequently ignored dimension of Durkheim's concept of anomie, bring out its critical edge, and refute the idea that he identified social health and normality with conformity to any and every kind of status quo. On the contrary, his normative and philosophically grounded idea of social normality enabled him to work out something like a con-

[18] *Ibid.*, pp. 284–287. In psychoanalytic terms, it may be observed that one case of anomie involved limitless ego ideals, while fatalism resulted from rigid and repressive superego demands. One form of anomic suicide may be fruitfully compared to what Herbert Hendin, in his *Suicide and Scandinavia* (New York: Doubleday Anchor, 1965) terms "performance suicide." Of one of his cases Hendin writes: "His dreams under hypnosis were of the most elemental kind. In one instance they revealed him running to catch a boat and just missing it. In his associations 'missing the boat' symbolized the low opinion which he had of his entire career. His legal ambitions were excessive and he found it impossible to compromise with his grandiose success fantasies. The aggressiveness which stemmed from this grandiosity interfered with his actual performance, a constellation frequently observed in patients with extremely high and rigid standards for themselves. What is seen as failure causes an enormous amount of self-hatred, and suicide amounts to a self-inflicted punishment for having failed" (p. 26). Hendin attempts to explain the Scandinavian suicide phenomenon of Sweden and Denmark with high rates but Norway with a low rate by patterns in child-rearing and their sociopsychological concomitants. His conclusions may readily be translated into Durkheimian terms. In Sweden, Hendin found a combination of anomie and egoism. Limitless ends in performance and achieving were combined with isolation and coldness in interpersonal relations. An expression in Swedish literally means "to kill with silence." In Denmark, he found a strongly integrated and excessively altruistic family structure which, with separation upon the children's reaching adulthood, gave way to uprootedness and feelings of dependency loss. In Norway, a greater balance was established, and the verbal expression of emotion functioned as a sort of safety valve.

cept of the pathology of normalcy within certain existing states of society.[19]

We are now in a position to understand better Durkheim's idea of the relation of anomie to egoism and the more cogent elements of his conception of the relation of sociology to psychology. Egoism, in the sense of atomistic individualism, obviously had a large area of analytic and empirical overlapping with individualistic forms of anomie, and both might be institutionalized or ideologically justified. But Durkheim's neo-Kantian assumptions made possible a distinction between anomie and egoism which, while allowing for events involving both anomie and egoism, was analytically "clear and distinct." In this sense, "anomie" referred to a pathology of practical reason and "egoism" to a pathology of theoretical reason.

Suicides of both types [anomic and egoistic] suffer from what might be called infinity sickness [*le mal de l'infini*]. But this sickness does not take the same form in the two cases. In egoism, it is conscious intelligence which is affected and which becomes hypertrophied beyond measure. In anomie, it is sensibility which is overexcited and unhinged.

[19] In his classical article "Social Structure and Anomie," Robert K. Merton posed the problem in terms of a contradiction between limitless cultural values and limited institutional means of attaining them. This was exemplified for him in the conflict in the United States between the pursuit of wealth and the available opportunities open to members of society for making "big money." After being subjected to criticism on the grounds that he was identifying normative conflict and anomie, Merton in a rejoinder admitted confusion in his earlier formulation and argued that structural conflicts might lead to anomie in the delimited sense of normlessness. The original article and the rejoinder may be found in *Social Theory and Social Structure* (rev. ed.; Glencoe, Ill.: Free Press of Glencoe, 1964), pp. 131–194. Whatever the semantic gain in this revision, it served to divert attention from the problem of institutionalized and ideological anomie which Merton seemed to perceive earlier in the American desire for "just a little bit more" of the good things in life regardless of how much one already had. In terms of Durkheim's formulation, the cases of normlessness, normative contradiction, and normatively constrained or praised limitlessness shared the irrational quality of an absence of an institutionally grounded sense of legitimate limits which was essential for reciprocity and solidarity.

In the former, thought, through constant turning back upon itself, no longer has an object. In the latter, passion, no longer recognizing any limits, no longer has a goal. The first loses itself in the infinity of the dream; the second, in the infinity of desire.[20]

Thus anomie, in this more special sense, was related to the "practical," appetitive, and active faculties: desire, passion, and will, especially the will to power. Egoism was related to the imaginative, intellectual, cognitive, and "theoretical" faculties.

In fact, the more philosophically special meanings of "anomie" and "egoism" were closest to Durkheim's conception of personality types and psychological expressions of his sociological variables. Despite its lack of empirical substantiation (e.g., through the analysis of case studies), Book II, chapter vi, of *Suicide* is proof of the inadequacy of the prevalent idea that Durkheim, even on a theoretical level, ignored the problem of social psychology and the internalization of social norms and conditions. Here he argued that anomie was expressed in anxiety and manic agitation, egoism in depression and melancholy. In fact, his conception of their sociopsychological manifestations helps to explain why he correlated anomie, but not the more effete, passive, and inner-directed egoism, with the possibility of homicide. And it was from literature and philosophy that he derived the examples of the relation of social factors to individual personality which he did not provide in the form of empirical case studies. He cited the cerebral and indecisive heroes of Lamartine as cases approximating the pure form of egoism. Drawing on classical philosophy, he distinguished between the more detached and introspective stoical, and the more disabused and skeptical epi-

[20] *Le Suicide,* p. 324. Compare Nietzsche on the relation of infinite desire to egoism: "From an infinite horizon he withdraws into himself, back into the small egoistic circle, where he must become dry and withered; he may possibly attain to cleverness but never to wisdom. . . . He is never enthusiastic, but blinks his eyes and understands how to look for his own profit or his party's in the profit or loss of somebody else" (Friedrich Nietzsche, *The Use and Abuse of History* [Indianapolis and New York: Library of the Liberal Arts, 1957], p. 64).

curean, variants of egoism. In a rare moment of tragic irony, he observed of the egoistic frame of mind: "However individualized each one may be, there is always something which remains collective: it is the depression and the melancholia which result from this exaggerated individuation. One communes in sadness when one has nothing else in common." [21] Later, in his *Moral Education,* Durkheim was even more bitter: "Human activity . . . dissimulates nothingness by decorating it with the specious name of infinity." [22] In *Suicide* he offered as an example approximating the pure form of anomie the outlook of René, the hero of Chateaubriand, who exclaimed: "Is it my fault if I find limits everywhere, if what is finite has no value for me?" [23] But, as we have already observed, Durkheim did recognize the possibility—and indeed the probability in certain states of society— of a combination of the ideal types of anomie and egoism in the "manic-depressive" personality which displays "an alternation of depression and agitation, dream and action, waves of desire and the meditations of the melancholic." [24]

Although he did not fully investigate its import for collective behavior, the problem of the relation of scarcity to aggression and conflict in society was basic to Durkheim's notion of anomie. He recognized two forms of scarcity relevant to social life. The first was *de facto* scarcity in the form, for example, of inadequate genetic endowment or, on another level, of insufficient natural resources in relation to population and the existing state of technology. The second was a form that depended on the cultural definition of scarcity, as well as on the institutional creation or social conditioning of scarcity effected by the apportionment of

[21] *Le Suicide,* p. 230.   [22] P. 42.

[23] *Le Suicide,* p. 325. Although Durkheim referred to Chateaubriand, it may be observed that a magnificent anatomy of anomie—indeed a myth of the times—was provided by Balzac in *Le Peau de chagrin.* See also *Education morale,* p. 35, where Durkheim refers to Goethe's Faust as the literary personage who may be viewed as "the incarnation par excellence of the sentiment of the infinite."

[24] *Le Suicide,* p. 326.

things of social and cultural value and, of course, of any economic surplus. The problem of social order and solidarity was concerned with the dialectical relation of these two types of scarcity, for instance the ability of the second to shape or distort the first— an ability which in certain ways might increase with the development of science and technology. Durkheim's initial conception of the problem implied the circularity and tendentiousness of arguments defending institutions, which themselves aggravated scarcity, by an indiscriminate reliance on the universal prevalence of scarcity. But, within limits, it also implied the relativity of exploitation and the ethnocentrism of arguments which restricted the possibility of plenitude to modern societies possessed of advanced technology. Definitions of what constituted legitimate expectation and need, beyond the requirements of biological survival, varied according to social type. One of Durkheim's contentions was that the relative poverty of traditional societies was itself often a basis for the limitation of desires and expectations to a level at which they could be institutionally satisfied with available resources. This was the basis for the correlation of poverty, in certain societies, with low suicide rates. And especially in archaic societies, the institutional definition of legitimate needs often seemed to be consensually accepted by all interested groups.

In societies undergoing a process of "modernization," the development of social order and solidarity amounted in large part to the creation of institutions and traditions which viably realized newer values and were consensually accepted as the basis for a definition of legitimate needs. In modern societies, partly because of the functional imperatives of the advanced degree of division of labor, achievement tended to replace inheritance as the basis of status in society. The problem of social order, however, resided in the relation of status to stratification, scarcity, and anomie. In *Suicide*, Durkheim seemed to assume the existence of some sort of stratification in all societies. But, as in *The Division of Labor*, his treatment of stratification was minimal and hesitant and tended to raise questions rather than furnish answers. Once again, he failed to inquire into the principles or principal causes of stratification in various types of society. And his focus was clearly on anomie. Durkheim relied on the truism that, whatever the elements of stratification in society, they would have to be complementary, rather than contradictory, to forms of reciprocity, and consensually accepted as just if solidarity was to prevail in society as a whole. If forms of stratification, e.g., in economic reward, were to be eliminated or even substantially reduced, a sense of legitimate limits enshrined in a *conscience collective* would be all the more necessary to induce the more talented or powerful to accept equal treatment with the mediocre or powerless.[25]

The elementary and reiterated point of Durkheim's argument was that anomie, including its institutionalized variety, made the problem of solidarity and social order insoluble, because it both maximized scarcity and eliminated the possibility of reciprocity in social relations. In a state of society in which desires were perpetually stimulated and status always in doubt, mutually invasive and aggressive relations were inevitable. A society which combined achievement values and anomie faced devastating problems, for it gave rise to the type of man who was constrained to be pre-emptively rapacious in his dealings with others and anxiously uncertain in his every action. Through a combination of institutional change and advanced technology, modern societies might be able to transcend the cruder forms of economic exploitation. But economic exploitation, despite its importance, was not the sole cause of restlessness and conflict in society. And affluence alone was not a solution to the social problem of scarcity. In the absence of consensually accepted norms which defined within flexible limits an optimal set of compatible alternatives in the just allocation of resources, any surplus—however great it might be in absolute terms—would be socially and psychologically experienced in terms of uncooperative competition

[25] *Ibid.*, pp. 278–279.

for scarce values. And anomie on this level would prevent the solution of the problem of creating social milieus and symbolic forms which would permit men to feel at home in the world.

To some extent, Durkheim tried to provide more concrete answers to these problems in his corporatist proposals and his theory of morality and religion. His underlying concern, however, was to transcend uncontrolled scarcity and anomie by creating appropriate institutional norms and cultural values. This transcendence required the divorce of achievement from limitless achieving, its identification with self-fulfillment, and its reconciliation with the humanistic ideal which asserted that human beings were equal in a sense more basic than all the senses in which they were unequal. Durkheim more than intimated that in a state of society marked by extreme anomie and egoism, men were in fact already equal in a respect perhaps more fundamental than all the respects in which they were unequal—i.e., in their common anxiety and isolation. The problem was to use this condition, which so easily lent itself psychologically to destructive compensatory reactions, as a motivation for the creation of a just society. Only through a sense of just institutional limits could society marry modern achievement values to the humane classical ideals of personal maturation and social plenitude as the coordinate foundations of self-fulfillment and solidarity. Indeed, in one of his very first articles Durkheim enunciated the idea that was to serve as the inspiration of *Suicide* and of his social philosophy of finitude in general: "How I prefer the words of the old sages who recommend before all else the full and tranquil possession of oneself. No doubt, the spirit as it develops needs to have before it vaster horizons; but for all that it does not change its nature and remains finite." [26]

[26] "La Science positive de la morale en Allemagne," *Revue philosophique*, XXIV (1887), 41. Of major French writers following Durkheim, the one with basic assumptions closest to his own was probably Albert Camus. A highly illuminating essay could be written comparing these two men. From the initial insight into modern society as one characterized by anomie and anxiety, through a consideration of the problem of suicide, to the ultimate

Society and personality as complementary integrated wholes whose finite fullness was activated and agitated by a marginal leaven of anomie: this was Durkheim's essential vision throughout his life. And he increasingly saw the healthy society as one which both institutionally constrained and spontaneously evoked the commitment of all but the incorrigibly criminal and the extraordinarily creative. It accomplished this feat by founding the dominant sense of solidarity and "wholeness" in a *conscience collective* that represented a culturally relative variant of substantive reason that flexibly disciplined the imagination and controlled desire and will.

Altruism and Fatalism

Durkheim began his discussion of altruism with the following general pronouncement:

In the ordering of life, nothing is good without measure [*mesure*]. A biological characteristic can fulfill the ends it must serve only if it does not go beyond certain limits. The same principle applies to social phenomena. If excessive individuation leads to suicide, insufficient individuation produces the same effect. When a man is detached from society, he readily kills himself; he also kills himself when he is too strongly integrated into society.[27]

Thus altruism, in contrast to egoism, was characteristic of a social context marked by excessive integration and solidarity, especially in extreme communal forms. Fatalism, in contrast to anomie, characterized a social context marked by "an excess of regulation through which subjects find their future pitilessly walled up and their passions violently inhibited by an oppres-

---

affirmation of a normative sense of limits, these two thinkers went furthest in defending the type of conventional wisdom which they believed had become highly unconventional in the modern world.

[27] *Le Suicide*, p. 233. Compare the early Nietzsche on the need for limiting horizons: "A living thing can only be healthy, strong and productive within a certain horizon; if it is incapable of drawing one around itself, or too selfish to lose its own view in another's, it will come to an untimely end" (*The Use and Abuse of History*, p. 7).

sive discipline." [28] But Durkheim believed that neither altruism nor fatalism was significant in modern society. In his view, modern society in the West was characterized by egoism and anomie, by a minimum of *communitas,* and by institutional structures which might be rigid and authoritarian but were often comparatively benign in nature. Moreover, oppressive or repressive features of modern institutions would be met, not by fatalistic resignation, but by militant, impatient protest that often attained by its demands anomic heights complementary to those of the dominant system. The peculiarly unstabilizing force of this combination of factors did not escape Durkheim, although he failed to relate it to the possible genesis of truly authoritarian regimentation in society.

Extreme altruism was a trait of traditional, and especially of archaic, societies. Durkheim's discussion of the possible extremism of institutionalized *communitas* made apparent the superficiality of interpretations which present him as the unconditional advocate of solidarity in society. All forms of excess were antipathetical to his basic philosophy, at least insofar as they became generalized in society.

In extremely altruistic contexts, suicide might in certain cases be obligatory (e.g., the practice of suttee among widows in India), be considered a supererogatory virtuous act, or simply be the result of a total involvement in the collectivity and its many religious customs. Another form of suicide classified by Durkheim as altruistic was the more negative type in which an offense against a deeply rooted value created a sense of guilt so strong that suicide became a mode of expiation. Examples of altruistic suicide in one form or another abounded in traditional societies. Similar to the obligation of suttee was the injunction that retainers not survive the death of their chief or patron. Danish warriors committed suicide to escape the ignominy of dying in bed. For the Goths, natural death was shameful; the mythical punishment for it was condemnation to eternal stagna-

[28] *Le Suicide,* p. 311.

tion in caves filled with venomous animals. The Visigoths had a high rock, named the Rock of Ancestors, from which old men threw themselves when they were tired of life and felt themselves to be a burden to the community. Among the Spanish Celts a future life of glory was reserved for suicides, while hell awaited those who died of illness or old age. These might be called suicides of strength. Altruistic suicide also had its appeal to the weak. Suicides expressing protest might be directed by the oppressed against a powerful oppressor and, in ritual form, be conceived as imposing upon the adversary a burden of guilt of crushing proportions. In a sense, ritual suicide might function as the symbolic vengeance of the weak, who "altruistically" conferred upon their enemies an imaginary gift of death.

Isolated instances of altruistic suicide of course occurred in modern society. There was, for example, the mother who sacrificed her life in order to save her child from harm. But the institutional context which Durkheim treated extensively as embodying a modern vestige of primitive morality was the military. In fact, this was the only section of his chapter on altruistic suicide in which Durkheim cited statistics. They showed higher suicide rates among military men than among civilians and a tendency for the suicide rate to increase with the duration of military service. The statistics indicated that the nature of military organization and the type of social psychology it fostered explained the rate differentials. As was the case among savages, the extreme spirit of abnegation and collective solidarity induced military men to place little value on their own individual existence and to be ready to risk their lives for a *point d'honneur*. The suicide rate of the military over time, however, was following a downward trend. Durkheim found the reason in the decline of the old military spirit and the influence of modern values and conditions in fostering a more flexible discipline and greater individualism within the military itself.[29]

The nature and significance of altruistic suicide were of course

[29] *Ibid.*, pp. 259–260.

quite different from those of egoistic or anomic suicide. Altruistic suicide was prompted by an affirmation of the norms and values of society and was at times even honored by the relevant group. Egoistic and anomic suicides were induced by despair, anxiety, and suffering and were generally condemned by society.

In his discussion of egoistic suicide, however, Durkheim touched on the possible genesis in modern society of extreme and, indeed, fanatical "altruistic" contexts which depressed the rate of suicides caused by egoistic conditions. His brief but pointed discussion—his only significant reference in *Suicide* to social conflict—reveals his awareness of the "integrating" function of social conflict.

Great social commotions, like great popular wars, inflame collective sentiments, stimulate party spirit and patriotism, political faith and national faith, and by concentrating activities toward the same goal, determine, at least for a time, a stronger integration of society. This salutary influence is not due to the crisis itself but to the struggles of which the crisis is the cause. Since they oblige men to come together to confront a common danger, the individual thinks less of himself and more of the common cause. Moreover, one understands how this integration may not be purely momentary but may at times survive the causes which were its immediate occasion, especially when it is intense.[30]

Earlier, in his discussion of the correlation of intellectual pursuits and egoism, Durkheim had applied the same principle of the integration of groups and personalities through shared social antagonism to the Jews, who avoided suicide by combining intellectualism with ethnic solidarity.

It is a general law that religious minorities, in order to be able to maintain themselves more securely against the hatreds of which they are the object, or simply through a sort of emulation, make an effort to be superior in knowledge to surrounding populations. Thus Protestants themselves show more taste for learning when they are a minority. The Jew seeks education, not to replace his collective prejudices with

[30] *Ibid.*, p. 222.

thought-out notions, but simply to be better armed in the struggle. For him this is a means of compensating for the disadvantageous situation which is created for him by opinion and at times by the law. Since learning in itself has little effect on vigorous traditions, he superimposes his intellectual life on his customary activity without having the former cut into the latter. Hence the complexity of his physiognomy. Primitive in certain ways, he is in other ways a cerebral and refined type. Thus he joins the advantages of little groups of the past with the benefits of the intense culture of our great contemporary societies. He has all the intelligence of moderns without sharing their despair.[31]

It would, of course, be difficult not to see an element of biographical nostalgia in this portrait, as well as a partial intimation of Durkheim's reformist hopes for professional groups.

Durkheim devoted only a brief footnote to "fatalistic" suicide, for he believed this type to be largely of historical interest. Although his concept of fatalism seems to hark back to the discussion of the constrained or forced division of labor in his first major work, Durkheim did not refer to this problem in the later book. In part, this was because the idea of fatalism in *Suicide* was not related to the existence of exploitative structures alone. It dialectically comprised both the oppressive or repressive nature of institutional norms and the nature of individual or collective response to them. Fatalism, in other words, implied the kind of resignation to "moral or material despotism" that led, not to spontaneous or organized protest, but to suicide (or perhaps to crime).[32] From history Durkheim drew examples of the suicides of slaves. From modern society, he cited the less institutionally pertinent instances of wives without children and of husbands too immature to assume the responsibilities of marriage; he did not raise the question of the relation of these cases to the sociocultural definition of the role of the married woman, the relation of the sexes, or the nature of the modern family.

Durkheim's brief discussion of fatalistic suicide has the merit

[31] *Ibid.*, pp. 169–170.   [32] *Ibid.*, p. 311.

of justifying the inclusion in the definition of suicide of a cognitive factor which implied the ability of the individual to assess the objective situation and to take a form of action that required a significant measure of initiative. For suicide to be a typical reaction to oppression, authoritarianism would have to be strong enough to check more effective forms of protest, but not strong enough to break down all self-control and spirit of resistance. It has been remarked that in situations approximating total oppression, the suicide rate, instead of rising, tends to drop. This was, for example, true of Nazi concentration camps.[33] In the context of extreme authoritarianism, conditions induce infantile attitudes, an inability to make objective assessments, a loss of the sense of personal identity and "ego boundaries," and what Freud termed "identification with the aggressor." Thus a situation of extreme social pathology might make the oppressor an object of distorted and servile hero worship that would exclude even the option of suicide as an existential response.

Although Durkheim failed to investigate adequately the genesis and nature of extremely authoritarian attempts at integration, it may be observed that his belief that modern Western societies would give birth, not to fatalistic suicides, but to a combination of liberalized institutional norms (or at least benign authoritarianism) and forms of protest shot through with anomie has been borne out by developments since his death. One instance has been the evolution of sexual norms and attitudes. Durkheim's own time was the period during which Freud treated female hysteria caused by extremely repressive sexual norms. Since that time, puritanical official morality has been increasingly undercut by a sexual revolution which has combined greater permissiveness with disorientation concerning its legitimate limits. Even prophets of liberation have been led to speak of "repressive desublimation." The confused status of sexual attitudes is only one

[33] Elie Cohen, *Human Behavior in the Concentration Camp* (New York: Norton, 1953), p. 158.

aspect of the modern crisis of legitimacy which Durkheim perceived. As Erik Erikson has observed: "The patient of today suffers most under the problem of what he should believe in and who he should—or indeed might—be or become; while the patient of early psychoanalysis suffered most under inhibitions which prevented him from being what or who he thought he was." [34] The "identity crisis" in its extreme forms is of course a psychological derivative of anomie. In a healthy or integrated society, much of the crisis would be taken out of the search for identity.

Durkheim and Weber

If asked to name the sociological classic par excellence, most sociologists would hesitate between *Suicide* and *The Protestant Ethic*. But the extent to which these two works are complementary as contributions to the analysis of modern social and cultural history has been little recognized.

Both Durkheim and Weber, in their conception of modern society, stressed the importance of the comparative method in investigating major processes of cultural transformation. Their foci converged on the relation of ideologies or value systems to institutions, a trait of Durkheim's work which became increasingly prominent with his growing interest in religion. In *The Division of Labor*, Durkheim treated anomie and a crisis of transition in terms of the breakdown of one type of social system under the impact of demographic pressure and the rise of newer institutions and values. But in comparison with Weber's elaborate investigation of feudal institutions, symbolic systems, urbanization, and bureaucracy, the level of discussion in Durkheim's first major work was of minimal historical interest. Despite the fact that it shared Durkheim's constant tendency to devote insufficient attention to the precise nature of symbolic beliefs and in-

[34] *Childhood and Society* (New York: Norton, 1950), p. 239.

stitutional practices, *Suicide* was often more to the point. *Suicide* attempted an analysis of the functions and consequences of institutions and values whose genesis and symbolic nature Weber later investigated in *The Protestant Ethic and the Spirit of Capitalism* (1920).

Indeed, the overall relationship between the ideas of Durkheim and Weber reveals an apparent paradox which would merit extensive investigation. The basic assumptions of these two thinkers were often diametrically opposed. Weber's thought rested on tragic and ironic assumptions. He combined a Nietzschean metaphysic with a neo-Kantian methodology. For Weber, as for Nietzsche, reality was anomic. Meaningful structures were fictive projections of the human mind. Any notion of a correspondence between concept and reality was out of the question. A concept did not represent reality; it actively shaped it. Knowledge, for Weber, thus had a highly problematic basis. Fundamental conflict, moreover, was an inescapable fact of life. Human values, which were crucial in the attempt to impose order on chaos, existed in a state of irreconcilable conflict with one another. The choice of values was, in the last analysis, the subjective, existential decision of the individual, and this ultimately irrational decision determined his entire perspective on reality. (Durkheim provided a largely critical appraisal of the thought of Nietzsche in his *Pragmatisme et sociologie*. But he seemed to know Nietzsche's ideas only from secondary sources.) Sociological method, for Weber, involved the elaboration of "one-sided" analytical models (or "ideal types") of the attempts of men to impose order on chaos. Weber maintained that research in social science was initially guided by subjective values, but once significant problems were selected, the results obtained might in some sense be objective and value-neutral. In terms of its conclusions, social science confronted an irrational universe with formally rational methods, but it remained silent about substantive values.

Durkheim oscillated between a Cartesianized neo-Kantian and a more Hegelian dialectical conception of science. History, for him, was the scene of a struggle between meaningful order and anomic chaos. But the prevalence of order was normal, and excessive anomie was pathological. In contrast to Weber, Durkheim did not find the knowledge of reality to be itself highly problematic. Durkheim's epistemology was a variant of the "correspondence" theory of truth. And it ultimately was subordinated to a very traditional kind of metaphysic. Except for an irreducible margin of anomie, essential reality was rationally structured, and science could discover its laws. Durkheim's idea of social science closely integrated cognitive and normative aspects. Values could be rationally known. And a viable harmony of values was possible in the normal society. From Durkheim's perspective, Weber was theorizing from within an anomic context and proposing, at best, a tenuous basis for rationality within the confines of anomie. From Weber's perspective, Durkheim was being irrelevantly traditional, hopelessly naïve, and possibly utopian. The apparent paradox, however, is that, on the basis of such antithetical assumptions, Durkheim and Weber arrived at largely complementary research interests and specific analyses in their investigation of culture and society.

Durkheim classified Protestantism under egoism and somewhat sketchily explained its correlation with relatively high suicide rates (in contrast with Judaism and Catholicism) by drawing attention to the absence of solidarity in a religious society that institutionalized individualistic free enquiry. Protestantism reduced to a minimum the nexus between symbolic cult and existential community which Durkheim was later to present as the essence of the religious phenomenon. Weber may not have shared the philosophically critical intent of Durkheim, but he did concur in the essentials of the analysis.

In its extreme inhumanity this doctrine [predestination] must above all have had one consequence for the life of a generation which surrendered to its magnificent consistency. That was a feeling of unprecedented inner loneliness of the single individual. In what was for the man of the age of the Reformation the most important thing in life, his eternal salvation, he was forced to meet a destiny which had been decreed for him from eternity. No one could help him. No priest. . . . No sacraments. . . . No church. . . . Finally, even no God. For even Christ had died only for the elect, for whose benefit God had decreed his martyrdom from eternity. This, the complete elimination of salvation through the Church and the sacraments (which was in Lutheranism by no means developed to its final conclusions), was what formed the absolutely decisive difference from Catholicism. The great historic process in the development of religions, the elimination of magic from the world [*die Entzauberung der Welt*—disenchantment], which had begun with the old Hebrew prophets and, in conjunction with Hellenistic scientific thought, had repudiated all magical means to salvation as superstition and sin, came here to its logical conclusion. The genuine Puritan even rejected all signs of religious ceremony at the grave and buried his nearest and dearest without song or ritual in order that no superstition, no trust in the effects of magical and sacramental forces on salvation, should creep in.[35]

Thus Dowden, whom Weber quoted, wrote: "The deepest community [with God] is found not in institutions or corporations or churches but in the secrets of a solitary heart." [36] The conception of the religious situation of man as that of a solitary individual whose salvation had been decided by a totally transcendent, hidden divinity might be seen as a symbolic representation which simultaneously made sense of, and functioned to sustain, a sense of isolation and anomic anxiety in a period of historical transition. This might have various consequences, e.g., the formation of extremely integrated groups under charismatic leaders, as in the case of Cromwell's "army of saints." Here men reacted to extreme isolation and anxiety, fostered by religious symbolism, by seeking demanding and militantly fanatical forms of social integration. But what concerned Weber was another historical possibility: the relationship of the religious doctrine of predesti-

[35] *The Protestant Ethic and the Spirit of Capitalism* (New York: Scribner's, 1958), pp. 104–105.
[36] *Ibid.*, p. 221, n. 16.

nation and *Deus Absconditus* ("Hidden God") to an ethic of "this-worldly asceticism" which combined anxiety about one's fate with a rigorous form of individualistic self-discipline and formally rational activity in occupational life. This relationship Weber, of course, conceived as vital in the formation of an elite of capitalistic entrepreneurs whose influence helped determine the shape of modern society in the West.

It is necessary to note, what has often been forgotten, that the Reformation meant not the elimination of the Church's control over everyday life, but rather the substitution of a new form of control for the previous one. It meant a repudiation of a control which was very lax, at that time scarcely perceptible in practice, and hardly more than formal, in favor of a regulation of the whole of conduct which, penetrating to all departments of private and public life, was infinitely burdensome and earnestly enforced.[37]

Thus, where Durkheim stressed the role of anomie in modern history, Weber emphasized the birth of a new "nomie" or ethic. But Weber himself tended to situate the new "nomie" on the formally rational level of the adjustment of means to ends; and he perceived a certain type of institutionalized anomie on the level of ends in modern activity. What were the relationships among the religious doctrine of predestination, the total investment of the sacred in the transcendent, the new formally rational "nomie" or ethic of self-discipline in a calling, capitalism, and the element of institutionalized anomie or limitlessness on the level of ends which, according to Durkheim, was the negation of substantive rationality? In a sense, the problem of the Protestant sectarian who believed in predestination decreed by a hidden God was for Weber the problem of objective indices. It was this need for a visible sign of a state of election which one could never directly know or be entirely sure of that provided the intelligible but unintended link between the Protestant religious problematic and the ethos of capitalism. Worldly success

[37] *Ibid.*, p. 36.

in the form of limitless competitive achieving pursued with ascetic rigor and functional rationality, and conceived as the structural motivation of work in an occupational calling, became the visible index of personal salvation. Although he noted the importance of other factors, it was the combination of institutionalized limitlessness on the level of ends and functionally rational discipline on the level of means which seemed to be the truly distinctive criterion of the capitalist ethos in Weber's mind.

The impulse to acquisition, pursuit of gain, of money, has in itself nothing to do with capitalism. This impulse exists and has existed among waiters, physicians, coachmen, artists, prostitutes, dishonest officials, soldiers, nobles, crusaders, gamblers, and beggars. . . . Unlimited greed for gain is not in the least identical with capitalism, and is still less its spirit. . . . But capitalism is identical with the pursuit of profit, and forever *renewed* profit, by means of continuous, rational, capitalistic enterprise. . . . We will define a capitalistic economic action as one which rests on the expectation of profit by the utilization of opportunities for exchange, that is on (formally) peaceful chances of profit.[38]

This conception of capitalism was not, it may be added, dependent upon the private ownership or even control of the means of production; it referred to the issues of how institutions functioned and the nature of control. Weber identified as traditional, in contrast with the capitalistic ethos, the attitude based on a sense of legitimate limits in the mutual adjustment of needs and institutionalized means of satisfaction. Weber's perspective enabled him to emphasize the new "nomie" involved in sober bourgeois self-discipline and rationality in the adjustment of means to ends. From Durkheim's perspective, this situation would appear as one case of a combination of a pathology of "practical" reason (institutionalized limitlessness or anomie) and a subsidiary pathology of "theoretical" reason (functional rationality directed to limitless ends).

Thus Weber believed he had found a genetic link between re-

[38] *Ibid.*, p. 17.

ligious and economic phenomena which in the epoch of classical
liberalism tended to separate into discrete institutional spheres.
Instead of elaborating a reformist project in the manner of Durkheim, Weber dispassionately and ironically observed of the
future:

No one knows who will live in this cage in the future, or whether at
the end of this tremendous development entirely new prophets will
arise, or there will be a great rebirth of old ideas and ideals, or, if
neither, mechanized petrification, embellished with a sort of convul-
sive self-importance. For of the last stage of this cultural development,
it might well be truly said: "Specialists without spirit, sensualists
without heart; this nullity imagines it has attained a level of civilization never before achieved." [39]

From Analysis to Reform

Suicide concluded with proposals for a corporatist reform of
modern society. In presenting his plea for corporative groups,
Durkheim was sensitive to the heritage of suspicion associated
with the idea of corporatism because of the evolution of corporative organizations in the *ancien régime*. Certainly, the uses
to which corporative establishments have been put since Durkheim's death have compounded this negative reputation. Yet the
continuing difficulty in resolving the problems discussed by
Durkheim, as well as the emergence of corporative features in
all advanced industrial societies, may be grounds for renewed
interest in the specific nature of Durkheim's idea of corporatism.

Suicide contained Durkheim's most pointed conception of the
problematic nature of modern society, and whatever one may
conclude about his notion of reform, this work will continue to
be remembered for its insight into modern social pathology. The
modern age, for Durkheim as for so many thinkers in the nineteenth century, was an age of transition. It was a period intervening between an earlier type of integrated society and an integrated society of the future. *The Division of Labor* included an

[39] *Ibid.*, p. 182.

exploratory and inconclusive conceptualization of these types of integration, and it concluded with a discussion of pathological phenomena in modern society. *Suicide* focused in a more explicit and central way on modern social pathology. In his key concept of anomie, Durkheim tried to account for the severe imbalances, dissociations, and contradictions of an age of transition. The concomitant of anomie in the lives of people was profound disorientation—what other social theorists discussed as alienation. The sociological study of suicide was for Durkheim a precise way to investigate the disruptive features of modern life. And his proposals for reform were based on the faith that modern society would in time achieve legitimate order.

In the concluding sections of *Suicide,* Durkheim remarked that the rise of synthetic philosophies of pessimism was one indication that the current of social malaise in modern life had passed all bounds and had attained a pathological state. In normal states of society, maxims and sayings which expressed the necessary element of suffering in life were not systematized into a dominant mood or *Weltanschauung.* They were counterbalanced in the collective psyche by sentiments of a different sort. But in modern society, pessimism had become the basis of philosophical systems, and this development was not restricted to isolated philosophers like Schopenhauer.

One must also account for all those who, under different names, start out under the influence of the same spirit. The anarchist, the aesthete, the mystic, the socialist revolutionary, if they do not despair of the future, at least agree with the pessimist in sharing the same feeling of hatred or disgust for the status quo and the same need to destroy or escape from reality. Collective melancholy would not have invaded consciousness to this point if it had not been subject to a morbid development. Consequently, the development of suicide which results from it is of the same nature.[40]

The primary intention of Durkheim was to grasp the over-all nature of the social system, both in its dominant institutions and

[40] *Ibid.,* p. 424.

the reactions evoked by them. Only on this basis could a rational conception of reform be elaborated. Moral issues were uppermost in Durkheim's idea of reform, but his understanding of morality was a special one related to the reconstruction of society. There is no more accurate introduction to his conception of reform and its relation to morality than his own words in the conclusion to *Suicide*.

Just as suicide does not proceed from man's difficulties in life, so the means of arresting its progress is not to make the struggle less difficult and life easier. If more people kill themselves today than formerly, this is not because we must make more painful efforts to maintain ourselves or because our legitimate needs are less satisfied; it is because we do not know the limits of our legitimate needs and we do not perceive the meaning of our efforts. It is indeed certain that at all levels of the social hierarchy, average well-being has increased, although this increase has not always taken place in the most equitable proportions. Thus the malaise from which we suffer does not come from an increase in the number and intensity of objective causes of suffering; it attests, not to a greater economic misery, but to an alarming moral misery.

But we must not deceive ourselves about the meaning of the word "moral." When one says of an individual or social problem that it is entirely moral, one generally means that it does not respond to any treatment but can be cured only through repeated exhortations, methodical objurgations, in a word through verbal action. But in reality the mental system of a people is a system of definite forces which cannot be deranged or rearranged through simple injunctions. It really corresponds to the way social elements are grouped and organized. It is far from the truth that, in analyzing as "moral" the sickness of which the abnormal progress of suicide is the symptom, we intend to reduce it to some sort of superficial illness which can be conjured away with soft words. On the contrary, the alteration of moral temperament which is thus revealed bears witness to a profound alteration of our social structure. To heal the one, it is necessary to reform the other.[41]

[41] *Ibid.*, pp. 444–445.

Durkheim was one of the first social thinkers to see clearly the crisis of legitimacy and meaning in modern society. His thought indicated an awareness of the real suffering and genuine values distorted in the ideological reactions of prophets of doom. But he did not advocate a "politics of cultural despair" based on indiscriminate and destructive criticism of modernity, romantic nostalgia for an idealized past, and utopian visions of a totally integrated and authoritative society.[42] The intent of his proposals for reform was to extricate the valid element in inchoate and possibly dangerous strivings for community and shared values and to embody this valid element in a rational conception of reconstruction in modern society.

[42] For an acute analysis of nihilistic social criticism in pre-Nazi Germany, see Fritz Stern, *The Politics of Cultural Despair* (first pub. 1961; Garden City, N.Y.: Doubleday, 1965).

5 »

Theory and Practice

It is not good for man to live on a war footing in the midst of his immediate companions. This sensation of general hostility, the mutual defiance which results from it, the tension which it necessitates are deplorable states when they are chronic. If we love war, we also love the joys of peace. And the latter have all the more value for men to the extent that they are more profoundly socialized, that is to say (for the two words are equivalent) more profoundly civilized.

—Preface to the second edition of
The Division of Labor in Society

Economic functions are not ends in themselves. They are only means toward an end and organs of social life. Social life is above all a harmonious community of efforts, a communion of minds and wills with a common end. Society has no *raison d'être* if it does not bring men a little peace—peace in their hearts and peace in their commerce with each other. If industry can be productive only by troubling this peace and causing war, it is not worth the trouble it costs.

—*Professional Ethics and Civic Morals*

Sociology, History, and Reform

An intense involvement in the Dreyfus Affair, the time-consuming preparation and editing of the *Année sociologique*, a growing interest in religious symbolism, and a related concern with elaborating his mystique-laden social philosophy—all these factors combined to prevent Durkheim from carrying to completion two studies in comparative history: a history of socialism and a history of corporatism. The intimate connection between these two unfinished projects has rarely been recognized. They were related both to each other and to his idea of necessary structural change in modern society. Indeed, they represented the concrete basis for his attempted *Aufhebung*—his dialectical synthesis—of radicalism, conservatism, and liberalism for the achievement of "normality" in modern society. Thus it makes sense to treat as a unit in the development of his thought those works in which he discussed corporatism and socialism: the concluding chapter, on "practical consequences," in *Le Suicide; Le Socialisme; Leçons de sociologie* (translated as *Professional Ethics and Civic Morals); L'Education morale;* and the important preface to the second edition of *De La Division du travail social.*

All these works were thought out in the period extending roughly from 1896 to 1902. This may be considered the middle period in the development of Durkheim's thought. Before it came *The Division of Labor* and *The Rules of Sociological Method.* The broader ambition of the latter methodological treatise was to provide a sociological version of Descartes's discourse on method. It approached general theory through the uncertain perspective implicit in Durkheim's first major work. From its conception of social facts to its mechanistic theory of causation, *The Rules of Sociological Method* was the explicit statement of the more analytically dissociated, Cartesianized neo-Kantian strand of Durkheim's thought. It presented society primarily as an "objectivated" action system which sociologists were to investigate by studying discrete, linear cause-and-effect relationships. In this book, Durkheim tended to focus upon the most reified aspects of social life, disregarding the problem of the internalization of social norms and the meaningful nature of human activity. He subsequently modified his narrow focus on the "exteriority" and "constraint" of social facts and provided greater insight into the meaning of his famous dictum that social facts should be treated like "things." After the turn of the century, he was preoccupied with preparatory studies for *The Elementary Forms* and with the revision of his theoretical assumptions to accommodate his more mature conception of the relation of theory to practice and of methodology to philosophy. Hence, the specifics of his notion of structural change in modern society are to be found primarily in the works of his middle period.

The architectonic goal of Durkheim's idea of structural reform was simple but ambitious: conscious and substantively rational social control of the economy and all forms of particularistic interest or power. The elementary social units in his proposed reform—corporative or occupational groups—would at some significant level be small enough to provide a communal, face-to-face milieu for their members. But the broader scope of regional, national, and international exchange in large and highly complex modern societies required more inclusive organization, planning, and social control. Absolutely fundamental at all levels was the existence of autonomously accepted and deeply internalized institutional norms which defined legitimate limits between differentiated functions, created the necessary conditions for reciprocity, and provided the basic structure for decisions in specific cases and controversies. This, in stark outline, was the motivating idea of Durkheim's venture in creative and historically informed social reform, which he explicitly refused to detail in the form of an itemized blueprint. Despite his feeling that social action involves unpredictable turns and creative élan, he did give certain directives for the attainment of social health in modern times.

In a critical review of a work which based its analysis of socialism upon the thought of Marx, Durkheim flatly asserted, "As for us, all that is essential in socialist doctrine is found in the philosophy of Saint-Simon." [1] This assertion might be taken as the leitmotif of Le Socialisme, Durkheim's only completed work on the history of socialism.[2] He had begun his study of socialism

[1] Review of Gaston Richard, Le Socialisme et la science sociale, Revue philosophique IV (1897), 201.

[2] First given as a lecture course in 1895–1896, this study was published posthumously in 1928 as Le Socialisme (Paris: Alcan). An excellent English translation by Charlotte Sattler has been published with an incisive introduction by Alvin Gouldner: Socialism (New York: Collier Books, 1962). The first translation was under the title Socialism and Saint-Simon (Yellow Springs, Ohio: Antioch Press, 1958). References throughout are to the Collier Books edition.

in part because some of his brightest students were being won over to Marxism. Polemical animus was not totally absent from his *Socialisme*. Brief but stringent criticism of Marx was played off against extensive and lavish praise of Saint-Simon. Marx's *Capital* was indeed recognized as the "strongest work" of socialist thought.[3] But this accolade was bestowed almost as a means of damning with faint praise. It prefaced an argument that *Capital* lacked convincing scientific proofs and stood out only because of the even greater deficiencies of other socialist works, judged from a scientific point of view. But this attitude was part of Durkheim's broader conception of socialism as a fervid ideology —"a cry of grief, sometimes of anger, uttered by men who feel most keenly our collective malaise."[4] Despite the apparent element of rash generalization in his estimation of socialist literature, Durkheim's argument did lead him to conclude that, at least on a symptomatic level, socialism had to be taken seriously. Scientific refutation of detailed points of socialist thought was merely a "labor of Penelope." A more dialectically adequate perspective was needed to discover the causes of socialist ideology in society and to assimilate the elements of truth socialism contained.

In certain respects, the thought of Saint-Simon had a privileged position for Durkheim as an approach to a more adequate perspective. Indeed, he stated that "aside from Cartesianism, there is nothing more important in the entire history of French philosophy. At more than one point these two philosophies can legitimately be reconciled with one another, for they were both inspired by the same rationalist faith."[5] Thus Saint-Simonism took its place beside Cartesianism and neo-Kantianism as a constructive force in shaping Durkheim's rationalist perspective.

This consideration helps to situate more precisely the influence of Comte on Durkheim's search for the laws of social life. Durkheim scored the injustice of Comte's reference to his association with Saint-Simon as a "morbid liaison in his early youth with a

[3] *Socialism*, p. 40.   [4] *Ibid.*, p. 41.   [5] *Ibid.*, p. 142.

depraved juggler." [6] According to Durkheim, Comte clearly owed
Saint-Simon much more than he sometimes acknowledged. But
Durkheim admitted that it was no easy task to discover unity in
Saint-Simon's thought. His work was "a loose series of papers,
innumerable brochures, plans and lists of articles forever outlined but never realized." [7] Durkheim was not one to underestimate the importance of organization and synthesis in relation
to outbursts of genius and beguiling digressions. In *Socialism* he
asserted that the honor of being the founding father of sociology,
currently ascribed to Comte, should in justice be awarded to
Saint-Simon. In a later article, Durkheim repeated the assertion
that "in a sense all the fundamental ideas of Comte's sociology
may already be found in Saint-Simon." [8] But he added the stric-
ture that the "truly creative act consists not in throwing out a
few beautiful ideas which beguile the intelligence but in grasping
ideas firmly in order to make them fecund by placing them in
contact with things, coordinating them, providing initial proofs
in a manner that makes ideas both logically assimilable and open
to verification by others. This is what Comte did for social science, . . . and it is why he deserves to be considered its father
and why the name sociology which he gave the new science remains definitive." [9]

Thus Saint-Simon was the charismatic inspiration for social
science, but Comte was its systematic organizer. In his own
analysis of Saint-Simon, Durkheim undoubtedly saw the earlier
prophet of Paris through the prism provided by the more disciplined thought of Comte. Aside from its relation to his Cartesianized neo-Kantianism, Durkheim's initial emphasis upon the
"exteriority" and "constraint" of thinglike "social facts" may have
owed a great deal to the leaden gray social world of Comte.
Comte, however, was explicit in expressing his penchant for

---

[6] *Ibid.*, p. 144.   [7] *Ibid.*, p. 124.

[8] "La Sociologie en France au XIXe siècle," *Revue bleue,* 4th series,
XIII (1900), 611–612.

[9] *Ibid.*, p. 612.

authoritarian hierarchies and bureaucratic structures for exercising control. His idea of consensus and order has been fittingly described as a Catholicism without Christianity. Even Comte's latter-day openness to the influence of brotherhood and love remained permeated with idiosyncratic fantasies, and it culminated intellectually in a "religion of humanity" which was often little more than an individualistic worship of heroes of the past. Durkheim increasingly moved away from this frame of reference in an attempt to combine institutional constraint with communal sentiment. This idea of social normality was also the point of departure in his interpretation of religion.

If Comte went to extremes in his *polytechnicien's* admiration for formal rationality and bureaucratic order, Saint-Simon, in Durkheim's opinion, went too far to the opposite extreme of romantic passion and spontaneity. This judgment was in fact the sole basis of the criticism of Saint-Simon in Durkheim's work on socialism. In one strand of his argument, Durkheim affirmed the mind-body dualism in uncompromising form. His reaction to Saint-Simon's insistence on the erotic aspect of love was to remark that his predecessor failed to appreciate the Christian message. The pantheistic, pagan thrust of Saint-Simon's *New Christianity* subverted the Christian idea that "the divine, bound and as if imprisoned in matter, tends to free itself to return to God, from Whom it came." [10] Such sentiments, which were prominent in Durkheim's social metaphysic, were strongly represented in the outlook of the *fine fleur* of republican spiritualistic philosophers who were often Durkheim's intended audience and reference group.

A second strand of Durkheim's argument applied to the fantasies of a total liberation of the erotic which were prevalent among one group of Saint-Simonians. It also applied to images of consumer bliss, eulogies of unlimited entrepreneurial drive, and the generalization of Promethean values. Indeed, Durkheim argued that the thought of Saint-Simon and the worldly philoso-

[10] *Socialism*, p. 233.

phy of the ideologists of capitalism—the economists—were different expressions of "the same social state" and shared "the same sensuous and utilitarian tendency" and the same "fundamental principle." [11] For Durkheim, this principle of endless need and limitless assertion as a dominant social force was pathogenic in all its manifestations, including the technocratic and the erotic. In his basic critique of Saint-Simon, Durkheim in fact uttered certain strictures which were to be repeated verbatim in his discussion of anomie in *Suicide*. He concluded that ultimately Saint-Simon offered "as a remedy an aggravation of the evil." [12]

What were the elements in Saint-Simon's conception of reform which Durkheim believed were to be detached from their anomic context and given new meaning in a healthy state of society? Durkheim's very definition of socialism depended primarily on the perspective of Saint-Simon: "We denote as socialist every doctrine which demands the connection of all economic functions, or of certain among them, which are at the present time diffuse to the directing and conscious centers of society." [13] In contrast with Comte, Saint-Simon did not believe that the division of labor necessarily led to social disintegration. Saint-Simon's idea of socialism embodied his conception of the manner in which organic solidarity among highly differentiated functions could be generated in modern society.

In accepting this conception of socialism, Durkheim rejected definitions based on the abolition of private property, collectivism, and the working class. On the subject of property, he observed that Marx himself envisioned the collective ownership only of the means of production. The basic question was the relationship of familial inheritance, collective ownership of the means of production, and individual property. Durkheim's own corporatist proposals would embody his specific answer to this question. But he noted in a prefatory manner that criticism of inheritance involved the most complete and radical affirmation of the right of private property in history. Inheritance was a

[11] *Ibid.*, p. 238.   [12] *Ibid.*, p. 245.   [13] *Ibid.*, p. 54.

vestige of "old familial communism." It had nothing to do with the achievement or work of the individual. "In order that property may be said to be truly individual, it is necessary that it be the work of the individual and of him alone." In this sense, "private property is that which begins with the individual and ends with him." Thus the decline of the importance of kinship had two institutional consequences which were yet to be fully realized: the restriction of private property to the individual who acquired it and the creation of a more significant social agency in modern society for the transmission of capital.[14]

Moreover, collectivism in general was not specific to socialism; according to Durkheim, "There has never been a society in which private interests have not been subordinated to social ends; for this subordination is the very condition of all community life." [15] To the charge that collectivism meant authoritarianism, Durkheim answered, "If there is an authoritarian socialism, there is also one which is essentially democratic." [16] Nor could exclusive concern for the fate of the working class be identified with socialism. The betterment of workers' lives was one goal of the organization of the economy, "just as class war is only one of the means by which this reorganization could result, one aspect of the historic development producing it." [17] Socialists were correct in arguing that "there is presently an entire segment of the economic world which is not truly and directly integrated into society." Members of the working class "are not full-fledged members of society, since they participate in the community's life only through an imposed medium"—the capitalist class which deprives workers of social justice.[18] Socialists were also right in arguing that the legitimate demands of the exploited could not be met by welfare doles or charity. "Charity organizes nothing. It maintains the status quo; it can only attenuate the individual suffering that this lack of organization engenders." [19] Only through structural change that would provide institutions for

[14] *Ibid.*, pp. 47–48.   [15] *Ibid.*, p. 48.   [16] *Ibid.*, p. 49.
[17] *Ibid.*, p. 58.   [18] *Ibid.*, pp. 59–60.   [19] *Ibid.*, p. 58.

the regulation of the economy and all groups involved in it—not through measures restricted to the working class alone—might social justice be created in modern society.

What was Durkheim's conception of the relation of sociology to history and ethnography, and what were the implications of the relationship for his idea of reform in modern society? A general answer to these questions is provided by the dual bases of Durkheimism: the tree of social life and the distinction between normality and pathology. Durkheim clearly rejected the conception of unilinear evolution in Comte's famous law of the three stages:

Whatever Pascal may have said—and Comte mistakenly took up his celebrated formula—mankind cannot be compared to a man who, having lived through all past centuries, still subsists. Rather, humanity resembles an immense family whose different branches, which have increasingly diverged from one another, have become little by little detached from the common trunk to live their own lives. Besides, what assurance is there that this common trunk ever existed? [20]

In his guiding model of the tree of sociocultural life, Durkheim combined a flexible theory of invariance with a notion of different "social species" or types. His conception of the common trunk and its relation to archaic societies owed much to Rousseau. His idea of typological branches and its relation to history derived in large part from Saint-Simon. He was also indebted to Saint-Simon in his specific conception of modern history, as well as in his more comprehensive ideas of social normality and pathology. Aside from the influence of earlier social theorists, this chapter of Durkheim's thought was of course also permeated with biological analogies, at times with confusing results. On the whole, however, Durkheim recognized the limitations as well as the value of the "organismic" metaphor.

The trunk of the tree of social life represented the elementary conditions or "functional prerequisites" of society. They were

[20] "Cours de science sociale: Leçon d'ouverture," *Revue internationale de l'enseignement*, XV (1888), 33.

approximated in the most clear and distinct form in archaic societies. And at times Durkheim, with some misgiving, converted his logical model into an evolutionary timetable by arguing that the "common trunk" was indeed present in its pure form in "totemic society." The more general methodological point was that archaic societies in their relative simplicity presented privileged cases for "crucial experiments" which attempted to deduce the universal bases of society and culture.

In this respect, Durkheim underwent a significant change of opinion. His early thought, e.g., in *The Rules of Sociological Method,* tended to denigrate the importance of ethnography in comparison with historiography.[21] Under the combined impact of better ethnographic research in the field and a shift in theoretical and philosophical focus, his later thought made ethnography the anchor point of general sociology (or, in the sense of Lévi-Strauss, of anthropology). In *The Elementary Forms,* Durkheim chided historians for ignoring the theoretical importance of ethnographic material for an understanding of the intemporal or universal bases of society which the objects of historical research would reveal in different manifestations.[22] One of the examples he was fond of citing was the relation of Polynesian taboo to Roman *sacer*—a point which Marc Bloch would develop in his study of royal rituals of healing, *Les Rois thaumaturges.*

But Durkheim never lost interest in the relation of sociology to history and its importance for the definition of social types. And this interest was especially marked in the works of his middle period. The problem of the relation of history to sociology gave rise, in Durkheim's France, to disciplinary squabbles and imperialistic posturing which accorded ill with his idea of "organic solidarity." However important these debates may have

[21] *Les Règles de la méthode sociologique* (15th ed.; Paris: Presses Universitaires de France, 1963), p. 132.

[22] *Les Formes élémentaires de la vie religieuse* (4th ed.; Paris: Presses Universitaires de France, 1960), p. 5.

been for the play of personality and the historical development of the disciplines, their intellectual foundation was often minimal.[23]

Indeed, it is significant that the debate over historicism never reached in France the heights of intensity and divisiveness that it did in Germany. One obvious reason was that historicism had not made as great an impact in France and, therefore, did not form as imposing an obstacle to thinkers more concerned with modes of experience oriented to the present or future. In France, realism in the novel had, in the works of such figures as Balzac, applied to contemporary realities principles of understanding which, in Germany, had been largely restricted to an appreciation of the past. And in someone like Balzac the result was a visionary realism that was sensitive to the role of symbol and myth in culture. Realism in the novel declined toward the end of the nineteenth century. To some extent, Durkheimian sociology, in its attempt to penetrate contemporary social realities, may be seen as the heir of the realistic novel. It is, however, true that Durkheim's early thought shared features of naturalism, while his later thought conceived values and symbols in a manner reminiscent of symbolism. To this extent, the development of his thought paralleled the division of literature into naturalistic and symbolist tendencies. But on its more dialectical or relational side, Durkheim's thought retained the intention to be found in the visionary realism of a Balzac. And it did this in a manner that indicated not only an increasing awareness of the role of myth in society but also some sensitivity to the problem of integrating a conception of modern society with an understanding of historical development. The goal of a totalizing social history was a feature of the Durkheimian heritage to be preserved and developed by the *Annales* school under Marc Bloch and Lucien Febvre.

[23] For an excellent account of this discussion, see H. Stuart Hughes, *The Obstructed Path* (New York: Harper & Row, 1968), chap. ii. For the attitude of a contemporary historian, see Lucien Febvre, *Combats pour l'histoire* (Paris: Colin, 1953), pp. 422–423.

On a theoretical level, Durkheim conceived the basic relationship between history and sociology to be one of interdisciplinary cooperation in the definition of significant problems. He observed that studies dealing with social phenomena presented a strange dichotomy. On one side, there was "a rather inchoate multitude of sciences or quasi sciences which had the same object but were ignorant of their kinship and the profound unity of the facts they studied, often only vaguely sensing their rationality." On the other side was sociology, "which was aware of this unity but which glided too high above the facts to have any effect upon the way in which they were studied." Thus the most urgent reform was "to make the sociological idea descend into the special techniques and in that way transform them into real social sciences." Only in this way could sociology become more than an "abstract metaphysics," and the works of specialists more than "monographs without either links to one another or explanatory value." [24]

Methodologically, traditional historiography approached the study of society through a narrative of events and the lives of individual men. Without a theoretical complement, narrative was not explanatory, because it did not address itself to the problem of comparison. "History makes all comparisons impossible, because it arranges facts in linear series and on different levels. Preoccupied with distinguishing phenomena from one another and marking the place of each in time, the historian loses sight of similarities." [25] The recounting of a series of disparate facts did not constitute a logical ordering principle. For chronology was, as a rule, merely a more familiar form of chaos.

The comparative method was for Durkheim the laboratory of a more analytic and explanatory approach to the study of society, for it represented the social scientist's analogue of experimentation: "Claude Bernard remarked long ago that the essence of experimentation is not the operator's ability to produce phenomena artificially. Artifice is only one means whose goal is to place the fact under study in different circumstances and to see it in different forms so that relevant comparisons may be made." [26] But Durkheim was especially wary of the formalistic temptations of an analytic and model-building sociology. In a direct criticism of Spencer and Comte, he remarked that the sociologist's "excessively general interpretations are impotent in contact with the facts" and that this impotence had "in part produced the distrust that history has often felt for sociology." [27] He also explicitly rejected Georg Simmel's conception of sociology as the elaboration of ideal-typical constructs (e.g., forms of community, differentiation, domination, stratification, and conflict). Durkheim recognized that a science had to be formed on the basis of abstract ideas. But he insisted: "It is necessary that abstractions be methodically elaborated and that they divide facts according to their natural articulations. Otherwise abstractions degenerate into imaginary constructs and a vain mythology." [28]

Methodologically, these ideas led to a focus upon institutions and to a desire for a close working relationship with history. "Institutions have to exterior incidents the same relationship as the mode and functioning of organs in the individual have to the various actions which fill our daily lives. Only through an institutional focus can history cease to be a narrative study and open itself to scientific analysis." Events like "wars, peace treaties, intrigues of courts or assemblies, or the acts of statesmen" seemed to follow no definite laws. In any event, "if these laws exist, they are the most difficult to discover." On the other hand,

[26] "Introduction à la sociologie de la famille," *Annales de la Faculté de Lettres de Bordeaux*, 1888, p. 262.

[27] *Règles de la méthode sociologique*, p. 110.

[28] "La Sociologie et son domaine scientifique" (first pub. 1900); in Armand Cuvillier, *Où va la sociologie francaise?* (Paris: Librairie Marcel Rivière, 1953), pp. 181–182. See also Emile Durkheim and P. Fauconnet, "Sociologie et sciences sociales," *Revue philosophique*, LV (1903), 481.

"institutions—while of course evolving—conserve their essential traits during long periods of time and sometimes during an entire collective existence, because they express what is most profoundly constitutive of any social organization." Institutions also presented "striking similarities" in different societies. "Thus typologies become possible and comparative history is born." [29]

Hence sociology was in essence a comparative study of the genesis, structure, and functioning of institutions. To the list in this definition, the later Durkheim would undoubtedly have added the problem of the relation of institutions to beliefs, values, and ideologies. Referring to his own professor of history, for whom this problem was a central issue, Durkheim observed in the preface to the first volume of the *Année sociologique:*

History can be a science only to the extent that it explains, and explanation cannot proceed except through comparison. Otherwise, even simple description is hardly possible; one cannot adequately describe a unique fact, or a fact of which one has only rare instances, *because one does not see it adequately.* . . . Fustel de Coulanges was fond of repeating that true sociology is history: nothing is more incontestable, provided that history is carried on sociologically.[30]

Sociology, as Durkheim once put it, was like the grammar of history.[31] Changing the metaphor, he observed that history played, "in the realm of social realities, a role analogous to that of the microscope in the study of nature." [32] In an important review of works by Gaetano Salvemini and Benedetto Croce, Durkheim argued that history as a "nomothetic" (law-seeking) science and history as an "ideographic" (particularizing) art were "destined to become inseparable." There was no opposition

---

[29] "Sociologie et sciences sociales," pp. 486–487.

[30] 1896–1897; in Kurt Wolff, ed., *Essays on Sociology and Philosophy* (first pub. 1960; New York: Harper & Row, 1964), pp. 342–343.

[31] "Sociologie et sciences sociales" (not the same article as the one written with P. Fauconnet), in *De la methode dans les sciences* (Paris: Alcan, 1909), pp. 281–282.

[32] *Ibid.*, p. 280.

between them, but "only differences of degree." Scientific history, or sociology, could not do without the "direct observation of concrete facts." And history had to become informed by the general principles of sociology. All history required selection among facts, and this, in turn, implied the use of criteria that made comparison possible. "In reality," Durkheim concluded, "there are not two distinct disciplines but two different points of view which, far from excluding one another, presuppose one another." [33]

We have already had reason to note that Durkheim's actual practice at times diverged from the above indicated theoretical position. Perhaps the one work in which his analysis came closest to the history of the historians was his little known and untranslated *Evolution pédagogique en France*.[34] This work was restricted to the development of education in France. But it clearly was based on broad "comparative" knowledge of different social systems. Its focus was the development of ideologies of education in the context of the evolution of institutions. The result was a remarkable social history of ideas which revealed a sense of illuminating detail and a sensitivity to the complexity of social life often absent in Durkheim's more famous works. Indeed, the highest accolade one can bestow upon this study is a criterion of all good history: its argument belies summary.

How were Durkheim's methodological views related to evaluation and reform? Durkheim apparently did not believe that the historical process as a whole had a meaningful plot or structure. He did not, for example, subscribe to Hegel's theodicy of history. History did not have a meaning. But men in society created meaning, which existed in a tense dialectic with anomic forces.

[33] *Année sociologique*, IV (1899–1900), 124–125. For an excellent analysis of Durkheim's conception of the relation of history and sociology, see Robert N. Bellah, "Durkheim and History," in Robert A. Nisbet, ed., *Emile Durkheim* (Englewood Cliffs, N.J.: Prentice-Hall, 1965), pp. 153–176.

[34] *L'Evolution pédagogique en France*, Introd. by Maurice Halbwachs (2 vols.; Paris: Alcan, 1938).

At least by implication, Durkheim seemed to envisage the historical process as one of oscillation between varying states of order and chaos—the "organic" and "critical" periods of Saint-Simon.

Yet Durkheim's idea of the relation of conscious human action to this process was never clearly stated. His evolutionary optimism seemed to imply that there was an impersonal or unconscious process that effected, over time, a development of society in the direction of integration and viable order. Most often, his tendency in historical analysis was to de-emphasize the role of intentional action in attempts to shape meaningful forms of existence. At times he did attribute some weight to individual deviance or exceptional performance as a force for social change. For example, he presented great philosophers, like Socrates, as individuals who crystallized with heightened perceptiveness the tendencies of an age and acted as heralds of the future. But he certainly rejected a "great man" interpretation of history. And generally he insisted in extreme fashion on the role of impersonal processes in a history devoid of proper names.

One problem was that Durkheim proved unable to integrate fully, or at least to relate intelligibly, a methodology geared to causal analysis and one sensitive to meanings. The question of meaning would have required closer attention to the role of concrete agents in history, both as individuals and in groups. In his later emphasis on internalized values and "collective representations," Durkheim recognized the importance of the perception and ideological interpretation of social and cultural phenomena. But he never worked out an adequate notion of the dialectical relation of these factors to impersonal processes and long-term structural causation. His only attempt to account for the genesis of "collective representations" was the vague idea that they somehow emerged from the "collective substratum" before attaining a relative autonomy in entering into combinations with one another.[35] This idea amounted at best to a re-

[35] See Emile Durkheim, *Sociologie et philosophie* (Paris: Presses Universitaires de France, 1963), pp. 42–43.

formulation of the notion that social existence preceded social consciousness—a reformulation which was vaguer than the Marxist variant, since it did not contain even a rudimentary theory of the formation of ideologies. Durkheim would have gained much from closer attention to the contemporary German controversy over methods (*Methodenstreit*), from which Max Weber benefited so greatly.

Durkheim's dominant position was well expressed in an exchange with the historian Charles Seignobos. Seignobos himself took an extreme Rankean position on the importance of individual will in history and of eyewitness reports in historiography. Durkheim asserted:

> The question is to know if in history one can really admit only conscious causes, those which men themselves attribute to the events and actions of which they are agents. . . . It is not a question of events but of inner motives which could have determined these events. How may one know these motives? There are only two possible procedures. Either one tries to discover them objectively by an experimental method: neither the agents nor the witnesses of the events were able to do this. Or one tries to arrive at them by an inner method of introspection. . . . Now everyone knows how much consciousness is full of illusions. For a long time, there has not been a psychologist who believes introspection can reach to profound causes. Every causal relation is unconscious, and it must be found after the event; by introspection one arrives only at facts but never at causes.[36]

One problem generated by this doctrinaire attitude was that it seemed to leave Durkheim's calls to action in the present suspended in mid-air, for it offered no basis for existential commitment to a collective project. But in his conception of social action in modern society, Durkheim did seem to see a greater role for consciousness related to the birth of sociology itself. A constant theme of his thought was that a historically informed sociology would give men some measure of control over the historical

[36] *Bulletin de la Société Française de Philosophie*, session of May 28, 1908 (Paris: Colin, 1908), p. 230.

process. How did a sociological consciousness offer this possibility?

Combined with the "crucial experiment," comparative history was a means of arriving at a notion of the tree of social life. Ethnography, when subjected to theoretical elaboration, was especially important for the development of an idea of the universal bases of culture and society. Comparative history illustrated and tested the results of this theoretical elaboration. More specifically, it made possible the delineation of social types or "species" and furnished test cases of ways in which types of social structure functioned in normal or pathological ways. Relevant comparison also illuminated genetic processes of "becoming," thereby providing knowledge of trends in various social situations. In accordance with Comte's dictum "Savoir pour prévoir; prévoir pour pouvoir" ("Know in order to foresee; foresee in order to be able to control"), knowledge offered effective insight into the dangers and possibilities of alternative courses of social action.

Aside from incorporating biological analogies falling somewhere between Darwin and Lamarck, Durkheim's concepts of normality and pathology were more sophisticated versions of Saint-Simon's idea of organic and critical periods in history. Like Saint-Simon, Durkheim believed modern society to be, in significant ways, pathological. He discussed at length and with apparent agreement Saint-Simon's model of evolution in Western Europe in terms of a growing conflict between a religio-military and a scientific-industrial type of society. In France, this had culminated in the great Revolution, whose nature, causation, and consequences Durkheim saw in a basically Saint-Simonian way:

A two-fold need gave rise to it: the need to be extricated from the past and the need to organize the present. The Revolution met only the first of these needs. It succeeded in striking the final blows at the old system. It abolished all that remained of feudalism—even royal authority—and all that survived from the old temporal power. But on the land thus cleared, the Revolution built nothing new. It asserted that one was no longer obliged to accept the old beliefs but did not attempt to elaborate a new body of rational beliefs that all minds could accept.[37]

The Revolution had destroyed the old order, but it miscarried in the creation of the new. It gave birth to the highest ideals of modern society, but it did not specify and establish these ideals in institutions and rational beliefs. At the start of the nineteenth century, after the Revolution had run its course, the basic problem of a new social order was presented in the same terms as in 1789. Only the problem had become more urgent. A stabilized revolutionary settlement was, for Durkheim, necessary "if one does not wish to see each crisis produce another, exasperation the chronic state of society, and finally, disintegration more or less the result." This was the way in which Saint-Simon had posed the social question, and for Durkheim it could not "be posed with greater profundity." [38]

Durkheim's later thought frequently revealed the influence of Bergson's ideas of creative evolution and *élan vital*. By means of these conceptions, he was able to integrate some of the Prometheanism of Saint-Simon into his perspective. Thus he stressed more often the creative side of anomie and its relation to newer cultural possibilities. This tendency can be found in *The Elementary Forms*. It is also evident in the only completed section of his projected *magnum opus* "La Morale":

Life, all life, is rich with an infinite number of seeds of every variety, of which some are at present developed and correspond especially to the present exigencies of the milieu but of which many are dormant, temporarily unused, and undeveloped. These will perhaps be awakened tomorrow under new circumstances. All life is change and is refactory to static states. A living being is not made for a single end; it may lend itself to very different ends and to multiple situations. . . . So much the more is this true of human nature: history is not only the natural framework of human life; man is a product of history.[39]

[37] *Socialism*, pp. 158–160.   [38] *Ibid.*
[39] "Introduction à la morale," *Revue philosophique*, LXXXIX (1920), 89.

In his *Evolution pédagogique,* Durkheim insisted that it was impossible at any given moment to draw up a blueprint of human nature:

For the wealth of past production does not in the least authorize us to assign a limit to the production of the future or to think that a day will ever come when man, having reached the end of his creation, will be condemned to repeat himself perpetually. Thus one arrives at a conception of man, not as a system of definite elements which may be numbered, but as an infinitely flexible and versatile force capable of taking on the most diverse aspects under the pressure of ever renewed circumstances.[40]

Thus Durkheim arrived at a very flexible idea of the trunk of the tree of social life: it represented an unlimited set of cultural possibilities. Each type of society would realize a limited subset of these possibilities in normal or pathological form. Although cultural possibilities were unlimited in theory, any combination of them in a normal state of society would itself be limited and would instill in members of society a normative sense of limits leavened only by a creative margin of anomie. Especially significant in *L'Evolution pédagogique* was Durkheim's conception of the Middle Ages. For Saint-Simon, of course, the sociological interest of the medieval period was its achievement of one possible form of organic integration. Although Durkheim never fully adhered to an idealized view of the Middle Ages, he did present it as a period based on a tense and creative balance between faith and reason, spontaneity and institutionally grounded constraint. There was for Durkheim "something exciting and dramatic" in the spectacle offered by "this tormented epoch tossed between respect for tradition and the call of free enquiry." This period was far from being "plunged in a sort of quietude and intellectual torpor." It was in fact "internally divided and drawn in contradictory directions." Durkheim's reaction to this state of affairs may come as a surprise to those who have presented him as the

---

[40] *L'Evolution pédagogique en France,* II, 199.

rigid, if not authoritarian, champion of Cartesian constraint, formal rationality, and still-life order in society.

This is one of the moments when the human spirit was most full of effervescence and creative of new things. . . . Men had not yet tried to separate these two inseparable aspects of human life [i.e., faith and reason]. Men had not yet undertaken the canalization and the damming up of these two great intellectual and moral currents in a vain attempt to prevent them from meeting! How much more living was this general and tumultuous melee of all ideas and all sentiments than the artificial and apparent calm of the centuries which followed! . . . . We must indeed modify our national humor. We must again find the taste for free and varied life with all the accidents and irregularities it implies.[41]

Images of organic growth and relatively slow evolution applied only to development within a normal state of society or organic period. The creation of normality in modernity was a collective project. And even within the normal state, society was not a static object but a living whole which overcame generalized anomie through a tense, dynamic balance of the essential elements of social health. Durkheim opposed neither the study of history nor the vital element of creative change in social life. His polemical animus was reserved for pathology in the sense of generalized anomie and runaway change; and it implied a repudiation of the type of "historicism" which legitimated anomie or its concomitants in a transitional period of uncontrolled change. Thus Durkheim observed of his interest in social structure:

This branch of sociology is not a science of the purely *static*. For this reason, we deem it improper to adopt this term [of Comte], which expresses poorly the point of view from which society ought to be considered. It is not a question, as has sometimes been said [by John Stuart Mill, following Comte], of considering society at a given moment, immobilized by an abstraction, but on the contrary, of analyzing its formation and accounting for it. No doubt the phenomena that have to do with structure have something more stable about

41 *Ibid.*, pp. 95, 124, 158–159.

them than have functional phenomena. But between these two orders of fact there are only differences of degree. Structure itself is encountered in *becoming* [*le devenir*], and one can illuminate it only if one does not lose sight of the process of becoming. Structure is formed and disintegrated continually. It is life that has arrived at a certain degree of consolidation. To distinguish it from the life from which it derives or from the life which it determines would amount to dissociating inseparable things.[42]

In his *Moral Education*, Durkheim returned to his conception of the state of modern society with a renewed sense of urgency: "We are at present passing through a critical period. Indeed there is not in history a crisis as grave as that of European societies during the past century." [43] In *Socialism*, Durkheim remarked upon the significant relationship among the rise of sociology, socialism, and religious revival in modern society. Along with other later works, *The Elementary Forms* offered insight into the role of this relationship in Durkheim's own thought, and it revealed a sense in which revolutionary turmoil harbored a positive component and a guide to the creation of social health. For *The Elementary Forms* contained a striking parallel between social revolution and the origins of collective life, which for Durkheim were coincident with the genesis of religion. Revolution apparently involved, in his mind, a return to the primordial passage from nature to culture in the modified form of a transition from one type of society to another. The very values and ideals which served as guides to future action were generated in liminal, revolutionary epochs of "collective effervescence." "Collective effervescence" itself meant, for Durkheim, not a manifestation of crowd psychology in general, but a spontaneous, sacralizing *élan vital* open to *communitas* and the quasi-religious possibilities in social life. As he put it in an important article, the revolutionary apogee of the critical period was evangelical, in the etymological sense of the word:

[42] "La Sociologie et son domaine scientifique," pp. 189–190.

[43] *L'Education morale* (Paris: Presses Universitaires de France, 1963), p. 41.

Life is lived with such intensity and with such abandon that it fills consciousness and clears it almost completely of egoistic and vulgar preoccupations. The ideal tends to become one with reality; this is why men have the impression that the time is at hand when it will become reality and when the kingdom of God will be realized on earth.[44]

But life at this millennial pitch of quasi-religious intensity could not be continued as the basis of a stable, ongoing social system:

The illusion is never durable because this exaltation cannot last: it is too exhausting. Once the critical moment has passed, the social fabric loosens up, intellectual and sentimental commerce slows down, and individuals fall to their ordinary level. Then everything which was said, done, and felt during the period of fecund torment survives only in the form of a memory—a prestigious memory to be sure, like the reality it recalls, but with which it is no longer confounded.[45]

The truly successful revolution, according to Durkheim, was one which gave birth in time to a normal society. The normal society would embody a twofold rhythm of collective life in which ordinary, day-to-day activities that contaminated ideals with ultilitarian concerns and self-interest would alternate with special symbolic activities. In these communal and festive activities, the "prestigious memory" and extraordinary intensity of value-creating revolutionary times would be revived. These "ritual" activities would themselves reinvigorate norms and symbols by making them immediately present in the experience of members of society and by generating a living force which could be carried into the daily round. Through ritual, the values created during the "great times" of the past would become available as a mythical foundation for life in the present. Most important, perhaps, the *communitas*—the perfect communal identity among

---

[44] "Jugements de valeur et jugements de réalité," in *Sociologie et philosophie,* p. 133. The essay was first given orally before the International Congress of Philosophy at Bologna and published in 1911 in the *Revue de métaphysique et de morale.*

[45] *Sociologie et philosophie,* pp. 133–134.

equals—realized in liminal events like revolution would be instituted in ritual as a component of social solidarity. Members of
society would ritually realize *communitas,* the substratum of all
stable society. And this realization would flow into daily life as a
living faith which mitigated the dangers of both structural differentiation and self-interest. Thus, paradoxically but understand-
ably, the most historically turbulent of events—revolution—
would be most successful, in Durkheim's opinion, when it gave
rise to the most stabilizing features of social life: ritual and myth.

This conception of the revitalizing and reinforcing function of
communal ceremonies and feasts indicates the sense in which
Durkheim believed that all healthy societies required rituals related to the "ritual attitude" of sacred respect for basic commitments and values. Needless to say, these special, ritual activities
would be compatible with reason only if the values and norms
they legitimated were neither fanatically irrational nor systematically contradicted by ordinary experience. His idea of the former
condition of ritual in a normal state of society is implied in Durkheim's analysis rather than fully elucidated. But it is at least
consistent with his over-all argument to observe that rituals which
exacerbate irrational policies and fantastic visions without moderating them simply reflect the unhinged and unbalanced nature of
social life in general. But, as long as they were limited, the outbursts of anomic excess or chaotic unity in ritual (incest, sacrile-
gious buffoonery, role inversion, and other forms of radical *communitas*) functioned cathartically within the total economy of
cultural life to assure viable balance. In a more explicit way,
Durkheim saw that, in the normal state of society, ordinary realities and operative institutions would not hypocritically or self-
deceptively contradict cultural values but represent only "standard
deviations" from them. In a pathological context where values
and normative expectations were systematically upset in practice, the ritual settings that did exist might function as purely
escapist illusions or be seen through as vulgar shams.

The task of structural change in modern societies marked by

significant pathology was to revive the ideals of classical revolutions of the past and to realize them viably through a sort of cultural revolution of good faith. The criterion of success in this
endeavor would be the genesis of a normal or healthy rhythm of
social life. Values and norms constitutive of the *conscience collective* would guide ordinary practice with an allowance for "standard deviations" due to normal human failings. The *conscience
collective* would be periodically recreated in pure form in "ritual" contexts of communal spontaneity and joy. Thus the normal
society would combine the "constraint" of obligatory institutional
norms with the "collective effervescence" of motivated commitment, communal spontaneity, and a dynamic leaven of anomic
openness. Normative constraint would not be incompatible with
charismatic expressiveness. Only in such a normal society could
quasi-religious symbolism function authentically as the sacred
canopy of legitimacy for the social order. Durkheim's correlation
of sociology, religious revival, and social change provided the
background for his reform proposals.

Corporatism

Durkheim's corporatism is frequently considered to be an example of personal predilection which was extraneous to the main
body of this thought. It was, on the contrary, an integral component of his perspective which applied his general idea of social
normality to the problem of structural change in modern society.
Essential to this vision of modern social normality was a triangu-
lar model of the state, the corporative group, and the individual,
existing in a dialectical balance.

Durkheim's conception of the situation and needs of modern
society was based upon an analysis of historical evolution in
Western Europe. Corporative groups such as the commune, the
guild, and the estate had become increasingly restrictive at the
same time that their importance declined with the growing power
of the central state. At first the conflict between the state and
corporative groups had a positive function. For it was the con-

crete historical basis of individual rights. "It is from the conflict of social forces that individual liberties are born." [46] But the extreme development of this process of rising state power and individual emancipation from increasingly oppressive secondary groups threatened to have negative consequences. It unintentionally culminated in a social situation in which the state, as the sole significant organized power, confronted the atomized individual. This confrontation "had long since been prepared by progressive centralization under the *ancien régime*." But "the great change which the French Revolution accomplished was to carry this leveling process to a point hitherto unknown." [47]

Without the countervailing protection of secondary groups, the individual liberties first won through the intervention of the state became both of dubious existential value for the individual and of uncertain duration in the face of state power. "Thus, by a series of endless oscillations, we pass alternatively from authoritarian regulation, which excessive rigidity makes impotent, to systematic abstention which cannot last because of the anarchy it provokes." [48] Simultaneously, the largely uncontrolled development of the economy gave rise to classes whose relations were not based upon consensually accepted norms but upon unequal market power.[49]

The problem of modern society, according to Durkheim, was to create consensual institutions which viably realized the democratic values brought to the forefront of consciousness during the classical revolutions of the past. Before proposing a normative triangle of state regulation, individual rights, and decentralized corporatism, Durkheim reviewed other conceivable options.

He explicitly rejected authoritarian state collectivism and rigidly centralized bureaucratic control. The state was "too distant from the complex manifestations" of economic and occupational

[46] *Leçons de sociologie* (Paris: Presses Universitaires de France, 1950), p. 78 (trans. under the title *Professional Ethics and Civic Morals*).

[47] *Le Suicide* (Paris: Presses Universitaires de France, 1960), p. 447. One may note the similarity of Durkheim's ideas to those of Tocqueville in his *Ancien régime*.

[48] *Le Suicide*, p. 437.   [49] *Socialism*, p. 437.

life. It was "a heavy machine . . . cut out only for general and simple tasks." Its invariably uniform actions lacked "the flexibility needed to adjust to an infinite diversity of particular circumstances." It was "always oppressive and leveling." [50] In brief, the state, through its centralized bureaucracy, maximized authoritarian structure; and through ideologies like militant nationalism, it provided *communitas* only in aggressively irrational ways.

The study of the family and kinship had an importance to Durkheim which is not adequately reflected in the relatively small amount of published material he devoted to the subject. In general, he saw a process of "concentration" of the family in the course of European history: over time the basic kinship unit had come to include fewer persons performing fewer functions. Although the modern nuclear family continued to have an important social role for Durkheim, he did not believe it to be a focal point for overcoming modern anomie. One problem area on which he, like the disciples of Saint-Simon, placed special emphasis was that of inheritance.

The institution of inheritance implies that there are rich and poor from birth. i.e., there are in society two great classes, linked, however, by all sorts of intermediaries; one is obliged, in order to live, to have the other accept its services at any price whatsoever; the other is able to do without these services, thanks to the resources it possesses, even though these resources do not correspond to services rendered by those who enjoy them. As long as an opposition as clear-cut as this exists in society, more or less successful palliatives will mitigate the injustice of contracts; but, in principle, the system will function under conditions which do not permit it to be just.[51]

[50] *Le Suicide*, p. 436.

[51] *Leçons de sociologie*, pp. 250–251. Durkheim saw in inheritance a general characteristic that could be used for the objective classification of types of kinship. "If one tries to distinguish and classify different types of the family according to the literary descriptions of travelers and, at times, historians, one is in danger of confounding the most different types. If, on the contrary, one takes as the basis of classification the juridical constitution of the family and especially the right of inheritance, one has an objective criterion which, without being infallible, nonetheless obviates many errors" (*Règles de la méthode sociologique*, p. 45).

Familial inheritance was a vestige from the past which inhibited equality of opportunity in education and in the choice of an occupation that was in keeping with one's talents. "It is evident that the education of our children ought not to depend upon chance, which determines their birth in one place rather than another, and to certain parents rather than others." [52] Indeed, Durkheim asserted that "a day will come when a man is no longer permitted to leave, even by testament, his fortune to his descendants, just as he is no longer permitted to leave them his functions and titles." [53] As a practical proposal, however, Durkheim seemed to advance a compromise formula which restricted familial inheritance to a percentage of the family wealth roughly proportional to the importance of the family as an institution in modern society. This idea both accorded with existing familial sentiment and allowed for a store of wealth which could be used for social purposes. But given the dangers of excessive state power and rigid bureaucratic control, this solution created the problem of establishing a repository for the transmission of wealth in society. And greater equality of opportunity in the access to education and the choice of occupations did not solve the problem of the nature of social structures or affect the primary source of generalized anomie in modern society: the economy.

According to Durkheim, education itself was powerless to act as a major lever for basic social change. It could play a role only within a broader movement for rational reform. Education was "only the image and reflection of society." It was "healthy when peoples enjoy[ed] a state of health." But it became "corrupted with them, without being able to modify itself through its own initiative." Education could reform itself only if society was reformed. To reform society, one had to attack "the causes of the evil" from which society suffered.[54] Here Durkheim did not do

[52] *Education et sociologie* (Paris: Alcan, 1922), p. 51.
[53] "La Famille conjugale," *Revue philosophique*, XCI (1921), 10.
[54] *Le Suicide*, pp. 427–428.

justice to the central position of educational institutions as media of selection and training in highly developed societies. But his conception of priorities in structural reform was cogent.

The state of the economy was the basic cause of modern social pathology. On this point, Durkheim seemed to agree with Marx. But Durkheim's largely moral conception of the problem was not grounded in anything comparable to Marx's attempt to provide a detailed institutional analysis of the source of "contradictions" in the economy.

The most blamable acts are so often absolved by success that the limit between what is permitted and what is prohibited, what is just and what is not, no longer has anything fixed about it; it seems susceptible to almost arbitrary change by individuals. Such an imprecise and inconstant morality is no longer able to constitute a discipline. The result is that this entire sphere of collective life is in large part deprived of the moderating action of regulation. It is this anomic state that is the cause of the incessantly recurrent conflicts and the various disorders of which the economic world offers so sad a spectacle. Since nothing restrains the active forces and assigns them bounds which they are obliged to respect, they tend to develop without limit and come into collision with one another, battling and weakening themselves. To be sure, the strongest succeed in completely crushing the weakest, or in subordinating them. But if the conquered must for a time resign themselves to subordination under constraint, they do not consent to it. Consequently, this cannot constitute a stable equilibrium. Truces imposed by violence are never anything but provisional, and they satisfy no one. Human passions halt only before a moral power that they respect. If all authority of this kind is lacking, the law of the strongest prevails. And, latent or active, the state of war is necessarily chronic. That such a state of anarchy is a morbid phenomenon is self-evident, since it contradicts the very end of all society, which is to suppress, or at the very least to moderate, war among men by subordinating the physical law of the strongest to a higher law.[55]

55 Preface to 2d ed., *De La Division du travail social* (7th ed.; Paris: Presses Universitaires de France, 1960), pp. ii–iii.

Durkheim saw the development of labor unions and management groups as an initial but inadequate step in the right direction. Procedures like collective bargaining did not overcome excessively anomic relations; the result was an extremely precarious stability which was quite compatible with egoism and power conflicts.

Syndicates of employers and labor unions are distinct from one another, *which is legitimate and necessary*, but there is no regular contact between them. There exists no common organization which brings them together without denying their individuality and in which they may elaborate in common a regulation that, by fixing their mutual relations, is imposed upon both with a common authority. Consequently, it is always the law of the strongest which settles conflicts, and the state of war prevails completely. Except for actions which fall under common morality, employers and workmen are, in their mutual relations, in the same situation as two autonomous states, but of unequal power. Like peoples through the medium of their governments, they can make contracts. But these contracts indicate only the respective state of military forces confronting one another. They are like treaties which indicate the respective state of military forces between two belligerents. The consecrate a *de facto* state; they cannot create a just state [*un état de droit*].[56]

The professional or corporative group was the crux of Durkheim's idea of a possible means of creating a tense balance among the elements of social justice and health in modern society. In a sense, Durkheim's corporative idea applied the principle of Occam's razor—to make only as many assumptions as necessary—to the intricate problem of social "normality" in the context of the advanced degree of the division of labor and the generalized exchange of goods and services. Through functional decentralization, the corporative group could simultaneously provide a counterweight to the central state and a social context in which *communitas* and a more cumulative articulation of social

[56] *Ibid.*, pp. vii–viii.

and cultural experience might develop. Acting in accordance with the fundamental economic and occupational functions of modern society, the corporative group would also have a role in the inheritance of wealth, education, economic regulation, welfare services, political representation, and artistic creation. Most important, it would be a center of genuine communal commitment —a real existential group—with the moral power to restrain anomie and transcend egoism. In the corporative group, people would come to know one another and enjoy what might be called a supplementary kinship.

Durkheim derived his idea of the need for corporative groups partly from a historical survey which his proposed comparative history of this form of social organization was to have detailed. On the basis of the lessons he drew from his investigation of comparative history, he felt justified in asserting that corporatism corresponded to a permanent functional need in societies which had passed beyond the stage of an agricultural economy. Comparison itself, however, did not solve specifically modern problems; it merely helped one to separate similarities and differences, revealed normal and pathological functioning in different social types, and enabled one better to situate specifically modern conditions, dangers, and possibilities.

In Greece, at least until the Roman conquest, corporations were unknown, because economic occupations were socially despised and consigned to foreigners. In Rome, on the contrary, they dated from the earliest times of the Republic. Significantly, the Roman corporative group during the period of the Republic was a religious confraternity. Under the Empire, however, corporative groups both reached their fullest development and, in part because of civil wars and invasions, fell under the domination of the state. "This was the ruin of the institution." [57] The central point here, for Durkheim, was that an adequate comparison had to consider societies at comparable stages of development. One

[57] *Ibid.*, p. x.

could not, for example, generalize about the viability of an institution on the basis of its decadence or abuse. After the fall of Rome, "if an economist had taken stock of the situation, he would reasonably have concluded, as economists later did, that corporative groups had not, or at least no longer had, any *raison d'être*, that they had disappeared once and for all, and he undoubtedly would have treated any attempt to reconstitute them as retrogressive and unrealizable." [58]

The rebirth of corporative groups in the Middle Ages showed that the hypothetical economist living in the "Dark Ages" would have been wrong. In fact, the importance of corporative groups in the medieval period was greater than in Rome. In Rome, the corporative group was not a public institution. But in the Middle Ages it became the very foundation of the commune. In a different form, it retained moral and religious functions and was a center of communal feasts and banquets. And, as in Rome, it provided a locus of intimacy less restricted than the family and more personal than the city. A point which would become increasingly relevant with the development of Durkheim's thought was that in both cases "all religious community constituted a moral milieu, just as all moral discipline tended in time to assume a religious form." [59] If the case of Rome revealed the danger of state domination, the *ancien régime* pointed to the danger of the possible domination of one socioeconomic group by another. In the medieval period, stratification within the corporative group was often not rigid or highly marked, since the apprentice could as a rule become a master in his turn. By the end of the *ancien régime,* corporations had become instruments through which masters exploited workers. This development led to the formation of trade unions outside the pale of the corporative organization.[60]

[58] *Ibid.*   [59] *Ibid.*, p. xvi.

[60] "It is far from a fact that the corporation had retained in the eighteenth century the beneficial effects it had in the Middle Ages. The line of demarcation between masters and workers was sharp. . . . Just as the bourgeois scorned the artisan, the latter scorned the worker who had no apprentice" (*Socialism*, p. 103).

But there is no institution which does not at some time degenerate, either because it cannot change and becomes immobilized or because it develops in a unilateral direction. . . . This may be a reason to reform it but not to declare it permanently useless and destroy it. . . . If from the origin of the city until the zenith of the Empire, from the dawn of Christianity until modern times, they have been necessary, it is because they answer permanent and profound needs. The fact that after having disappeared the first time, they were reconstituted by themselves and in a new form rebuts any argument that their violent disappearance at the end of the last century is a proof that they are no longer in harmony with the new conditions of collective existence.[61]

One problem which the corporative group failed to meet in early modern times was that the commune proved to be too restricted a framework for the regulation of commerce, which was becoming national and international. A second and more difficult problem had to do with the structure of authority in the corporative group itself—a problem which subsequent history has exacerbated, along with the question of relations between the corporative group and the state. Although Durkheim was not as clear or as comprehensive as he might have been, his conception of the structure of authority in corporative groups was essentially democratic, and it included industrial democracy.

Specialized regulations can be made only by elected assemblies charged with representing the corporation. In the present state of industry, these assemblies, as well as the tribunals which apply professional regulations, obviously ought to include representatives of employers and employees . . . in proportions corresponding to the respective importance attributed by opinion to these two factors in production. But if it is necessary that both be present in the directing councils of the corporation, it is no less indispensable that they form at the base of the corporation distinct and independent groups, for their interests are too often rival and antagonistic. For them to be able to take positions freely, they must take positions separately. The

---

[61] *Division du travail social,* pp. xvi, xi.

two groups thus constituted could subsequently designate their representatives to the common assemblies.[62]

Durkheim argued that "the already so powerful and so clumsy hands of the state" were incompetent and dangerous instruments for the provision of social welfare and the detailed regulation of the economy. Thus, he concluded that the problem of the anomie and egoism fostered by the antipathy between centralized bureaucratic rigidity and atomized individualism could be resolved only by forming, "outside the state, but subject to its action, a cluster of collective forces whose regulative influence can be exercised with more variety." [63] But he readily acknowledged the tendency of secondary groups to develop in the direction of closed societies characterized by "the despotism of routine and professional egoism." [64] To check this tendency and to protect the rights of the individual, the democratic state was to retain limited but crucial functions. "Only the state can oppose to the particularism of each corporation a consciousness of general utility and the necessities of organic equilibrium." [65]

A defining feature of the democratic state, for Durkheim, was its achievement of conscious awareness of the needs of all social groups through the open communication assured by representative institutions.[66] His conception of the democratic state in the normal society was both legislative and moral. Using his peculiar philosophical vocabulary, he designated the state as the representative (but not the incarnation) of the *conscience collective.* Its specific function was to elaborate "collective representations" in the form of laws valid for society as a whole.

A striking defect of Durkheim's political sociology in such works as *Professional Ethics and Civic Morals* was the neglect of executive leadership and political parties. His neglect of executive leadership might be seen as a reflection of the do-nothing nature of the state in his own Third Republic. But he was not, in fact, advocating the reduction of government to the status of a

---

[62] *Ibid.*, p. xxix n.   [63] *Le Suicide*, p. 437.   [64] *Ibid.*, p. 439.
[65] *Ibid.*, p. 442.   [66] *Leçons de sociologie*, pp. 108ff.

debating society in a context marked by severe social problems. Nor was his neglect of political parties related to an attempt to discredit parliamentarism in the manner of more reactionary advocates of corporatism. Durkheim was a firm supporter of parliamentary government and did not advocate a "one party" state. But at times he did seem close to an idea of a "no party" state, or at least to a vision in which parties, like interest groups, would play a very subordinate role. Basically, Durkheim was presenting a normative conception of the role of the state in the normal society. Here all particular interests and agencies would be regulated by limiting norms. And the state would be a legal entity whose laws applied the norms and values of the *conscience collective*. Early in his life, Durkheim criticized Montesquieu for theoretically separating law and ethics.[67] In Durkheim's normal society, both law and ethics would find their unitary source in normative principles embodied in the *conscience collective*.

Indeed, according to Durkheim, self-government would most adequately fill social needs and the general conditions of normative pluralism be best realized if corporative groups themselves became the basic units of political representation. This idea was in keeping with his general view that in modern society territorial units lacked both cultural identity and the means to cope with problems stemming from advanced technology and industrialism. "The only decentralization which, without breaking up national unity, permits the multiplication of centers of common life is what might be called *professional decentralization*." [68] Regional and local groupings corresponding to problems which could be handled at these levels would continue to exist, but the brunt of

[67] *Montesquieu and Rousseau: Forerunners of Sociology*, trans. Ralph Manheim, Foreword by Henri Peyre (Ann Arbor: University of Michigan Press, 1960), pp. 22–23. Durkheim traced one line of French social thought leading from Montesquieu and Rousseau through Saint-Simon and Comte to himself and his school. It is interesting to contrast this tradition with the less optimistic strand leading from Montesquieu through Tocqueville and Comte to thinkers like Raymond Aron.

[68] *Le Suicide*, p. 449.

activity within a structurally transformed society would fall upon professional or corporative groups.

Thus corporative groups, internally characterized by a democratic structure of authority and related to one another by normatively controlled, amiable rivalry under the general auspices of the democratic state, were for Durkheim the sole means of overcoming anomie and assuring solidarity in modern society. In essence, the goal Durkheim indicated in his idea of the corporative group was that of raising society above the mundane level of the merely economic.

If we judge them [i.e., corporative groups] to be indispensable, it is not because of the economic services they could render but because of the moral influence they might have. What we see above all in the professional group is a moral power able to restrain individual egoism, maintain in the hearts of workers a livelier sentiment of their common solidarity, and prevent the law of the strongest from being applied so brutally in industrial and commercial relations.[69]

Durkheim admitted that it was difficult to see how occupations "could ever be elevated to the dignity of moral powers. Indeed, they are formed of individuals which nothing attaches to one another, who are even disposed to treat one another like rivals and enemies rather than like cooperators."[70] But he nonetheless remained optimistic. In his mind the professional group represented the "functional equivalent" through which there could be instituted what he saw as the essence of socialism. Corporatism would make socialism more than a bread-and-butter issue. It would respond to the socialist "aspiration for a rearrangement of the social structure, by relocating the industrial set-up in the totality of the social organism, drawing it out of the shadow where it was functioning automatically, summoning it into the light and the control of the conscience." Through corporatism the social question would become, "not a question of money or force," but "a question of moral agents."[71]

[69] *Division du travail social*, pp. xi–xii.   [70] *Le Suicide*, p. 438.
[71] *Socialism*, pp. 61, 62, 247.

The conception of Durkheim as a militant nationalist and "fiery jingo" came from his wartime pamphlets and a misconception of the nature of his more serious thought.[72] Whether or not his propagandistic pamphlets actually justified these characterizations is debatable. In his conception of the state and the nation in his more serious works, Durkheim showed himself to be a liberal patriot who applied to the relations among states the same principles of social solidarity that he applied to group relations in the "normal" domestic context. He was attracted to the ideal of world government. But he found it so far distant from the realm of feasibility that he proposed instead a slightly less utopian goal of reconciling humanism with the state system. His idealistic expression of patriotism was close to the ideas of a Mazzini.

If each state adopted as its essential task not to grow or to extend its frontiers but to deal with its own autonomy as best it could, to call to an ever greater moral life the vast majority of its own members, then all contradictions between national and human morality would disappear. If the state had no further goal than to make its citizens men in the full sense of the word, then civic duties would be only a particular form of the general duties of humanity. . . . This patriotism does not exclude all national pride. Collective personalities, like individual personalities, cannot exist without having a certain sentiment about themselves and what they are. And this sentiment always has something personal about it. As long as states exist, there will be social self-esteem, and nothing is more legitimate. But societies can see their self-esteem, not in being greater or wealthier, but in being more just, better organized, and in having a better moral constitution. Needless to say, we have not yet reached the time when this patriotism reigns supreme, if ever such a time can come.[73]

What may one conclude about Durkheim's proposed reforms? In one sense, his corporatist proposals required basic, structural

[72] George Simpson, Introd. to Emile Durkheim, *The Division of Labor in Society*, trans. George Simpson (New York: Macmillan, 1933), p. xxvii. See also the interpretation of George Catlin, Introd. to Emile Durkheim, *The Rules of Sociological Method*, trans. Sarah A. Solovay and John H. Mueller (Chicago: University of Chicago Press, 1938).

[73] *Leçons de sociologie*, pp. 90–91.

reform. They enjoined social control of the economy related, however vaguely, to democratic values. In addition, they implied a qualitatively different form of relationship among men in modern society. But Durkheim's formulations remained entirely theoretical. They were indeed vague and, for this very reason, open to conflicting interpretations. His conception of politics was often excessively high-minded and impractical. His hatred of the "political kitchen" inhibited a full understanding of political interests and an attempt to relate them cogently to his own ideas. Nor can his reforms be judged adequate to the severe problems which he at least partially perceived. And Durkheim offered no insight into the question of means of realizing his proposed reforms. This was an especially disabling omission in a case where the means employed would help to shape the envisaged end. Durkheim's attempt to relate theory and practice broke down at the most vital point. His vision tended to shade off into a pious hope about an indeterminate future which bore little relation to social realities or their apparent developmental tendencies. At a crucial juncture of the argument, optimism took the place of hard thinking. Nor did Durkheim in later life return to the issues raised by his reform proposals. Rather, he increasingly devoted himself to the investigation of religion and to the development of his own highly idealistic social philosophy.

The Individual and Society

What was Durkheim's conception of the role of the individual in society? Which type of individualism did he attack and which type did he defend? And how were these questions related to Durkheim's key distinction between social normality and pathology?

The specific type of individualism which Durkheim attacked was excessive individuation, or atomistic individualism. *Suicide* analyzed the pathogenic effects of *de facto* and institutionalized egoism and traced its relation to anomie. Durkheim saw utilitarianism as the ideological legitimation of extreme individualism.

One function of comparative studies and "crucial experiments," he thought, was to provide the perspective which permitted him to argue that utilitarianism (and other variants of atomistic individualism) attempted to transform a transitional aberration into a universal moral and cultural truth. For Durkheim, utilitarianism was "contradicted by everything which history and comparative ethnography teach us about the moral life of humanity." [74]

Essential to Durkheim's own position was a basic model of man. Durkheim conceived of man in the "state of nature" as an isolated individual outside all society. This conception reduced man to his organic and psychophysical givens. The psychological capacity of the individual in the "state of nature" was limited to sensation. But his needs were limited as well by organic functioning and instinct.

The role of society and symbolism in human life depended, in the most general sense, on whether social structure assumed normal or pathological form. At this point, Durkheim's sociology and his value theory were united. Central to both was the institutionalized norm or value enshrined in the *conscience collective.* The *conscience collective* became Durkheim's analogue for Kant's practical reason and Rousseau's *volonté générale.*

Social structure and *conscience collective* were aspects of the same reality. In the normal state of society, institutionalized norms and values would be both objectively structured and subjectively internalized. In their objective aspect, institutions were characterized by exteriority and constraint. In the normal state of society, however, constraint was identical with obligation and duty. It was related to the sense of legitimate limits and *mesure* which for Durkheim was essential for all morality and solidarity in society. This role of institutional norms was well expressed in a statement Durkheim quoted from Rousseau's *Emile:* "If the laws of societies, like those of nature, became so inflexible that no human force could ever bend them, dependence upon men

---

[74] *Année sociologique,* X (1905–1906), 354.

would become dependence upon things." [75] In his *Moral Education*, Durkheim expressed in his own way the meaning of the "thinglike" quality of inhibitions imposed by institutions in the normal state of society: "When a man with a healthy moral constitution tries to commit an act which morality blames, he feels something which stops him just as if he tried to pick up a rock which is too heavy for him." [76] Thus the moral inhibitions created by institutional norms would be as weighty as rocks in the personality.

Exteriority and constraint as criteria of institutional norms were stressed by Durkheim in his early thought. He came to see in time that in the normal state of society these aspects of institutions would be combined with their desirability. In the preface to the second edition of *The Rules of Sociological Method,* he observed: "Institutions may impose themselves upon us, but we are attached to them; they put us under obligations, and we love them; they constrain us, and we find our welfare in their functioning and their very constraint. Moralists have often pointed out this antithesis between the two concepts of 'the good' and 'duty' which present the two different and equally real aspects of moral life." [77]

The desirability of institutions was dependent on their provision of viable ways and means of realizing values. Ideals formed the soul of legitimate institutions. And such works as *Moral Education* made explicit the relationship between the desirability of institutions and the existence of communal groups. Through communal life, institutionalized activity approached the ideal and took on overtones of spontaneity and charismatic élan. In a sense, the desirability of institutions was to community as obligatory constraint was to differentiation and a sense of legitimate limits.

In the normal state of society, there was no fatal antagonism between society and the individual. With reference to the rela-

[75] Quoted in *Montesquieu and Rousseau,* p. 88.
[76] *Education morale,* p. 36.
[77] *Règles de la méthode sociologique,* pp. xx–xxi, n. 2.

tion between institutional norm and organic need, Durkheim argued that discipline was "the means by which nature normally realizes itself and not the means of reducing or destroying it." [78] This idea mitigated the antipathy between mind and body (*homo duplex*). More generally, Durkheim argued that there was no "total antagonism which makes total or partial abdication of his own nature the price of an individual's attachment to society." On the contrary, "the individual is truly himself and able to realize his own nature only if he attaches himself to society." The individual's need for normative limits and communal attachments was shown in Durkheim's study of suicide. Man was more prone to kill himself when he was "detached from all collectivities" and lived "more like an egoist." [79]

The nature of institutions in the normal state of society was to combine a constraining sense of normative limits with an internalized sense of commitment. Their function was to create moral solidarity, which was as vital to the life of the individual as it was to the ordering of society. This notion of institutions in the normal state of society was implicit in Durkheim's assertion, which has often been quoted out of context:

Never has the qualification of moral been applied to an act which has for its object only the interest of the individual or the perfection of the individual understood in a purely egoistic manner. If the individual who I am does not constitute an end which has *in itself* a moral character, this is necessarily true also of individuals who are my equals and who differ from me only in degree. From this one may conclude that, *if there is a morality*, it can have as its objective only the group formed by a plurality of individuals, i.e., society, under the condition that society may be considered as a personality qualitatively distinct from the individuals who compose it.[80]

Durkheim's mode of expression was not devoid of ambiguity, and the ambiguity was related to social metaphysic. But the relation of this argument to his theory of value can be clearly formu-

[78] *Education morale*, p. 44.   [79] *Ibid.*, p. 58.
[80] *Sociologie et philosophie*, p. 52.

lated: Self-seeking or slavish subservience to the particularistic interest of another individual constituted aspects of social pathology. Authentic moral regulation depended upon the existence of a *conscience collective* which was logically distinct from a sum of atomistic individuals in that it was formed by a rational structure of institutional norms and values.

In the pathological state of society, the nature and function of institutions changed, for they might be part of the problem instead of part of the solution. In the pathological state, the social status quo distorted the instinctual balance of the "state of nature" and added newer dislocations of its own. Anomie converted culture into a lever for an infinite well of organic or more sublimated responses which knew no limits. Man was prey to unlimited desire or to the hunger for power over others. Will, the spiritualized passion, was like desire in that it became unhinged when it was detached from rational commitment to limiting norms. The concept of anomie confined to a specific sociological context the "state of nature" in Hobbes's sense: man was a wolf to his neighbor because of the distrust and dislocation engendered by the absence of substantively limiting norms. Anomie also revealed the way in which the Freudian id was not a purely organic force but instead a drive impelling an organism disoriented by a certain state of society and culture.

One prominent aspect of social pathology was (to use the apt phrase of T. S. Eliot) a "dissociation of sensibility"—a dissociation which Durkheim's own narrowly analytic tendencies at times reflected. The crucial case of dissociation which Durkheim transcended in his conception of social normality was that between constraint and what was desirable in social life and in the personality. This dissociation might, for example, be seen in the anomic contradiction between institutions and the cultural values or ideals which institutions were supposed to embody. To the extent that institutions were houses of constraint alone, they were alienating and oppressive. At most, they were objects of ambivalent internalization which led to compulsive performance by "hollow men" internally divided against themselves. Institutions which constrained without eliciting genuine commitment were soulless; they helped to instigate anomic idealism, romantic excess, and often misguided quests for *communitas* in alienated segments of society.

The contrast between constraint and desirability was in certain ways similar to Weber's opposition between bureaucratization and charisma. Extreme bureaucracy was a social form based upon constraining structures dissociated from *communitas*. And the maximization of structure typically fostered movements which tried to maximize *communitas*. Charismatic break-through involved not only the heroic virtuosity of the individual leader—a trait which Weber tended to overemphasize—but also the charismatic *communitas* of his followers. Indeed, there was often a puzzling relationship between anomie, *communitas*, and individualism in radical movements. And the maximization of *communitas* typically gave way, in history, to the "Thermidorian reaction" of a maximization of structure and constraint. As we have already noted, the successful revolution—or the successful social movement in general—according to Durkheim, was one which broke this tragic cycle by integrating constraining structure and "desirable" *communitas* in the same ongoing social system.

Attempting to specify his own vision of the intimate bond between constraint and desirability in the normal state of society, Durkheim himself referred to Hobbes and Spencer. Hobbes, recognizing the anomic and destructive nature of dissociated spontaneity, had become the theorist of pure constraint. Rejecting a despotic order based on constraint alone, the utilitarians and classical economists had come forth as the theorists of spontaneity, often presenting "all collective discipline as a sort of more or less tyrannical militarism." They failed to see that "in reality, when discipline is normal, when it is everything it ought to be, it is entirely different. It is both the summing up and the condition of all common life, which means as much in the hearts of individuals as their own lives." [81] Theorists like Hobbes and Spencer opted for one horn of a dilemma. But the problem of

[81] *Leçons de sociologie*, p. 36.

legitimate social order could be resolved only by eliminating the dilemma itself.

These words "constraint" and "spontaneity" do not have in our terminology the meaning which Hobbes gives to the former and Spencer to the latter. . . . The principle we expound would create a sociology which sees in the spirit of discipline the essential condition of all common life, while at the same time founding it on reason and on truth.[82]

Durkheim's mature thought itself provided the theoretical tools to situate and transcend the controversy which earlier had divided Gabriel Tarde and himself. Earlier, Durkheim seemed to champion pure constraint and formal obligation. Working within the same over-all frame of reference, Tarde in equally one-sided fashion espoused the cause of inner spontaneity and the exceptional individual. Durkheim seemed to be the official advocate of the formal, public, external, "false" self, and Tarde the devil's advocate of the nonconformist, private, inner, daring self, which in modern French cultural history had usually been taken as the "real" self and the untouchable core of the personality. Both, in effect, had seized upon one dissociated element of society and the personality in one type of social pathology. This context did seem to posit a total antipathy between society and the individual in the form of an opposition between mass conformity and individual affirmation. But, in Durkheim's later conception of social normality, this dichotomy would be eliminated. Genuine commitment would replace mass conformity. And the antagonism between self and society would be reduced to marginal proportions and perhaps assume more creative meaning for all concerned.

It has already been observed that Durkheim's concepts of social normality and pathology did not go far beyond the point of tentative formulation. His notion of social pathology especially suffered from inadequate theoretical elaboration. A closer examination of Marx's thought—and of Marx's own use of Saint-Simon—

---

[82] *Règles de la méthode sociologique*, p. 123.

would have been most informative. For example, some distinction between prerevolutionary, revolutionary, and postrevolutionary periods seemed necessary. Durkheim himself seemed to believe that revolution might be inevitable when society found itself in a certain sort of structural bind. Revolution itself, he thought, was effective in its elimination of certain vestiges of an old order, valuable in the genesis of social ideals, and generally unsuccessful in the realization of ideals in a new institutional order. Revolution appeared to be on the borderline between social pathology and normality. Modern society—and especially his own France— seemed for Durkheim to represent a postrevolutionary context which suffered from an afterbirth of disorientation and runaway change. Its pathology was in some ways postrevolutionary. And this seemed to imply that in modern society violence would generally be self-defeating and that a different type of social action was mandatory. But precisely how these ideas related to his conception of normality and pathology and to other aspects of modern society—e.g., industrialization—remained unclear.

Let us return to Durkheim's idea of the relation of the individual to society. At times Durkheim was led by both mechanistic dualism and an emergent social mystique to present a dissociated notion of the "whole man" as a mere composite of the organic and the social self. This tendency was apparent in such important articles as "Représentations individuelles et représentations collectives" ("Individual Representations and Collective Representations," 1898) and "Le Dualisme de la nature humaine et ses conditions sociales" ("The Dualism of Human Nature and Its Social Conditions," 1914). At other times, the more dialectical or relational aspect of his thought—while maintaining a primary emphasis upon collective norms and shared symbols—led to a more complex conception of the individual that resisted reducing him to a mechanical combination of a bodily organism and a social self. This allowed Durkheim to provide further insight into the question of the individual in various types and states of society.

At all times, the individual had a *de facto* cultural status which

derived ultimately from ontological and epistemological sources.
"From the time there is consciousness, there is a subject who con‧
ceives himself as distinct from all that is not himself—a subject
who says 'I.'" [83] The pathological state of society carried the inevitable degree of existential tension between the individual and
society to unnecessary historical proportions. In contrast, the
normal state of society maintained the degree of existential tension which corresponded to the margin of anomic indeterminacy
in the social structure. But it complemented this with founding
social structures on consent. As early as *The Division of Labor*,
Durkheim had asserted that "social life is spontaneous wherever
it is normal, and if it is abnormal it cannot last." [84] Consent, however, was not identical with a sum of *ad hoc* acts of individual
will. Its primary object was a *conscience collective* combining
limiting norms and communal values essential for moral solidarity
in society.

A specific characteristic of modern society was that the *conscience collective* itself in certain ways institutionalized individualism. This became pathogenic when it reached the extreme of
atomistic individualism. But there was a valid core in modern
liberalism. It was embodied in the idea of personal dignity and
individual rights. "Human personality is a sacred thing; we do
not dare violate it and hold ourselves at a distance from the
sanctuary of the person; at the same time, the good par excellence
is communion with another." [85] The basic goal of Durkheim's
corporatism was to establish a normative triangle of community,
individual rights, and state regulation under the general guidance
of universal, humanistic values.

Durkheim even furnished a rudimentary theory of the genesis
of various types of relationship between the individual and
society. In *The Division of Labor*, he made reference to the "in-
determination of the *conscience collective*" in modern society. In
archaic societies, norms often had a ritual articulation which

---

[83] *Education morale*, p. 83.   [84] *Division du travail social*, p. 180.
[85] *Sociologie et philosophie*, p. 51.

directly structured concrete events. "The very simplicity of moral practices make them take the habitual form of automatism and, in these circumstances, automatism suffices. Since social life is always the same and differs little over space and time, unself-conscious habit and tradition cover almost everything." Tradition had a prestige and authority which left little room for reasoning and inquiry. As societies became more complex, it was "more difficult for morality to function through a purely automatic mechanism." In highly complex modern societies, circumstances were never identical, and norms had a conceptual structure which required the exercise of judgment in their application to concrete cases and events. Moreover, society was in "perpetual evolution." This implied that morality had to be "supple enough to be transformed when it became necessary." The distance between conceptual norm and concrete event created an interval of in-determinacy in moral life which necessitated reflection, personal responsibility, initiative, and choice in individuals. When anomic indeterminacy was extreme, the "desire to get ahead" might expose the individual to "excitation beyond all measure until he knows practically no limits." [86]

When Durkheim spoke of the need for the "ritual attitude" of sacred respect in modern society, he seemed to believe that the object of this attitude would be norms and values autonomously accepted as legitimate. Durkheim did not envision a concrete ritualization of modern life, except, perhaps, in periodic ritual contexts (whose nature he did not really specify). Moreover, he argued that criticism would be both necessary and functional in a highly complex social order. "The sacred character of morality ought not protect it from criticism as it did in the case of religion." [87] Constructive criticism would not impair basic commitments insofar as they were rationally justifiable. Indeed, it might serve as a "feed-back" mechanism in the application of norms to concrete cases. With reference to one of Saint-Simon's

[86] *Education morale*, pp. 45, 129, 42–43.
[87] *Sociologie et philosophie*, p. 69.

disciples, Durkheim observed: "What escaped Bazard is that the further one advances in history, the more one sees the traits of the critical period prolonged into the organic period. In fact, the more cultivated a people, the less does the dogma which unifies it bar free examination. Reflection, criticism exist next to faith, pierce that very faith without destroying it, and occupy an always larger place in it." [88]

The individual rights defended by Durkheim included private property as a material basis of moral autonomy.

This individual liberty which is so dear to us supposes not only the faculty to go about as we please; it implies the existence of a circle of things which we may dispose of as we will. Individualism would only be a word if we did not have a material sphere of action in which we exercise a sort of sovereignty. When one says that individual property is a sacred thing, one only states in symbolic form an indubitable moral axiom; for individual property is the material condition of the cult of the individual.[89]

Durkheim related these ideas to the notion that legitimate property in modern society was increasingly the property acquired by the individual through his own effort rather than through inheritance. He did not draw the seemingly obvious inference that a certain minimum of property was necessary for all individuals in a society based upon individual liberty. He did have a conception of a ceiling on property, but it was quite moralistic. He interpreted the labor theory of value as a concept of distributive justice which required that individuals be recompensed according to their social contributions. In this sense, distributive justice might require stratification because of the value system in terms of which functions and contributions were appraised. But counterbalancing this idea was that of the norm of community, which required equalization of rewards. The concepts of distributive justice relative to differentiated functions and of equality based on communal values were among the bases for Durkheim's distinction between socialism and communism in

<hr/>

[88] *Socialism*, p. 258.   [89] *Leçons de sociologie*, p. 202.

Socialism. The idea that Durkheim leaned more toward communism is justified by his apparent conception of community as a higher principle which both mitigated the "harshness" of distributive justice and represented its limiting ideal in a healthy society. In a statement which was entirely in keeping with his growing emphasis on the importance of community in all normal societies, he observed: "Charity [in the biblical sense] is the feeling of human sympathy freeing itself from the last inegalitarian considerations and effacing or denying the particular merit of this final form of heredity transmission—the transmission of mental capacity. It is thus only the apogee of justice." [90]

Durkheim's notion of the role of the individual in society also recognized aesthetic considerations. The response of the individual to shared norms and values might involve imaginative creativity and uncommon sensitivity above and beyond the call of duty. Indeed, in a *mot* in the epigrammatic tradition of the French *moralistes,* Durkheim asserted: "There are virtues which are acts of madness, and it is their madness which constitutes their grandeur." [91] His central point here as elsewhere, however, was that the daily bread of moral life was to be found in institutional norms in the broadest sense. These deserved first-order attention before a discussion of subjective variations made sense.

In a word, we do not support the exclusive thesis that moral life has no individual aspect but that the social aspect is the principal part and that one must first investigate it if one wishes to know what the individual aspect consists of. It is not a question of denying one of the two points of view for the benefit of the other, but of reversing the order of priority ordinarily recognized between them.[92]

Thus, from Durkheim's perspective, the essential rationale for individual resistance to social pressure was not individual opin-

[90] *Ibid.,* p. 258.   [91] *Sociologie et philosophie,* p. 125.
[92] Review of Alfred Fouillée's *Les Eléments sociologiques de la morale,* Gustave Belot's *En quête d'une morale positive,* and Adolphe Landry's *Principes de morale rationnelle,* in *Année sociologique,* X (1905–1906), 361.

ion. It was informed judgment which contrasted the existing state of society to the way society ought to be.

The very principle of rebellion is the same as the principle of conformism. An individual conforms to the *true* nature of society when he obeys traditional morality. And he conforms to the *true* nature of society when he rebels against this morality. . . . In the moral realm as in all other realms of nature, the reason of the *individual* is not privileged because it is the reason of the *individual*. The only reason for which one may legitimately, here as elsewhere, claim the right to intervene and to elevate oneself above historical moral reality in order to reform it is not my reason or yours; it is impersonal, human reason, which is truly realized only in science. . . . What I oppose to the collectivity is the collectivity itself, but more and better conscious of itself.[93]

In the context of Durkheim's concepts of normality and pathology, the idea expressed somewhat ambiguously in the quoted passage can be more clearly formulated: The individual had the right and duty to oppose a pathological state of society. But he did this, not in his own interest, but in the interest of furthering the emergence of a normal state of society. Durkheim's extreme mode of affirmation seemed to deny that there was any subjectivity in this action, even in the making of a committed decision. But his essential purpose was to deny that there was a purely "perspectival" or subjectivist position in morality. Instead, he affirmed morality to be scientific, in the sense that it involved rational argument about objective considerations. Nowhere else did Durkheim come closer to a sociological reformulation of the idea of natural law. He contended that, at the very least, one could reason about value judgments and that a sociological conception of the problem gave content to the reasoning process. Essential to morality was the consensually accepted norm and value which created solidarity in society. One's awareness of the validity of the "normal" state endowed moral action with an

[93] *Sociologie et philosophie,* pp. 95–96.

overriding goal—the creation or maintenance of social "normality."

One dimension of Durkheim's conception of the relation between society and the individual deserves special mention. In time, Durkheim provided some insight into the problem of psychopathology. In his early thought, his desire to establish a methodologically autonomous foundation for sociology led him to emphasize the distinctions between sociology and psychology. Later, he broached the problem of social psychology. He also touched at least peripherally on the problem of the relation between normality and pathology in society and the personality.

In *The Rules* and elsewhere, Durkheim observed that social normality and psychological normality were not identical concepts.[94] Social normality and pathology were related to the nature and functioning of social structures. Psychological normality was a type of social conformity, and psychopathology amounted to a type of social deviance. The normal society would contain a marginal number of psychopathological individuals, just as it would contain a marginal number of other types of deviants. In a pathological state of society, the extreme structural faults in the organization of social life would give rise to a distorted rate of psychopathology.

In Volume IV of the *Année sociologique,* Durkheim used the title "Madness as a Social Fact." In a book review, he argued that "social states are reflected in mental alienation" and observed that rates of psychopathology varied with social context.[95] As might be expected, Durkheim was more suggestive on the level of structural causation than he was on that of psychological description. He provided nothing comparable to the recent studies of R. D. Laing, to which Durkheim's type of thought is an obvious and necessary complement. Nor did he investigate the shifts

[94] *Règles de la méthode sociologique,* p. 66. See also "Crime et santé sociale," *Revue philosophique,* XXXIX (1895), 523.

[95] Review of G.-L. Duprat's *Les Causes sociales de la folie,* in *Année sociologique,* IV (1899–1900), 475–476.

in the very meaning of psychopathological phenomena with changing sociocultural states and contexts in the richly suggestive manner of Michel Foucault.[96] But he did see the possibility of a study which would treat madness in the same manner in which he had treated suicide. In *Suicide* itself, Durkheim discussed the psychological manifestations of anomic anxiety and egoistic withdrawal. In examining the psychology of egoism, he underscored the possibility of a schizoid split between inner and outer reality.

In turning away from the external world, consciousness folds in upon itself, takes itself as its own unique object, and undertakes as its principal task self-observation and self-analysis. But by this extreme concentration it merely deepens the chasm dividing it from the rest of the universe. . . . If it individualizes itself beyond a certain point, if it separates itself too radically from other beings, men or things, it finds itself unable to communicate with the very source of its normal nourishment and no longer has anything to which it can apply itself. It creates nothingness within by creating it without, and has nothing left to reflect but its own misery. Its only remaining object of thought is its inner nothingness and the resulting melancholy.[97]

---

[96] See R. D. Laing, *The Divided Self* (first pub. 1960; Baltimore: Penguin Books, 1965); and Michel Foucault, *L'Histoire de la folie a l'âge classique* (Paris: Plon, 1961). Laing provides a sensitive phenomenological description of schizoid and schizophrenic dissociation of the personality in response to a state of "ontological" insecurity. The most obvious deficiency in Laing's thought is the absence of an adequate sociological dimension both in explaining the genesis of psychopathological phenomena and in proposing reforms. Except for his investigation of the "schizophrenogenic" family, his conception of society is disappointingly vague. On the level of reform, Laing has increasingly advocated what might be called a mind-blasting technique. He looks to the psychopathological experience itself under controlled conditions as a deviant force that can shake people loose from mad conformity in a pathological society. As a social solution, the dubiousness of this proposal is evident. In addition, the basically private or, at most, small-scale communal approach of Laing does not address itself to the problem of large-scale social transformation affecting major institutions. Despite his penchant for obscurantist formulations, Foucault is more relevant for a sociological and historical understanding of madness.

[97] *Le Suicide*, pp. 314–315.

One conclusion that Durkheim himself did not draw was that the concept of psychopathology was methodologically easier to apply but philosophically more dubious than his own concept of social pathology.[98] As a form of social deviance, psychopathology often seemed to be readily detectable. But its relation to other things, such as criminal responsibility, might be problematic, and its very availability made tempting an identification of all unusual phenomena as psychologically aberrant. The notion of social pathology was more difficult to define. This difficulty, as well as ideological reasons, may explain the ill repute of the concept among social scientists in contrast with the better

[98] Freud made a similar point. See his *Civilization and Its Discontents,* trans. J. Rivière (London: Hogarth Press, 1953), pp. 141–142: "If the evolution of civilization has such a far-reaching similarity with the development of an individual, and if the same methods are employed in both, would not the diagnosis be justified that many systems of civilization—or epochs of it—possibly even the whole of humanity—have become 'neurotic' under the pressure of the civilizing trends? To analytic dissection of these neuroses, therapeutic recommendations might follow which would claim a great practical interest. . . . The diagnosis of collective neurosis, moreover, will be confronted by a special difficulty. In the neurosis of an individual we can use as a starting point the contrast presented to us between the patient and his environment which we assume to be "normal." No such background as this would be available for any society similarly affected; it would have to be supplied in some other way. And with regard to any therapeutic application of our knowledge, what would be the use of the most acute analysis of social neuroses, since no one possesses the power to compel the community to adopt the therapy? In spite of all these difficulties, we may expect that one day someone will venture upon this research into the pathology of civilized communities." The "background" for the analysis of social pathology was, according to Durkheim, to be found in comparative studies and the investigation of the relation of conditions, institutional structures, and cultural values. One of the "uses" of this type of diagnosis would be the heightening of critical consciousness, including the understanding of "mental illness" and the role of those who do have the power or influence to enforce conformity in a significantly pathological sociocultural context. On the "therapeutic" level of social reform, Durkheim was less adequate and only intimated the potential and dangers of a mass movement and political action. For a sometimes simplistic development in a direction comparable to that of Durkheim but within the Freudian tradition, see the works of Erich Fromm, especially *The Sane Society.*

fortune of psychopathology. Yet from a philosophical viewpoint, Durkheim's concept of social pathology had a stronger critical basis and was, in a sense, logically prior. From Durkheim's perspective, it would seem that the normal person would have to be conceived normatively with reference to the normal society. He would be the person who lived in accordance with meaningful, legitimate norms, applying them with the requisite flexibility and harboring within himself a marginal minimum of anomie. He would be a "conformist" in a very special sense of the term. And even in the normal state of society, the ideological deviant would not be unequivocally in the wrong. In fact, Durkheim seemed to attribute a greater causal importance to the exceptional individual in the normal state of society, for in this context his *hybris* would correspond to the element of possibly creative anomie in experience. And it would bear a more positive relation to society as a whole: it would evoke a shared sense of the tragic which ritual and other symbolic forms would simultaneously heighten and mitigate. The right kind of social integration would itself help save the creative exception from neurosis.

In the pathological state of society, the unquestioning conformist might retain some semblance of mental balance at the price of furthering disintegrating forces in society at large. The person with a psychopathological adaptation might be more or less off course than the conforming sociopath: he might experience in exaggerated form the causes of anxiety in his society or reveal in oblique and distorted fashion the symbolic bases of social normality missing in the status quo. The schizophrenic lived in limiting form the dualism between inner self and outer reality; the compulsive neurotic performed rituals which had lost their significance. Durkheim never gave to his own conception of social psychology and its relation to the individual a truly convincing formulation, and we have extended his thought in a certain direction. Despite the dangers of overinterpretation, it might not be stretching his thought too far to see it as tending toward a cultural conception of psychopathology which provided the basis for a critique of the very concept of "mental illness." For within the framework of his thought, mental illness might well appear as a defensive response to disconcerting and dangerous phenomena in a formally rational, bureaucratized society which had good institutional reasons to fear for its own social sanity. In this sense, a different appreciation of certain phenomena would itself require their reduction to marginal status and their insertion into a significantly different sociocultural context.[99]

The central point is that Durkheim's idea of the relation of sociology to moral philosophy was based upon the coordinate axes of his thought: the tree of social life and the concepts of normality and pathology. The distinctive task of the comparative method was to arrive at types situated midway between the extreme nominalism of traditional historiography and the extreme realism and quest for universals of traditional philosophy. Toward the end of his life, however, Durkheim turned to the concern with human nature which characterized traditional philosophy. This concern was central to his *Elementary Forms*. From Durkheim's sociological and cultural perspective, the concept of human nature could be reformulated: "human nature" referred to the possibilities of symbolic experience corresponding to the trunk of the tree of social life. These possibilities could take normal or pathological form.

In the most general terms, what characterized the normal society? First and foremost, it was based upon a *conscience collec-*

[99] A similar interpretation is applied to the thought of Marcel Mauss by Claude Lévi-Strauss in his very important introduction to Mauss's *Sociologie et anthropologie* (first pub. 1950; Paris: Presses Universitaires de France, 1968), pp. xviii–xxii. Even Michel Foucault, in his early, excellent *Maladie mentale et psychologie* (Paris: Presses Universitaires de France, 1954), commits the error of identifying Durkheim's concept of social pathology with psychopathology and mental illness (p. 75). Within the *Année* school, the problem of the relationship between social pathology and psychopathology was explored by Maurice Halbwachs in *Les causes du suicide* (Paris: Alcan, 1930). And the problem was a central concern in the work of Charles Blondel.

tive which embodied a tense balance of institutional norms and cultural symbols. The core of the *conscience collective* was a variant of practical reason which Durkheim termed *la morale*, or the collective type. In their application to concrete events by average individuals, the norms and values of the *conscience collective* suffered a "falling off" from ideal perfection. To ask more of ordinary social life would be to fall prey to anomic idealism, fanatically demanding perfection from all people at all times. But to remind members of society in a dramatically forceful way of their obligation to show sacred respect for shared values, special "ritual" activities were necessary. In ritual, the *conscience collective* was expressed and revitalized in intense and purified forms which transcended the inevitable compromises of everyday life. And through ritual, *communitas* would be institutionally realized and controlled. The normal society would also contain a dynamic leaven of anomie—including more anomic displays of *communitas*. But anomie would be limited to a marginal aspect of the average personality and to marginal groups in society. Either extreme of the bell-shaped curve of moral practice would reveal marginal categories of culture-bearing idealists (or perfectionist deviants) at one end and of criminal deviants at the other. In the normal society, deviants presenting ideological challenges to the existing order might attain ritual status and, invested with ambivalent sacred values, become the objects of dangerous fascination.

The universal function of the *conscience collective* in the normal state of society was to strike a viable balance between structure and *communitas*—the dual bases of solidarity in society. Objective and internalized at the same time, the *conscience collective* would create a meaningful sense of legitimate limits. "All life . . . is a complex equilibrium whose diverse elements limit one another, and this equilibrium cannot be broken without suffering and sickness." [100] Common to the biological organism and society was a structure whose normal functioning depended

[100] *Education morale*, p. 34.

on a dynamic equilibrium of mutually limiting parts. The elementary postulate of Durkheim's philosophy was the finite nature of all life. Indeed, one interesting aspect of his naturalistic metaphors representing his understanding of society was the mediation of the dualism between nature and society, matter and mind, which another tendency of his thought affirmed in extreme form. One may detect here a cosmological undercurrent which was more expansive than his social metaphysic. Moreover, Durkheim in time became sensitive to the dangers of excessive formal rationality and constraint as principles of social life; this sensitivity coincided with his growing awareness of the need for significant community in all society and his sense of the importance of the content of norms and values. One of his criticisms of Kant was of his predecessor's failure to recognize that all human nature required limitation, "our rational nature as well as our passionate nature." "Our reason is not a transcendental faculty. It is part of the world and, consequently, it must follow the law of the world. The universe is limited, and all limitation presupposes forces which limit." [101]

In his early thought, Durkheim saw little future for religion in modern society. With the expansion of his concept of reason, his view of the future of religion changed. He came to argue that a ritual attitude of sacred respect was at the root of all commitments and that periodic, festive ritual observances would be necessary to revive and reinvigorate these commitments. Hence the modern scientific and critical consciousness seemed to require only a newer definition of the relationship between faith and reason. For Durkheim, moreover, the basic nexus existed, not between religion and the categorical imperative, but between religion and communal spontaneity. The sacred did not serve primarily to enforce the strictness of obligations; it seemed to make men overcome a sense of compulsion by giving them a feeling of being at home in the world. "It is far from true that the notion of the imperative is the true characteristic of the re-

[101] *Ibid.*, pp. 95–96.

ligious side of morality. On the contrary, one could show that the more a morality is essentially religious, the more the idea of obligation is effaced." [102] Here Durkheim did relate religion to the overcoming of tragic antipathies in human existence.

With the idea of the potential of community and the sacred in modern society, Durkheim at least partially re-evaluated the nature of myth and its relation to reason. He seemed to imply that, insofar as myth did not contradict the substantive rationality of the *conscience collective,* it might well serve to convey forms of understanding which complemented literal truth.

There is and there will always be a place in social life for a form of truth which will perhaps express itself in secular form but which will, despite everything, have a mythological and religious foundation. For a long time to come, there will be two tendencies in every society: a tendency toward objective and scientific truth and a tendency toward truth seen from the inside, or mythological truth.[103]

A problem with mythologies in a state of social pathology was that they often intensified unnecessary contradictions and destructive forces which outraged reason instead of atoning for its necessary defects. Liberated from rational control, myth and ritual gravitated toward irrationality and maniacal agitation. The basic goal of Durkheim's thought was to retain rationality and the modern critical consciousness while opening society to repressed forms of human experience. The attempt to reconsider the sacred and assess its possible role in a revitalized modern society was one of the basic motivations of Durkheim's masterpiece, *The Elementary Forms of the Religious Life.*

[102] *Sociologie et philosophie,* p. 102.
[103] *Pragmatisme et sociologie,* ed. and Introd. by Armand Cuvillier (Paris: Librairie Philosophique J. Vrin, 1955), p. 184; reconstructed from students' notes for a course given in 1913–1914.

6«

The Sacred and Society

A seeking, a searching.
To seek whither?
To search the land, to seek the origin,
To seek out the base, to search out the unknown,
To seek out the *atua* [spirit].
May it be effectual.

—A Maori diviner's spell

By common accord, *The Elementary Forms of the Religious Life* is Durkheim's most ambitious work. But consensus disintegrates in the evaluation of Durkheim's achievement. Most scholarly opinion falls somewhere between the two extremes represented by the reactions of Robert Lowie and Talcott Parsons. Lowie condemned Durkheim with faint praise: "While by no means inclined to join in the paeans of praise that have been intoned in Durkheim's honor, I repeat that his essay is a noteworthy mental exercise and would rank as a landmark if dialectic ingenuity sufficed to achieve greatness in the empirical sciences." [1] Parsons, on the other hand, praised Durkheim with but faint reservation:

While ostensibly studying only a narrowly technical empirical material which might be thought to be of little general interest, he manages to make it the vehicle for unusually far-reaching theoretical reasoning. So, while *Les formes élémentaires de la vie religieuse* is in one aspect a technical monograph on Australian totemism, it is at the same time one of the few most important works on sociological theory. . . . In fact only when a monograph is at the same time an

[1] Robert Lowie, *Primitive Religion* (first pub. 1924; New York: Universal Press, 1952), p. 157.

essay in theory can it be the highest type of empirical study. Durkheim had the faculty of combining the two aspects in a way which provided models for future sociologists. Unfortunately, it is unlikely that many will attain this preëminence in the combination.[2]

There is more to this difference of views than the standard opposition between the empirical fieldworker and the theoretical concept builder. Both because it carried prominent tendencies of Durkheimian sociology to their extreme logical conclusion and because it exacerbated the permanent ambiguities of Durkheim's thought, *The Elementary Forms* has lent itself, not only to contradictory evaluations, but to divergent interpretations. Its argument merged various currents of thought into an encompassing, oceanic form of discourse which at times seemed to subvert differences among scientific theory, mythology, and philosophy. Thus the initial problem is how to come to terms with this singular work—this almost sacred text—which has had the power to allure and repel at the same time. Instead of tracing Durkheim's points in the exact order in which he made them, I believe it is analytically useful to approach *The Elementary Forms* under three overlapping but distinct headings: the theory of religion, sociological epistemology, and social metaphysic. In this way, one may attempt to grasp the nature of the argument as a whole, its place in Durkheim's thought, and its relation to the shape of modern culture and Durkheim's reformist hopes.

The Theory of Religion

By the time he wrote *The Elementary Forms*, Durkheim was convinced that religion was the matrix of civilization and the

[2] Talcott Parsons, *The Structure of Social Action* (first pub. 1937; Glencoe, Ill.: Free Press, 1949), p. 411. More recently, Parsons has made a similar evaluation: "Anthropological research has enormously enriched our knowledge in this field, though Durkheim's codification and analysis of Australian totemism remains perhaps the most eminent single monographic contribution, because it is both a great monograph and much more than that" (Introd. to Max Weber's *The Sociology of Religion* [Boston: Beacon Press, 1963], p. xxvii).

pre-eminent form of social life. In a preface to the *Année socio-logique*, he explained why sociology should accord priority to religion in its investigation of culture and society:

Religion contains in itself from the very beginning, even if in an indistinct state, all the elements which, in dissociating themselves from it, articulating themselves, and combining with one another in a thousand ways, have given rise to the various manifestations of collective life. From myths and legends have issued forth science and poetry; from religious ornamentations and cult ceremonials have come the plastic arts; from ritual practice were born law and morals. One cannot understand our perception of the world, our philosophical conceptions of the soul, of immortality, of life, if one does not know the religious beliefs which are their primordial forms. Kinship started out as an essentially religious tie; punishment, contract, gift, and homage are transformations of expiatory, contractual, communal, honorary sacrifices, and so on. . . . A great number of problems change their aspects completely as soon as their connections with the sociology of religion are recognized. Our efforts must therefore be aimed at tracing those connections.[3]

In *The Elementary Forms*, Durkheim's object was to trace the connections between religion and society on the highest level of generality by seeking the essential constituents of religion which represented a permanent aspect of human nature in society. "What we want is to find a means to discern the ever present causes on which depend the most essential forms of religious thought and practice."[4] In other words, Durkheim was working at the most basic level of the tree of sociocultural life. He sought the common trunk of specifically human experience, which would be differentiated according to varying conditions in different types of society. Moreover, it was contextually clear that he was primarily concerned with the nature and role of religion in the normal form of social life. Thus his last major

[3] II (1897–1898); in Kurt Woolf, ed., *Essays on Sociology and Philosophy* (first pub. 1960; New York: Harper & Row, 1964), pp. 350–351.

[4] *Les Formes élémentaires de la vie religieuse* (4th ed.; Paris: Presses Universitaires de France, 1960), p. 11.

work, like the studies which preceded it, was at least implicitly conceived with reference to the two coordinate bases of Durkheim's thought: the paradigm or model of the tree of social life and the root distinction between the normal and the pathological.

The method Durkheim employed was that of the "crucial experiment." Through concentrated analysis of a limited range of related facts, he attempted to arrive ultimately at the formulation of general laws. Durkheim's "crucial experiment" focused on archaic society and, more specifically, on Australian societies and used the American Indians as a sort of control group. The principal analytic reason for this choice was methodological. The relative simplicity of archaic societies made them the most plausible objects of study in the attempt to define the essence of religion and the permanent in human nature. It may be observed, moreover, that the general methodological viewpoint was analytically independent of the specific theory of totemism, the evolutionary tendencies, and the social metaphysic with which it became associated in the course of Durkheim's argument.

The problem of initial definition which was always significant in Durkheim's work assumed paramount importance in *The Elementary Forms*. The definition of the religious phenomenon was much more than a preliminary step in the orientation of research. It embodied a summary of what was essential in religion and permanent in human nature. Definition was thus related to subsequent argument in accordance with the Cartesian dictum that a chain is as strong as its first link.

Durkheim began by rejecting general definitions of religion in terms of a personal divinity or radically transcendental mysteries. As he had put it in an earlier article, the notion of divinity was only a "secondary episode" in the history of religions.[5] Buddhism offered a prominent example of a major religious system without

[5] "De La Définition du phénomène religieux," *Année sociologique*, II (1897–1898), 13.

divinities. In addition, many religions provided cases of rituals without gods or, indeed, of gods who were conceived as the products of ritual action. From these considerations Durkheim derived the general principle that the meaning, efficacy, and social function of cult were independent of the idea of divine intervention.

Durkheim's discussion of transcendental mysteries was more theoretically elaborate than his comments on the notion of divinity. The notion of the inexplicably mysterious was reciprocally related to the notion of an autonomous realm of nature. Both notions were alien to primitive man. Instead, he had an experience of *le merveilleux*—the wondrous—which comprehended both the processes of nature and the doings of men.

For him there is nothing strange in the power of voice or gesture to command the elements, to stop or hasten the motion of the stars, to bring rain or cause it to cease, etc. The rites which he employs to assure the fertility of the soil or the fecundity of animal species on which he is nourished do not appear more irrational in his eyes than the technical processes of which our agriculturalists make use, for the same purpose, do to ours. The powers which he puts into play by these diverse means do not seem to him to have anything especially mysterious about them. . . . That is why the miraculous interventions which the ancients attributed to their gods were not to their eyes miracles in the modern sense of the word. For them, they were beautiful, rare, or terrible spectacles, or causes of surprise and wonder (*thaumata, mirabilia, miracula*); but they never saw them as glimpses into a mysterious world which reason cannot penetrate.[6]

Durkheim conceded that the feeling of supernatural mystery had considerable importance in certain religions, notably Christianity. But it could not be conceived as a basic element of Christianity itself since it was subject to significant variations and even total eclipse in Western history. A fortiori, it could not be seen as the essence of all religion.

This conception of the supernatural and transcendental mys-

[6] *Formes élémentaires de la vie religieuse*, pp. 35–36.

tery was highly significant. Durkheim's thought was a forerunner of modern "death of God" theologies, insofar as they use "God" to refer to the radically transcendental divinity of Christianity. In addition, he seemed to indicate the possibility of a transcendence (in the Hegelian sense) of positivistic conceptions of science through a philosophy which integrated modern rationalism into a more comprehensive vision of valid experience. And he shifted the center of gravity in religious interpretation from the supernatural to a notion of *le merveilleux* intimately bound up with the sacred and *communitas*.

Durkheim defined religion thus:

A religion is an integrated system of beliefs and practices relating to sacred things, that is to say, things set apart and forbidden—beliefs and practices which unite into one and the same moral community called a church all those who adhere to them. The second element which thus finds a place in our definition is no less essential than the first; for by showing that the idea of religion is inseparable from that of a church, it shows that religion must be an eminently collective thing.[7]

The definition comprised two related elements, one substantive, the other functional. The substantive element asserted that religion involved a perception of the world in terms of the distinction between the sacred and the profane. The second element asserted that religion functioned to create moral community in society.

The second element of Durkheim's definition is more controversial than the first. In one sense, Durkheim's conception had a critical edge that was related to his idea of social normality. Implicitly, it seemed to deny religious legitimacy to churches based on extreme bureaucratization. More explicitly, it impugned the validity of religious systems which functioned to atomize men in society. Moreover, it did not consider the context in which religion or quasi-religious ideologies might integrate a

[7] *Ibid.,* p. 65.

group internally but intensify conflict in the broader society. Obviously, Durkheim's definition applied only to the function of religion in the normal state of society; it applied to pathological states only as an expression of evolutionary optimism or an indication of projected goals.

It might be observed, however, that a more "value-neutral" and predictive line of argument was open which Durkheim did not take. He might have argued that religion in a context of extreme bureaucratization or atomistic individualism served the interest of relatively small and privileged elites but that a more communal experience of the sacred had greater mass appeal. This approach would have led to the problem of the relationship between certain conceptions of the sacred and certain social functions. The case of Protestantism was significant in this respect. Sectarian Protestantism, which arose in part as a reaction against bureaucratic corruption (e.g., the commercialization of indulgences), conceived the sacred in radically transcendental and supernatural terms which functioned to create a direct link between a hidden divinity and atomized individuals. As Weber observed, this attitude was maintained only among a select elite, while the larger population, especially in rural areas, fell back upon more cosmic and archaic forms of religious experience which included elements of magic. Thus Durkheim's notion of the relationship between the sacred and community might have been associated with popular or mass religion and perhaps with developmental possibilities in modern secular societies. In this sense, he might have supplemented Weber's idea of the "bureaucratization of charisma" with a countervailing idea of the tendency of popular movements to react against routinization and atomization in a charismatic quest for a more communal experience of the sacred. To the extent that the correlation held between a communal conception of the sacred and popular devotion—or between its absence and mass unrest—plausibility would be lent to the claim that Durkheim had at least discovered a permanent aspect of human nature in society. In one form or another, the bond between the sacred and community would make its relevance felt in all social contexts.

Like his definition of religion, Durkheim's attempt to distinguish religion from magic had both substantive and functional components. And it too seemed most problematic on the sociofunctional level which received the bulk of his attention.

Substantively, Durkheim held that both religion and magic depended upon the distinction between the sacred and the profane. They differed, however, in their orientations to the sacred. Religion presented a "ritual attitude" toward the sacred experienced in purely symbolic terms. If religion involved an experience of the sacred as, so to speak, an end in itself, magic took the sacred as a means. It placed "sacred forces" in a causal circuit geared to the achievement of practical, utilitarian effects. In extreme forms, this manipulation of the sacred brought about its profanation. It may be parenthetically noted that this point of view was applied by Hubert and Mauss, in their "Théorie générale de la magie," to the relationship between magic and technology.[8]

Durkheim's distinction between religion and magic paralleled the opposition, in his moral philosophy, between the normative and the utilitarian. Magic, for him, almost seemed to imply a misappropriation of the public fund of sacred values for private and particularistic interests. This aspect of his argument was especially pronounced in the more sociofunctional element of his distinction. Here, however, he proposed differential characteristics which were not universal in incidence and which, furthermore, harbored internal contradictions in their application to differentiated types.

In considering social functions, Durkheim argued that religion

---

[8] Henri Hubert and Marcel Mauss, "Esquisse d'une théorie générale de la magie," *Année sociologique*, VII (1901–1902); reprinted in Marcel Mauss, *Sociologie et anthropologie* (first pub. 1950; Paris: Presses Universitaires de France, 1968), pp. 3–141.

was inconceivable without a church but that "there was no church of magic."

Between the magician and the individuals who consult him, as between these individuals themselves, there are no lasting bonds which make them members of the same moral community, comparable to that formed by believers in the same god or the observers of the same cult. The magician has a clientele and not a church, and it is very possible that his clients have no relations with one another, even to the point of not knowing one another; even the relations which they have with him are generally accidental and transient; they are like those of a sick man with his doctor.[9]

Thus the magician might provide services for individuals whose personal problems were not adequately resolved in the dominant system. Yet Durkheim's argument harbored a number of difficulties. These related both to the nature of symbolic systems and to their social functions in a "church" of believers. In the context of *The Elementary Forms* as a whole, a church obviously meant a solidaristic corporative group which especially emphasized the existence of moral community among its members. But Durkheim did not attempt to relate this notion to the problem of highly bureaucratized churches or highly individualistic sects.

In order to appreciate Durkheim's conception of religion and its relation to magic, it is useful to distinguish between (1) symbolic systems which integrate religion and magic as elements of a more inclusive paradigm, (2) symbolic systems which dissociate religion from *some* forms of magic, and (3) symbolic systems which dissociate religion from *all* forms of magic. These three types of symbolic systems may then be related to the existence and strength of a church, in the limited sense of a solidaristic corporative group.

In archaic societies, magic and religion were, typically, inte-

---

[9] *Formes élémentaires de la vie religieuse*, pp. 61–62.

grated elements of the same over-all paradigm. Durkheim at times seemed to recognize this. But he did not see the ways in which both religion and magic served to integrate the same corporate group (or "church"). A rain ritual which insured a good crop for the group as a whole did not work invidiously for the benefit of special or private interests. And it was in archaic societies, where the integration of the meaningful content and social function of religion and magic was strongest, that the element of moral community was most marked.

The history of Christianity in the West, which was often Durkheim's implicit frame of reference, revealed different developments. As it became increasingly bureaucratized and less communal, Catholicism did dissociate religion and certain forms of magic. White magic was assimilated into the dominant symbolic system as miracle. Black magic was relegated to the sphere of diabolical forces. In missionary territories, elements of other symbolic systems which could not be integrated into the established paradigms were frequently dismissed as black magic. And charismatic deviants who upset the bureaucratic administration of sacred values were often condemned as witches or sorcerers. The strongest communal bonds in such a context might well be generated between selfless disciples and the charismatic deviant who used magical prowess as an instrumental support for a revolutionary prophetic message. Within the dominant organization, community was subordinated to the imperatives of a bureaucratic, hierarchical structure.

In sectarian Protestantism, the tendency was to purge all magic from religion and to brand all magical elements as signs of witchcraft. The denigration of visible symbolism and its efficacy was attendant upon the establishment of an unmediated nexus between the "inner" self of the individual and a transcendental, hidden divinity. The degree of community derived from religion was decreased to a minimum. The religious group was a sect in which membership was voluntary on the part of the individual and subject to approval of his personal qualifications by members of the sect. Magic was entirely a matter of extrareligious and irreligious private consultation; it was highly suspect in the light of the radical secularization of "this-worldly" experience and the idea that worldly success was related to religious election only as an external index. But tension was created between a radically transcendental theology, which could be used as a basis of existence only by an elite, and the tendency of the common man (and the common in all men) to fall back upon paradigms which allowed an ambivalent fascination with the symbolism of magic and sorcery. Indeed, even private consultations with a magician might give rise to feelings of dependency which contrasted sharply with the individualistic nature of the established religious system.

In brief, it would seem that when the conditions of Durkheim's definition of religion applied, the conditions of religion's distinction from magic did not, and vice versa. It was in systems with a high degree of integration between the meaningful content and social functions of religion and magic that moral community was most marked. One basic difficulty in his attempt to distinguish sharply between religion and magic in the archaic context was his failure to see that genuine belief in a symbolism involved a belief in the causal efficacy of that symbolism. The difference between the "merely" symbolic and the symbolic as an object of genuine belief was set forth by Durkheim himself in an earlier work:

Contemporary ideas make us inclined to see mere symbols or modes of allegorical figuration. But it is a general rule that practices do not take on at first merely symbolic characteristics. This type of symbolism is a form of decadence and it comes only when their primitive sense is lost. Symbols begin not as external signs but as efficacious causes of social relations.[10]

The problem, of course, was that from a critical standpoint Durkheim recognized the illusory aspects of magic. If he was to

[10] *Leçons de sociologie* (Paris: Presses Universitaires de France, 1950), p. 222.

save religion and make it compatible with rationalism, he seemed obliged to dissociate it from magic and its discredited falsehoods. The antipathy between the collectively normative and the particularistically utilitarian, which was essential to his own moral philosophy, served this need. As we shall see, however, the issue left open by his social metaphysic was whether his salvaging operation was untenably reductionistic and whether it adequately accounted for the dimension of causal efficacy in sacred symbolism.

At this point one might have expected Durkheim to turn directly to a study of the sacred and the profane in belief and ritual practice, using an in-depth analysis of a small set of archaic societies as a basis of generalization. A highly significant exploratory study in this direction had already been completed by Hubert and Mauss in their "Essai sur la nature et la fonction du sacrifice" ("Sacrifice: Its Nature and Function").[11] In line with the earlier work of Durkheim and his school, the primary problem would have been the relationship and ramifications of two sets of correlated oppositions: sacred-profane and communitas–differentiated structure. This focus would have provided insight into the key question of how religious beliefs and practices constituted the ultimate source of legitimation in society and how they functioned in relation to solidarity.

Instead, Durkheim at this point turned to the evolutionary problem of the earliest known form of religion. This preoccupation was one basis for the exaggerated importance he attributed to totemism in the history of religions. Indeed, it inhibited him from analyzing objectively both the extent to which totemism

[11] Henri Hubert and Marcel Mauss, "Essai sur la nature et la fonction du sacrifice," Année sociologique, II (1897–1898); in Mauss, Oeuvres, I: Les Fonctions sociales du sacré, ed. Victor Karady (Paris: Les Editions du Minuit, 1968), pp. 193–301. See also Roger Caillois, L'Homme et le sacré (Paris: Gallimard, 1950), and Mircea Eliade, The Sacred and the Profane (first pub. 1957; New York: Harper & Row, 1961). All of Eliade's works, especially his Cosmos and History (first pub. 1954; New York: Harper & Row, 1959), are important in this respect.

did or did not have religious aspects and the problem of other facets of religion in the societies he investigated. But the concentration upon totemism had another basis in Durkheim's thought. In the course of his argument, the term "origin" took on three senses: the evolutionary sense of a historical starting point; the analytic sense of a permanently applicable paradigm or a model of "ever present causes"; and the sense of a legitimating mythical source or *fons et origo*. The evolutionary signification was in fact the least important, since Durkheim himself was very cautious concerning its pertinence. On the other hand, the analytic and mythical meanings seemed to merge in his mind and to become the primary basis for his interest in origins. Insofar as it was not simply an adjunct of the contemporary anthropological quest to find the "secret of the totem" (in the phrase of Andrew Lang), totemism was important in *The Elementary Forms* largely because it proved convenient for Durkheimian social metaphysic and for the myth of origins which helped to legitimate it.

Durkheim prefaced his account of totemic belief and ritual with a refutation of competing theories of the original form of religion. Naturism derived religion from the primitive personalization of awesome forces of nature. In the linguistically oriented formulation of Max Müller, this conception of natural processes was attributed to the metaphoric power of language. In this sense, according to Durkheim, religion was "an immense metaphor without objective value." [12] Animism, which received its most influential formulation in the works of E. B. Tylor, maintained that the minimal definition of religion rested on a belief in spirits or souls. The origin of this belief was the reliance of the primitive mind on the idea of spirits in order to interpret dreams. The reasons for Durkheim's rejection of both naturism and animism were identical: they either ignored the sacred or reduced it to a groundless illusion. "Not only would the symbols through which religious powers are conceived mask in part

[12] *Formes élémentaires de la vie religieuse*, p. 114.

their true nature, but, furthermore, behind these images and figures there would be only the nightmares of uncultivated minds. Religion would in the last analysis be only a systematized and lived dream without any foundation in reality." [13]

Despite its partial validity, Durkheim's elaborate and somewhat tedious critique of naturism and animism had all the qualities of a refutation of heresies. He did not ask what the role of the relationship between man and nature might be in religious systems or what part metaphor might have in articulating this relationship. And, although the Australians referred to the mythical past as "dream time," he did not inquire into the place of the "night side" of life in religious experience. In fact, he seemed to conceive dreams in a narrowly Cartesian manner which denied them all cognitive value. Nor did he reject reductionism as a mode of interpretation. Prefacing his own reductionistic interpretation of totemism, he simply denied the validity of specific forms of reductionism in naturism and animism. The refutation of heresies in short was a prerequisite of apologetics. The style of argument became increasingly theological.

Certain aspects of Durkheim's treatment of totemism were analytically independent of his social metaphysic. But the growing interpenetration of his theory of totemism and his social metaphysic certainly contributed to his impermeability to mounting evidence which falsified some of his elementary assumptions. Durkheim believed that totemism was a global institution which combined kinship and religion. In other words, he assumed that the same group (the clan) shared both kinship and religion and that the same object (the totem) was the family name or emblem and the object of religious symbolism.

The primary source for facts on the Australian tribes which were the presumed object of Durkheim's crucial experiment was the exemplary monograph by Sir Baldwin Spencer and Francis James Gillen, *The Native Tribes of Central Australia*.[14]

[13] *Ibid.*, p. 97.
[14] London: Macmillan, 1899. This work was reviewed in detail by Durkheim (in its political and social aspects) and Mauss (in its religious aspects) in *Année sociologique*, III (1898–1899), 330–336, 205–215.

The Arunta (or Aranda) tribe received extensive treatment by Spencer and Gillen and by Durkheim. What were the *faits cruciaux?* There was no identity of the patrilocal territorial group, the partilineal exogamic group, and the totemic group with a territorial base. Religion was dispersed through various elements of cultural life, including religious confraternities not identical with the former groupings. The totemic groups, moreover, were not strongly constituted as corporate entities. The central role of the *intichiuma* ceremony of the totemic groups, which Durkheim attempted to interpret in predominantly religious terms as a primitive sacrifice involving oblation and communion, did appear to be predominantly magico-economic in nature. To Durkheim's dismay, Sir James Frazer had already observed this fact. Indeed, Mauss himself had argued in the *Année sociologique* that the seeming act of "communion" in the "totemic sacrifice" was performed by the totemic group in order to consume the sacred element of the totem and thereby free it for profane consumption by other groups.[15] This consumption created a metaphoric link between the *intichiuma* ritual and the ordinary economic life of society. The manifest purpose of the ritual was to assure the reproduction of the animal species. Moreover, exogamic marriage rules applied to patrilineal moieties (or phratries) and to marriage classes within them determined by generation. The totemic affiliation, in contrast, did not regulate exogamy and was determined by the ancestral totemic spirit mythologically associated with the spot at which the mother believed herself to have conceived the child.

In the face of similar evidence which could not be integrated into the paradigm of a global totemic institution, Durkheim resorted to ingenious and factually gratuitous evolutionary arguments. Evolutionary ideas were more important in Durkheim's attempt to relate the "original" totemic institution to known facts about archaic societies than in his attempt to relate archaic to other types of societies. In such *Année* articles as "La Prohibition de l'inceste et ses origines" (1896), "Sur le totémisme"

[15] III (1898–1899), p. 215.

(1900), and "Sur l'organisation des sociétés australiennes" (1903), he had laid the groundwork for *The Elementary Forms* by attempting to explain away counterevidence by imaginative accounts of the "original" totemic institution and how it had evolved into one known form or another. The primary impression left by these efforts is comparable to that left by Ptolemaic astronomy when it was compelled to resort to increasingly intricate epicycles in order to account in some way for increasingly hostile evidence.

It might be maintained that even if one concedes that Durkheim failed to provide an adequate general theory of totemism, this failure did not invalidate his general theory of religion. Objectively, totemism would be relevant to a general theory of religion only insofar as it provided in certain cases an illustration of religious symbolism. After all, Durkheim himself was primarily interested in religion and its relation to society. And in *The Elementary Forms,* he argued that the selection of the totem as a religious symbol was at first arbitrary. From an objective point of view, this line of argument is convincing, and it even makes one wonder why Durkheim was so insistent about the importance of totemism. The reason for his interest in totemism becomes less puzzling only in the context of his social metaphysic. Once totemism was implicated in his metaphysic of society, it became contaminated with all the symbolic values that follow in the train of a basic commitment. In this sense, Durkheim's steadfastness in the defense of an "original" totemic institution was much more than a case of senile hardening of the interpretive categories or psychological involvement in a pet theory.

To develop an idea of Durkheim's theory of religion, let us try to disentangle the elements of Durkheim's discussion which were not altogether subservient to his social metaphysic. Beliefs and rituals constituted the complementary modes through which men in society related to the sacred. Although he recognized the intimate relationship between ritual and myth in religious cults, Durkheim did not balance his treatment of rituals with a theory of myths. His analysis of beliefs concentrated in rather Platonic fashion upon conceptual paradigms or ideas which were presumed to be basic to religious beliefs.[16]

Durkheim divided rituals into the following types (which are perhaps more adequately conceived as elements present in varying combinations in specific rituals): the ritual interdict, or taboo; the sacrifice, comprising the elements of oblation (offering) and communion through consumption; the mimetic ritual, which had special relevance for beliefs about causation; the representative or commemorative ritual; and the piacular ritual relating to sorrowful events like death. The negative cult involving taboos served generally as a preparation for the positive cult (sacrificial, mimetic, commemorative, and piacular rituals) by setting men and things off from the profane world. Either in periodically recurrent form or as a reaction to potentially unsettling critical events, the role of ritual was to maintain and dramatically re-create the meaningful symbolic universe which functioned to integrate society.

Thus, for Durkheim, the center of religion as an operative force was the cult. And central to the cult was the nexus between symbolic manifestation and solidarity, especially in its intensely communal forms. Men experienced the strongest bonds with one another when they demonstrated that they held the same things sacred.

[16] As Durkheim put it: "It is not our intention to retrace all the speculations into which religious thought, even of the Australians alone, has entered. What we wish to reach are the elementary notions at the basis of religion; but there is no need to follow them through all the developments, sometimes very intricate, which mythological imagination has given them since primitive times. We shall make use of myths when they enable us to understand these fundamental notions, but we shall not make mythology itself the object of our study. Moreover, insofar as mythology is a work of art, it does not fall within the jurisdiction of the science of religions alone. Also, the mental processes which underlie it are too complex to be studied indirectly and tangentially. It constitutes a difficult problem which must be treated in itself, for itself, and with a method peculiar to itself" (*Formes élémentaires de la vie religieuse*, pp. 141–142).

From our point of view, it is readily seen how the group of regularly repeated acts which form the cult assume once again all their importance. In fact, whoever has really practiced a religion knows quite well that it is the cult which gives rise to the impressions of joy, of interior peace, of serenity, of enthusiasm which are, for the faithful, like an experimental proof of their beliefs. The cult is not simply a system of signs by which the faith is outwardly translated; it is a collection of the means by which faith is created and re-created periodically. Whether it consists of material acts or mental operations, it is always this which is efficacious.[17]

Hence the primary importance Durkheim attributed to the alternation between ordinary profane activities and ritual occasions in the normal rhythm of social life. Indeed, it was only in *The Elementary Forms* that his conception of the normal society came to full fruition. In and through festive celebration, the symbolic values which guided social life would be reinvigorated and receive the power to prevent unwanted historical change. Anomie could be kept within tolerable bounds only if men were periodically reminded in intense ways of the bases of their common cultural world and their solidarity.[18]

Durkheim's interpretation of religious beliefs was in one sense influenced by this conception of cult. He began with the assumption that the totem was in fact a religious symbol. But his subsequent argument could be applied to any religious symbol. For he went on to affirm that the figurative representation of the sacred object was more sacred than the object (e.g., the plant or animal species) itself. From this point on, Plato was

---

[17] *Ibid.*, p. 596.

[18] One aspect of ritual which Durkheim's own devotion to *la vie sérieuse* prevented him from treating adequately was its tolerance of comic relief. He gave little attention to rituals which included buffoonery and even obscene raillery or which inverted established principles of moral sobriety, authority, and hierarchy. Yet these aspects of ritual, which provided controlled and limited outlets for immoral, subversive, and at times unconscious desires, functioned to maintain the solidity of normative paradigms in the rest of social life. They also indicated ways in which religion went beyond moral notions of good and evil.

Durkheim's *maître de penser*. The figurative representation of a sacred object derived its religious quality from a higher source. The totemic emblem received its sacredness through partaking of an archetypical totemic principle. On a still higher level of abstraction, the totemic principle, in turn, related to the Maori concept of mana. Especially in Durkheim's ultimate and essentially moral conception of it, mana might well be compared to Plato's concept of the Good or to the analogous Christian idea of the indwelling of the Holy Spirit in the hearts of the just.

The meaning of the concept of mana and analogous concepts in all cultures remains a point of contention among anthropologists. Robert Henry Codrington, whom Durkheim followed in this respect, defined "mana" thus:

There is a belief in a force altogether distinct from physical power, which acts in all ways for good and evil; and which it is of the greatest advantage to possess or control. This is mana. I think I know what our people mean by it. . . . It is a power or influence, not physical and in a way supernatural; but it shows itself in physical force, or in any kind of power or excellence which a man possesses. This mana is not fixed in anything. . . . All Melanesian religion consists, in fact, in getting this mana for one's self, or getting it used for one's benefit.[19]

[19] Quoted in *Formes élémentaires de la vie religieuse*, pp. 277–278. In his introduction to *Sociologie et anthropologie*, by Marcel Mauss (first pub. 1950; Paris: Presses Universitaires de France, 1968), Claude Lévi-Strauss has given an extremely operational and rather demystified interpretation of mana as a concept similar to what the linguists term the "point zero" of communication. In other words, mana would be a filler concept which indicated a blank space in communication that required further specification for meaning to be imparted. In this sense, mana would be similar to the French *espèce de truc* ("something or other"). This interpretation is a good example of the excessively operational side of Lévi-Strauss and of his tendency to stress similarities among archaic and modern societies, often at the price of reducing things to their lowest common denominator. In the mystique-filled interpretation of Durkheim, on the contrary, mana came close to being the "point infinity" of communication. An interpretation by R. Godfrey Lienhardt comes closer to Durkheim's sense of the term: "*Virtus*, prestige, authority, good fortune, influence, sanctity, luck, are

Mana thus corresponded, in the first instance, to an impersonal force immanent in the world and yet beyond ordinary capacities or processes. It could be related to the notion of cosmic unity and to the feeling of *le merveilleux*. Manifesting itself in exceptional events and powers, it was nonetheless behind the order of the universe, which was not extraordinary in its daily manifestations but wondrous in its totality—and even epiphanous in its details when they were seen in a certain light. In brief, mana represented the unitary source of the sacred, the ecumenical core of all religion. In specific events, beliefs, and rituals, mana became differentiated and separated from the profane. And the reality for which mana stood was the primary object of the ritual attitude of sacred respect and the magical belief in symbolic efficacy. As Durkheim observed:

A Dakota Indian . . . expressed this essential consubstantiality of all sacred things in a language full of relief. "Everything which moves stops here or there at one time or another. The bird which flies stops at one place to make its nest, at another to rest from its flight. The man who walks, stops when he wishes. It is the same with the god [*la divinité*]. The sun, so bright and magnificent, is one place where he stopped. The trees, the animals are other places. The Indian thinks of these places and sends a prayer to them in order to reach the place where the god has stopped and receive assistance and blessings." In other words, the wakan [a term similar in meaning to "mana"] (for

all words which, under certain conditions, give something near the meaning. . . . Mana sometimes means a more than natural virtue or power attaching to some person or thing, different from and independent of the ordinary natural conditions of either. . . . I once had a tame pig which, before heavy rain, would always cut extraordinary capers and squeak and run like mad. . . . All the Maori said that it was a pig possessed of mana: it had more than natural powers and could foretell rain. The mana of a priest . . . is proved by the truth of his predictions. . . . Mana in another sense is the accompaniment of power but not the power itself. . . . This is the chief's mana. . . . The warrior's mana is just a little something more than good fortune" ("Religion," in H. Shapiro, ed., *Man, Culture, and Society* [first pub. 1956; New York: Oxford University Press, 1960], p. 316). Weber's notion of charisma was similar to mana insofar as the latter received expression in an exceptional individual.

this is what he was talking about) comes and goes through the world, and sacred things are the points upon which it alights.[20]

Even more than his analysis of ritual, his interpretation of religious belief revealed the primacy, for Durkheim, of *communitas* in religion. *Communitas* was the living warmth, the effervescent élan which motivated a vision of the world in sacred symbols. And a legitimate structure was a crystallization of *communitas*—its very legitimacy depended on the conservation, in a structured universe, of *communitas* and the *foi vive* it inspired. For it was only through a regulated alternation of *communitas* and structured activity that society achieved normal integration and legitimate stabilization. Just as structure was the stopping point of *communitas*, so *communitas* was the moving force of structure. This was the elementary truth contained in myth and ritual. Once Durkheim's argument reached this point, however, it did not conclude that the root of primitive religion and the essence of all religion was a cosmic intuition of the solidarity of all existence—including the communal identification of man with all "others" in the cosmos. Rather, it turned to the question of the origin of mana (and analogous concepts like wakan) in a fashion which led to the development of a social metaphysic.

Sociology and Epistemology

For the most part, Durkheim's sociological epistemology was a corollary of his social metaphysic. But, as in the case of his theory of religion, one may attempt to extricate other elements of the argument and situate them in the context of his thought as a whole.

The sociology of religion had, in Durkheim's mind, an integral relation to epistemological problems, since he believed that the first "collective representations" were religious in nature.

If philosophy and the sciences were born of religion, it is because religion itself began by taking the place of the sciences and philoso-

[20] *Formes élémentaires de la vie religieuse*, pp. 284–285.

phy. But it has been less frequently noticed that religion did not confine itself to enriching the human mind, formed beforehand, with a certain number of ideas; it contributed to forming the mind itself. Men owe to religion, not only a notable part of the content of their knowledge but also the form in which this knowledge has been elaborated.[21]

In all societies, moreover, the collective representations which formulated elementary types of legitimation had at least a quasi-religious character. Indeed "collective representation," in Durkheim's usage of the term, seemed to cover the gamut from shared verbal behavior based on deeply rooted beliefs, through elaborate "ideologies," to more or less sophisticated theoretical reflections. It primarily referred, however, to the shared model or paradigm which functioned as a mode of explanation and justification in society, especially as the core of the *conscience collective* which he treated in his moral philosophy as *la morale*. It comprised both cognitive and normative elements. With the development of theoretical reflection, and notably with the emergence of sociology, cognitive and normative elements became increasingly differentiated. But they were never entirely disjoined. In his own sociology, for example, the higher-order paradigms of normal and pathological states embodied his idea of the intimate relation of the cognitive and the normative.

One question which Durkheim did not raise was that of the relationship between epistemology and the sociology of knowledge. In one way, this failure was due to his thoroughly classical subordination of epistemology to metaphysic. In another way, however, it was related to the continuity in his thought between epistemology and social psychology. Today the sociology of knowledge is increasingly seen as a branch of social psychology. And its relationship to epistemology has become increasingly problematic. Generally, the following distinction is made: The sociology of knowledge tends, for its own purposes, to identify reality with objects of belief recognized by members of society

[21] *Ibid.*, p. 12.

as exercising constraint over the will. Knowledge is equated with a sense of certainty about empirical beliefs. Epistemology, in its culturally relevant forms, operates at a deeper level of analysis. It might, for example, pose the problem of the foundations of sociology itself. In other words, its paradigms are applicable at the level of the presuppositions that are implicit in the articulation of experience. This might be seen as a matter of degree. A second distinction is more qualitative. Epistemology poses the problem of validity.[22]

Thus one might differentiate between epistemology and the sociology of knowledge in terms of levels of analysis and the problem of validity and truth. But the attempt to escalate a distinction into a disjunction or even a working division of labor —e.g., by conceiving the sociology of knowledge as an empirical science and epistemology as a philosophical concern—runs into difficulty in such concepts as alienation and false consciousness. Moreover, epistemological problems are implied in such matters as the social and historical conditions which favor the emergence of truth. The Marxist tradition, which prompts certain comparisons with Durkheim's thought concerning the dialectic of the sociology of knowledge and epistemology, has generated notorious conundrums in this respect. Yet the sociologist who disavows epistemological problems either avoids concepts like alienation and false consciousness (often with conservative implications) or surreptitiously introduces through the back door philosophical issues which he showed out through the front.

Durkheim was avowedly preoccupied with a very elementary kind of analysis, and he was even more palpably concerned with the problem of validity. Indeed, perhaps the central issue treated in a course he gave after the publication of *The Elementary Forms* (and subsequently reconstructed in the book *Pragmatisme et sociologie*) was epistemological. Here he opposed a

---

[22] For a similar formulation of the relationship between epistemology and the sociology of knowledge, see Peter Berger and Thomas Luckmann, *The Social Construction of Reality* (Garden City, N.Y.: Doubleday, 1966).

classically "hard" conception of truth to the "logical utilitarianism" of pragmatists who equated truth with practical success or the satisfying illusion. He asserted the impersonal and compelling nature of truth, which imposed itself with rational conviction. "Truth is a norm for thought, just as the moral ideal is a norm for conduct." [23] Moreover, he flatly rejected an invariant correlation of truth with happiness.

Truth is often painful. It may disorganize thought and trouble the serenity of the spirit. When a man recognizes it, he is at times obliged to transform his entire mental organization: this provokes a crisis which leaves him disconcerted and disabled. If, for example, in adulthood he suddenly realizes that his religious beliefs lack solidity, he may collapse morally. His intellectual and emotional life is paralyzed. . . . Thus it is far from the case that truth is always attractive and seductive. Quite often, it resists us, opposes our desires, and has a hard quality about it.[24]

In his own sociology, the basic distinction between normality and pathology provided a critical apparatus which involved the problem of validity. In Marxian terms, a pathological state was

[23] *Pragmatisme et sociologie* (Paris: Librairie Philosophique J. Vrin, 1955), p. 197.

[24] *Ibid.*, p. 155. Within the context of his social metaphysic, Durkheim retained an emphasis upon the role of truth in his conception of things. "If society is a specific reality, it is not an empire within an empire. It is a part of nature, and indeed its highest manifestation. Now it is impossible that nature should differ radically from case to case in regard to what is most essential. The fundamental relations that exist among things—those which it is precisely the function of the categories to express—cannot be essentially dissimilar in the different realms. If . . . they are more clearly disengaged in the social world, it is nevertheless impossible that they should not be found elsewhere, though in more disguised forms" (*Formes élémentaires de la vie religieuse*, pp. 25–26). As a defense of the universal applicability and truth of categories which were presumed to be specifically social in origin, this piece of argument was unfortunately about as cogent as the idea that a photographer takes good photographs because he is himself photogenic. Within the context of Durkheim's social metaphysic, however, the problem was similar to the theological question about whether something is true because it comes from God or whether God created it because it is true.

an alienated empirical reality which gave rise to ideology as a form of false consciousness. In *The Rules,* Durkheim formulated the conception of false consciousness in terms of Descartes's notion of *praenotiones* and Bacon's idea of *idola.* "As products of ordinary experience, their object is to place our actions in harmony with the environing world. They are formed by practice and for it. Now a representation can play this role usefully while being theoretically false." [25]

Unlike Marx, however, Durkheim did not relate ideology as a form of false consciousness to class domination and exploitation. Thus, he did not discuss the continuity between normative legitimation and cognition in the distorted form of collective misrepresentations which attempted to present a pathological state as if it was normal, e.g., by construing the interest of one group as the good of society as a whole. As a consequence, he failed to treat the function of ideology in the stabilization of a pathological social order. This failure was especially significant in

[25] *Les Règles de la méthode sociologique* (15th ed.; Paris: Presses Universitaires de France, 1963), p. 16. Compare Karl Mannheim's conception of ideology as false consciousness: "The concept 'ideology' reflects the one discovery which emerged from political conflict, namely, that ruling groups can in their thinking become so intensively interest-bound to a situation that they are simply no longer able to see certain facts which would undermine their sense of domination. There is implicit in the word 'ideology' the insight that in certain situations the collective unconscious of certain groups obscures the real condition of society both to itself and to others and thereby stabilizes it" (*Ideology and Utopia* [New York: Harcourt, Brace, 1936], p. 40). Robert Paul Wolff provides this pertinent gloss: "Ideology is thus self-serving in two senses. First, and most simply, it is the refusal to recognize unpleasant facts which might require a less flattering evaluation of a policy or institution or which might undermine one's claim to a right of domination. For example, slave-owners in the antebellum South refused to acknowledge that the slaves themselves were unhappy. The implication was that if they were, slavery would be harder to justify. Secondly, ideological thinking is a denial of unsettling or revolutionary factors in society on the principle of the self-confirming prophecy that the more stable everyone believes the situation to be, the more stable it actually becomes" ("Beyond Tolerance," in *A Critique of Pure Tolerance* [Boston: Beacon Press, 1965], pp. 39–40).

view of Marx's conception of religion as a prominent form of ideological distortion and mystification in an exploitative society.

Certain things, however, seemed clear in the development of Durkheim's thought as a whole. The truth would be unsettling and subversive in a pathological situation which had been ideologically accepted as legitimate. But it would be essential to an objective analysis of that situation and to the reconstruction of society on a normal basis. Rational means to effect a passage from pathology to normality varied with historical conditions. Durkheim found modern society to be significantly pathological, but he did not believe violent revolution to be necessary or desirable for the achievement of structural change. In a state of normality, moreover, the knowledge of the truth would offer the most authentic basis for legitimation of the existing order and the means to confine anomie to a marginal status. For in the normal state, the normative and cognitive paradigms which constituted a coherent world view and integrated society as a whole could be justly conceived as an applied function of the truth. In all societies, this state would involve an optimal combination of community and reciprocity, and a relationship between values accepted as sacred and average performance in daily living which did not pass beyond the limits of "standard deviation."

Durkheim's epistemological assumptions revealed the most profound sense in which he was both a structuralist and a conservative. In his mind, there existed a comprehensive correspondence between the foundations of truth and knowledge in general and the prevalence of order and solidarity in society. Essential to human existence was the institution of normative and interpretive paradigms which made sense of shared experience and simultaneously provided the background against which to evaluate change.

These considerations make possible an estimation of Durkheim's relation to Bergson and the pragmatists. Early in his life, Durkheim was cast in the role of the archenemy not only of Tarde but of Bergson. His insistence on formal structures of obligation and, more broadly, his Cartesianized, neo-Kantian brand of rationalism were often developed with implicit reference to Bergson as the modern exemplar of mysticism and anti-rational intuitionism. In his later thought, however, Durkheim was partially influenced by Bergson in two restricted but important ways. First, Durkheim recognized the role of "collective effervescence" as an ambivalent *élan vital* which was necessary in the passage from pathology to normality. Second, he saw that in the normal state itself, communal spontaneity was to be reconciled with duty, just as "collective effervescence" retained its relevance as a spiritual milieu for a generous and expansive rationalism. But Durkheim always rejected the ideological glorification of change, mobility, empirical fluidity, individual transcendence, existential turmoil, and "buzzing confusion"— in brief, the symptoms of anomie—as mystical ends in themselves. In a pathological state of society, the primary function of rational change was to put a stop to uncontrolled, rampant, runaway change. In a normal state, the value of change was dialectically related to the predominance of order, and it had value only insofar as it remained marginal in incidence and significance.

In *The Elementary Forms of the Religious Life,* Durkheim's manifest goal was to define the elements of truth in religion.

In fact, it is an essential postulate of sociology that a human institution cannot rest upon error and lies. Otherwise it could not last. If it were not founded on the nature of things, it would have encountered in things a resistance over which it could not have triumphed. So when we commence the study of primitive religions, it is with the conviction that they hold to reality and express it. This principle will be seen to recur time and again in the course of the analyses and discussions which follow, and the reproach which we make against the schools from which we have separated ourselves is that they have ignored it. No doubt, when only the letter of the formulae is considered, these religious beliefs and practices seem disconcerting, and one is tempted to attribute them to some sort of deep-rooted aberration. But one must know how to go underneath the symbol to the reality which it represents and which gives it its true meaning.[26]

Within his own frame of reference, this conception of religion meant that Durkheim was defining religion and its role in terms of the normal state of society. At times, however, he seemed to generalize his viewpoint so that it applied to all states of society. At the very least, he placed his conception of the truth of religion within the context of his optimistic belief in an emergent evolutionary straining toward consensual normality in all society. Thus *The Elementary Forms,* taken as an isolated work, might be interpreted to have either orthodox conservative or liberal implications, although its conclusion made it obvious that Durkheim conceived normality in modern society as a goal of action. One basic reason for the imprecision of *The Elementary Forms* in its treatment of concrete problems was the increasing importance of abstract social metaphysic in Durkheim's thought. In the context of his thought as a whole and its application to modern society, however, he may be seen as employing his study of archaic religions to complete his idea of the normal state and to derive a general conception of ends in basic structural change.

The most significant and influential general feature of Durkheim's approach was his interpretation of epistemology as the analysis, on the most fundamental level, of the structural articulations of cultural experience (and their relation to anomie). The object of epistemological analysis in this sense was to unearth the more or less related set of paradigms or categories which, in varying combinations, informed symbolic experience expressed in word and action. The intimate link between an epistemologically oriented sociology and philosophy was manifest. Sociology would culminate in what might be termed (in the expression of Ernst Cassirer) a philosophy of symbolic forms.

[26] *Formes élémentaires de la vie religieuse,* p. 3.

The promise in this conception of epistemology as the archae-
ology of cultural experience was formulated by Marcel Mauss:
"We must first of all draw up as complete as possible a catalogue
of categories, beginning with those which mankind is known to
have employed. It will then be seen that there have been, and
that there still are, many dead moons, and others pale or obscure,
in the firmament of reason." [27]

This perspective enjoined a correlation of epistemology with
society and culture. The attempt to limit epistemological inquiry to an investigation of the mind of the isolated individual
was a symptom of ideological distortion. From Durkheim's point
of view, solipsism and the problem of other minds might be
seen, not as components of an epistemological theory, but as
problems for epistemological investigation and philosophical
criticism. They were elements of the same pathological context
of atomistic individualism that included utilitarian ethics, economic self-interest, and narrowly empiricist methodology. Isolation was the limiting case of the common medium of all symbolic
systems: communication. Only sensation was confined to the
individual organism; but symbolism, and especially the concept,
was an object of communication.

A concept is not my concept. It is common to me and other men or,
in any case, it can be communicated to them. But I cannot make a
sensation pass from my consciousness into the consciousness of
another; it is narrowly bound up with my organism and my personality, and it cannot be detached from them. . . . By themselves individual consciousnesses are closed to one another. They can communicate only by means of signs which translate their internal states.
For the commerce which is established among them to be able to
culminate in communion, i.e., in a fusion of all particular sentiments
in a common sentiment, there must be signs expressing these sentiments which themselves are fused in a sole and unique resultant. It
is the appearance of this resultant which enables individuals to know

[27] "Psychologie et sociologie: Extrait de la conclusion du débat," in
Sociologie et anthropologie, p. 309.

that they are united and which makes them conscious of their moral unity.[28]

This viewpoint gave special importance to the socialization process in epistemological investigations. For in the flow of communication which made the individual a member of society, there would be transmitted in operative form the basic categories of experience and the anomic inconsistencies which typified social life. This did not necessarily imply that the individual was a passive receptacle of traditional paradigms and creative interaction. But it did mean that he could form his own ideas only against the background of common experience or common disorientation. And those ideas would have to be addressed to common problems and assume assimilable form if they were to have more than idiosyncratic or psychopathological meaning.

Crucial for Durkheim was the basis in society of all major symbolic systems and modes of communication. This idea, which raised problems at the intersection of epistemology and social psychology which Durkheim did not treat, applied to the natural sciences as well as to religion or morality.

In reality, science is something pre-eminently social, however great the role of individuals may be in it. It is social because its methods and techniques are the work of tradition, and they constrain the person with an authority comparable to that of rules of law or morals. They are truly institutions which apply to thought, just as juridical and political institutions are obligatory methods of action. In addition, science is social because it utilizes notions which dominate all thought and in which all of civilization is condensed: the categories.[29]

The role of neo-Kantianism in Durkheim's thought was revealed in the significance he attributed to the categories. "If the mind is a synthetic expression of the world, the system of categories is a synthetic expression of the human mind." [30] The cate-

[28] Formes élémentaires de la vie religieuse, pp. 619, 329.

[29] Review of Wilhelm Jerusalem's "Soziologie des Erkennis," in Année sociologique, XI (1906–1909), 44.

[30] "Sociologie religieuse et théorie de la connaissance," Revue de métaphysique et de morale, XVII (1909), 757.

gories, for Durkheim, were the fundamental logical institutions of the human mind conceived as a sociocultural reality with an organic base. By identifying the category with his own notion of the collective representation, he simultaneously grounded it in culture and society and expanded its range of application to encompass all forms of symbolic experience. "De quelques formes primitives de classification" (*Primitive Classification*, 1901), written by Durkheim in collaboration with Mauss, had the virtue of demonstrating, with some oversimplification, the systematic and meaningful character of classificatory systems in archaic societies. Despite the tendentiousness of his own ultimate scheme of interpretation, the fundamental step Durkheim took was to open up to epistemological reflection the entire gamut of human cultures and symbolically informed systems, including social structure and religion.

Although the postulates of his own social metaphysic jeopardized his effort, Durkheim further intended his conception of epistemology to serve as a transcending (in the Hegelian sense of *Aufhebung*) of empiricism and apriorism.

The rationalism which is immanent in a sociological theory of knowledge is an intermediary between empiricism and classical apriorism. For the first, the categories are purely artificial constructions; for the second, they are, on the contrary, natural givens. For us, they are in a sense works of art, but of an art which imitates nature with a perfection susceptible of growing without limit.[31]

The category, in other words, was neither a purely nominalistic label nor the natural scaffolding of the mind. It was simultaneously a sociocultural given and the product of human activity— a historical monument built to withstand the erosive pressure of anomie. On the whole, however, Durkheim remained closer to the apriorist side of the classical antagonism, and his social metaphysic revealed the extent to which he was unable to transcend dualism through a more dialectical mode of thought. He

---

[31] *Formes élémentaires de la vie religieuse*, p. 26, n. 2.

was possessed of an inordinate sense of the conceptual presence of categories. This was indicated in his specific interpretation of structural analysis and the importance of the concept. "To conceive a thing is simultaneously to grasp more adequately its essential elements and to situate it within a whole; for each civilization has its organized system of concepts which characterize it. Before this system of notions, the individual mind is in the same situation as the Nous of Plato before the world of Ideas." [32]

In *The Elementary Forms,* the problem of determining the essential constituents of religion joined that of comparing science to symbolic systems prevalent in archaic societies. Yet in this respect Durkheim's argument was almost entirely subordinated to his social metaphysic. As a preface to the discussion of the metaphysical chapter of Durkheimism, it is interesting to compare the recent attempt of Claude Lévi-Strauss to address himself to problems similar to those of Durkheim.

Although Lévi-Strauss refuses to admit a philosophical intention, his book *La Pensée sauvage* (*The Savage Mind*) might well be taken as a study in epistemology. In this work, Lévi-Strauss sought out a structure of the mind which was pre-eminently characteristic of archaic societies but which represented a permanent given, or at least an ever present possibility, in human experience. Thus the object of investigation was not the thought of the savages but savage thought as a symbolic form or archetypical mode of articulating experience. The English term "savage thought" (and even more so, "the savage mind," with its resurrection of Lucien Lévy-Bruhl and his penchant for unbridgeable antipathies between the primitive and the modern) obviously fails to capture the relevance and symbolic weight of the French expression. *La pensée sauvage* refers ambiguously to culture (a structure of the human mind) and to nature (to a species of flower, the wild pansy). Thus it not only literally denotes, but metaphorically expresses, the type of comprehensive paradigm that correlates culture and nature.

[32] *Ibid.,* p. 622.

Within *la pensée sauvage,* one may distinguish two dialectically related levels, or (in the Hegelian sense) "moments." *La pensée sauvage* constitutes *une théorie du sensible* or a structure of perception, but it operates simultaneously on two levels: the literal and the metaphoric. Often its meticulous classifications of natural phenomena can be correlated with those of positive sciences like botany, which approach reality on the same strategic level of perception. In all cases, it manifests a close and sustained attention to natural phenomena and processes which are open to sensory perception. Moreover, its technology, e.g., in metal working, reveals the product, not of chance discovery, but of experimentation. In this sense, the "Neolithic revolution," which brought the arts of civilization like agriculture, pottery, and weaving which still remain as a foundation of modern culture, was an achievement of *la pensée sauvage.*

But observation, within the context of *la pensée sauvage,* is not separated from other levels of experience to result in a positivistic notion of nature. Nor is technology seen as an expression of unilateral domination over nature by man; it is rather a mediator between culture and nature. In other words, both observation and applied knowledge are implicated in more encompassing structures which place them within a broader scope of normative regulation, imaginative mutuality, and emotional response. "Enveloping terms, which confounded in a sort of surreality the objects of perception and the emotions they aroused, preceded analytic reduction in the strict sense."[33] Notions are "ensnared" in images like birds in quicklime, and they imply an intricate network of correlations and correspondences among various levels of experience. The ulimate logical intention of this mode of thought is cosmic. And prominent in the attempt to classify the elements of the known universe in a meaningful manner are correlations between social and natural phenomena. "The mythical system of representations serves to establish relations of

[33] Claude Lévi-Strauss, *Le Totémisme aujourd'hui* (Paris: Presses Universitaires de France, 1962), p. 146.

homology between natural conditions and social conditions. Or more exactly, it defines a law of equivalence among meaningful contrasts which are situated on several levels: geographical, meteorological, zoological, botanical, technical, economic, social, ritual, religious, philosophical." [34]

From this point of view, the intimate relations between religion and magic within the context of *la pensée sauvage* become manifest. They represent complementary directions taken by the imaginative mutuality of man and nature.

If it can in a sense be said that religion consists of a *humanization of natural laws* and magic of a *naturalization of human actions*—the treatment of certain human actions *as if* they were an integral part of physical determinism—this is not to say that these are alternatives or stages in an evolution. The anthropomorphism of nature (of which religion consists) and the physiomorphism of man (by which we have defined magic) constitute two components which are always given, and vary only in proportion. . . . Each implies the other. There is no religion without magic, any more than there is magic without at least a trace of religion. The notion of a supernature exists only for a humanity which attributes supernatural powers to itself and in return ascribes the powers of its superhumanity to nature. [35]

We have already observed that for Lévi-Strauss totemism is not the global institution invariably combining kinship and religion that it was for Durkheim. It is an instance of the general logical principle of differentiation and integration. Within the context of *la pensée sauvage*, totemism posits a metaphoric homology between a binary opposition of natural species (the totems) and a binary opposition of human groups. This ordering principle is available for a complex variety of uses in society. But its usage as a principle of kinship may not coincide with religious belief, and vice versa. From Lévi-Strauss's viewpoint, the attempt to explain away facts by unfounded evolutionary hypotheses has no relation to scientific theory. The theoretical problem, at a

[34] Claude Lévi-Strauss, *La Pensée sauvage* (Paris: Plon, 1962), p. 123.
[35] *Ibid.*, pp. 292–293.

higher level of understanding, is to discover the higher-order paradigms which account for the actual correlations among aspects of cultural life or represent possible variations of them.

For Lévi-Strauss, all thought employs the same formal logical principles, such as opposition and correlation. In this sense, no thought is "prelogical." But significant differences do exist both between symbolic forms and between their actual prevalence in different societies. In the principal fields of modern life characterized by technology and bureaucracy, *la pensée sauvage* is rather wilted; it flourishes largely in marginal areas, such as certain forms of art. The level of concrete perception has diminished importance, and it is difficult to conceive of truly credible paradigms which integrate or at least relate the literal and the metaphoric in shared experience. Positive science appears as a "domesticated" form of thought which approaches reality on a more sophisticated strategic level—that of conceptual formulation and mathematical notation—and it results in a more operational knowledge of nature. But the price it often pays is the alienation of man from more inclusive structures of experience. Symbolism, in general, tends to become formally rationalized and emotionally neutralized.

This brief discussion of Lévi-Strauss's thought is intended merely to indicate the areas of vital interest touched upon in Durkheim's idea of a sociological epistemology. The problems which I have superficially treated did receive some attention from Durkheim, but his ideas remained disparate and were given a semblance of coherence only through the medium of his social metaphysic.[36]

[36] Durkheim recognized the possibility of a symbolic logic which focused upon the common formal principles of all thought. (See *Les Règles de la méthode sociologique,* p. xviii.) But, as early as *The Division of Labor* and *The Rules,* he asserted the particular importance of concrete and informed observation in symbolic systems that were prominent in archaic societies. (See *Les Règles,* p. 15, and *De La Division du travail social,* 7th ed., p. 275.) At times he recognized the existence of correlations between society and nature in the symbolism of archaic societies. In *The Elementary Forms* itself, he observed that the "confusions" in archaic thought did not stem from an animistic, anthropomorphic instinct which immoderately

Yet Durkheim combined qualities which have become rare in influential sectors of recent French thought: an aversion for the obscure and a capacity for true belief. In a thinker like Lévi-Strauss, one at times senses an unresolved tension between hu-

extended features of humanity to all of nature: "Primitive men . . . have not conceived the world in their own image any more than they have conceived themselves in the world's image: they have done both at the same time. Into the idea they have formed of things, they have undoubtedly made human elements enter; but into the idea they have formed of themselves, they have introduced elements coming from things" (*Les Formes élémentaires de la vie religieuse*, p. 337). See also *De La Division du travail social*, p. 273, and *Formes élémentaires*, p. 320. Durkheim apparently did not sense the contradiction between these ideas and his own social metaphysic which interpreted religious symbols and the categories as derivative projections or "superpositions" of the specifically social. Yet he was always clear about the systematic quality of thought in archaic societies. (See his and Marcel Mauss's *Primitive Classification* [Chicago: University of Chicago Press, 1963], pp. 77–78, 81, a translation of "De quelques formes primitives de classification," *Année sociologique*, VI [1901–1902].) With some inconsistency in his formulations, Durkheim also saw the integration of cognition, practice, imagination, and emotion in comprehensive forms of symbolism. (See, for example, *Pragmatisme et sociologie*, p. 161; *Primitive Classification*, p. 85–86; and *De La Division du travail social*, p. 69.) The notion of a comprehensive ordering or codification of experience in certain symbolic systems was the most important and valid element of his idea of a "primitive nebula," which is treated in another context in Chapter 3, above. Moreover, Durkheim rejected Lévy-Bruhl's notion of the "pre-logical" character of primitive thought. For Durkheim, there was no gap between primitive and modern thought or between the logic of religious thought and that of scientific thought. The contents or terms employed might differ, but the mental processes were essentially the same. "The explanations of contemporary science are surer of being more objective because they are more methodical and because they rest on more carefully controlled observations, but they do not differ in nature from those which satisfy primitive thought" (*Formes élémentaires*, pp. 340–341). Finally, Durkheim conceived the difference between the experimentalism and theoretical falsifiability of scientific propositions, on the one hand, and the symbolic necessity and "impermeability to experience" (or circularity) of myth and ritual, on the other, not in strictly logical, but in psychological terms. Between the commitment to a ritual and the unwillingness to abandon a well-tested scientific theory in the face of initial counterevidence, there was, for him, only a difference of degree (see *Formes élémentaires*, pp. 515–516).

man warmth and formalism, clarity and obscurantist preciosity, a feeling for the interplay between the literal and the metaphoric, and a somewhat technocratic fascination for the manipulation of analytically reduced "logical operators." [37] Durkheim's social metaphysic was his surrogate for religious belief. Unfortunately, in confiding in something as palpably ineffective as social metaphysic, Durkheim dissipated both his massive intelligence and his genuine spiritual intensity. From him one might have expected a more convincing attempt to forge a synthesis between uncoordinated elements of the modern experience and the heritage of devaluated symbolic forms.

Social Metaphysic

Like other comparable systems of the time—e.g., those of Marx or Freud—Durkheim's social metaphysic ultimately conceived of interpretation in the form of reductionism. It presented a truncated and impoverished notion of reality which identified adequate analysis with the sacrifice of the richness and diversity of human experience on the altar of a unilateral fixation. To all problems in history and philosophy, Durkheim felt justified in offering what came in time to be a prefabricated and mechanical "sociological" solution whose very predictability and facile applicability were indications of superficiality and circularity. The operational upshot of Durkheimian social metaphysic was the methodology of social functionalism. This interpretive schema accounted for all symbolically informed phenomena in terms of the contrast between social reality and cultural "dress." In other words, human experience was interpreted as if society (often a vague concept in itself) was the basic reality and all other

[37] Compare the criticism Edmund Leach has made of Lévi-Strauss: "He fails to allow for the fact that, whereas the symbols used by mathematicians are emotionally neutral—ix is not more *exciting* than x just because i is an imaginary number—the concrete symbols used in primitive thought are heavily loaded with taboo valuations. Consequently psychological factors such as 'evasion' and 'repression' tend to confuse the logical symmetries" (*New York Review of Books*, IX [Oct. 12, 1967], 8).

aspects of culture were derivative or secondary manifestations.

The methodology of social functionalism was to be found even in theorists who rejected other elements of Durkheim's heritage, e.g., the relative de-emphasis of social conflict and its functions. For example, Edmund Leach, as late as 1954, felt justified in prefacing his important work, *The Political Systems of Highland Burma*, with the declaration:

My view here is that ritual action and belief are alike to be understood as forms of symbolic statement about the social order. . . . Culture provides the form, the "dress" of the social situation. As far as I am concerned, the cultural situation is a given factor, it is a product and an accident of history. I do not know *why* Kachin women go hatless with bobbed hair before they are married, but assume a turban afterwards, any more than I know *why* English women put a ring on a particular finger to denote the same change in social status; all I am interested in is that in this Kachin context the assumption of a turban by a woman does have this symbolic significance. It is a statement about the status of the woman.[38]

The lasting achievement of Lévi-Strauss in anthropology was the awareness that symbolic systems, especially in archaic societies, might have meaningful status and coherence; that their reduction to social factors (or utilitarian needs, economics, biology, and so forth) might itself be a reflection of modern ethnocentrism; and that the problem was, rather, the relation-

[38] Boston: Beacon Press, 1964 (first pub. 1954), pp. 14, 16. Leach has changed his position, largely under the influence of Lévi-Strauss. A. R. Radcliffe-Brown, who is himself largely responsible for the influence of Durkheim in Anglo-American social anthropology, nonetheless criticized Durkheim's theory of religion in these terms: "In every human society there inevitably exist two different and in a certain sense conflicting conceptions of nature. One of them, the naturalistic, is implicit everywhere in technology, and in our twentieth century European culture, with its great development of control over natural phenomena, has become explicit and preponderant in our thought. The other, which might be called the mythological or spiritualistic conception, is implicit in myth and in religion, and often becomes explicit in philosophy" (*Structure and Function in Primitive Society* [London: Cohen & West, 1952], p. 130).

ships among various levels of experience. But social functionalism was the operational "rationalization" (in the Weberian sense) of Durkheim's thought, which consciously employed the language of perspectives, interests, and arbitrary initial definitions. Durkheim conceived of social functionalism as a subordinate part of a genuinely metaphysical view. Durkheim not only retained the classical commitment to truth and realistic definition, but his search for the reality of things was conveyed in an increasingly mystical form of discourse which he used to recount an elaborate myth of origins and an ideology of modern society.

In *The Elementary Forms of the Religious Life,* the argument that religion was the origin of culture culminated in the idea that society was the origin and essence of religion. Since the first ideas of men were representations of religious reality, society was consequently also the origin of the categories. In *The Elementary Forms,* the piece of argument directly addressed to the identity of God and society was little more than a form of *pars pro toto* legerdemain followed by a string of rhetorical questions:

[The totem] is the outward and visible form of what we have called the totemic principle or god. But it is also the symbol of the determinate society called the clan. It is its flag; it is the sign by which each clan distinguishes itself from the others, the visible mark of its personality, a mark borne by everything which is a part of the clan under any title whatsoever, men, beasts, or things. So if it is at once the symbol of the god and of the society, is that not because the god and the society are only one? How could the emblem of the group have been able to become the figure of this quasi divinity if the group and the divinity were two distinct entities? The god of the clan, the totemic principle, can therefore be nothing else than the clan itself, personified and represented to the imagination under the visible form of the animal or vegetable which serves as totem.[39]

Thus Durkheim felt entitled to conclude, not only that religious belief and ritual had social functions, or even social aspects,

[39] *Formes élémentaires de la vie religieuse,* p. 236.

but that they were specifically, or *sui generis*, social in essential reality and origin. Of ritual, he wrote:

Everything leads us back to the same idea: it is that rituals are above all else the means by which the social group reaffirms itself periodically. From this, we may perhaps arrive at a hypothetical reconstruction of the manner in which the totemic cult must primitively have been born. Men who feel themselves united in part through bonds of blood but still more through a community of interests and traditions assemble and become conscious of their moral unity. . . . The moral efficacy of ritual, which is real, led men to believe in its physical efficacy, which is imaginary. . . . The truly useful effects which ceremonies produce are like the experimental justification of the elementary practices of which they are composed.[40]

The full sweep and nature of the argument in *The Elementary Forms* are better understood if one sees it in the light of Durkheim's preparatory articles on related problems, especially his study of the incest taboo.[41] Durkheim began with the root assumption that social solidarity and social structure were ultimate realities and explanatory principles. Continuity with his earlier thought was embodied in the belief that community was prior to the structural differentiations which stemmed from it. Beginning with the idea of a group of men who had some sense of their moral and social community, Durkheim introduced the idea of "collective effervescence" as a transitional force which led to the genesis of religious cults. Collective effervescence was in this sense a sacralizing, mana-like élan which intensified the sense of community until it attained religious proportions and propelled men from the state of nature into that of culture and society. In his article on the incest taboo, Durkheim was even more specific in his elaboration of a sociologistic myth of origins. Seized by an intensified sense of their own solidarity, the group

[40] *Ibid.*, pp. 553, 513.
[41] "La Prohibition de l'inceste et ses origines," *Année sociologique*, I (1896–1897), 1–70; trans. Edward Sagarin, *Incest: The Origins and the Development of the Incest Taboo* (New York: Lyle Stuart, 1963).

selected a totem to serve as its emblem. Its unity was solidified by the myth of a common totemic ancestor whose blood was imagined to flow in the veins of the clan. The association between the imaginary mythical blood of the communal clan and the very real menstrual blood of its female members provoked horror at the idea of clan endogamy. Thus, although totemism was in fact a restricted phenomenon and the prohibition of incest a universal phenomenon, the myth of origins which led from social solidarity to totemism caused Durkheim to believe that incest derived from a specific totemic taboo. Evolutionary ideas, in this way, took on a fully mythical cast.

Apparent in Durkheim's social metaphysic of religion was the extent to which his argument depended on modern presuppositions which in fact were typical of one important dimension of his thought as a whole. From the very outset, Durkheim analytically dissociated intelligible reality into a realm of material nature and an autonomous realm of social facts. He conceived this realm of social facts in "hyperspiritual" terms and identified it increasingly with the object of idealistic philosophy. In the extremely dualistic Cartesianized neo-Kantian tendency of Durkheim's thought, man was *homo duplex*—a composite of a body and an ideal social self.

Durkheim did not devote sufficient attention to the interactions between body and mind, even when they could be formulated literally, e.g., genetically or psychosomatically. Possible metaphoric relations often seemed to be completely beyond his ken. And his analysis of the symbolic efficacy of ritual neglected to consider the very real effects of religion and magic on the organic and psychological processes of the believer.

Epistemologically, Durkheim's dualistic conception of human nature led him to restrict his attention to sensation, which he correlated with the "individual" body, and the concept, which he correlated with the specifically social. This frame of reference was fully developed in his 1898 article, "Individual Representations and Collective Representations." The "individual representation" was the sensation. The "collective representation" was the concept. Durkheim devoted no attention in his idea of epistemology to perception, imagination, emotion, personal uniqueness, and the relation of thought to action. This omission created a logical gap between his epistemological presuppositions and such of his methodological notions as "social morphology" (which in general was comparable to the anthropological notion of "material culture"), sentiment, anomie, the role of the individual in culture, and the relation of theory and practice in the passage from pathology to normality. It also accounted for his curious conception of economics as the study of the individual and the material—a notion which did little justice to the problem of economic institutions. In brief, the extremely dualistic assumptions of his social metaphysic and its epistemological corollaries subordinated a dialectical conception of experience to a rigid idea of disjunctive antinomies.

When Durkheim came to devote special attention to the sacred, he was faced with a problem of classification created by the presuppositions of one element of his thought. He solved it by placing the sacred in the category of the specifically social and interpreting its various manifestations as "superpositions" of the social and the "hyperspiritual." In his "Le Dualisme de la nature humaine et ses conditions sociales" (1914), which he first presented as a speech to his spiritualistic, neo-Kantian peer group at the Société Française de Philosophie, Durkheim argued that the basic contribution of *The Elementary Forms* was to show that the sociology of religion provided confirmation for the traditional idea of a dualism between body and spirit in man. In other words, Durkheim asserted that his interpretation of religion revealed that the mind-body dualism was an essential characteristic of human nature—a viewpoint which seems to raise the specific (if not the pathological) to the universal. Thus Durkheim's primary line of development in an increasingly idealistic direction was to be found in his growing reliance on antinomies—a reliance which culminated in the idea of *homo duplex.* He conceived of the passage from nature to culture as the spiritual arousal of the group, like the conglomerate body of some incredible Frankenstein monster, through the electric charge of "collective effervescence" which mysteriously generated the "hyperspiritual" ideals of civilization.

But both in his emphasis on sacred community and in his sociological (or sociologistic) reformulation of the idea of *homo duplex,* Durkheim's thought represented a reaction against extreme secularization in modern culture. Metaphors and imagination, excluded from other spheres of his experience, flooded Durkheim's idea of the social through the narrow channel left open by his conceptualistic and spiritualistic tendencies. With increasing abandon, Durkheim gave himself, not to developing concrete images of social life, but to composing abstract conceptual prose poems about the true nature of society. The sacred was society expressed metaphorically. Incarnation found its reality in the process of socialization. Roles assumed the quality of sanctified callings. And the educator had a truly priestlike function as the intermediary between society and its members.

The believer bows down before God because it is from God that he believes he receives his being, and particularly his mental being, his soul. We have the same reasons to feel this sentiment for the collectivity.[42]

What indeed is discipline if not society conceived as what commands us, dictates orders, and gives us laws? And in the second element of morality—the attachment to a group—it is again society that we find, but conceived this time as a good and desirable thing, an end which attracts us, an ideal to be realized. In the former sense, it appears to us as an authority which contains us, fixes limits which resist our infringements, and before which we bow with religious respect; in the latter sense, it is a friendly and protecting power, a nursing mother, from whom we receive the principal part of our intellectual and moral substance and toward whom our wills are turned

[42] *Sociologie et philosophie* (first pub. 1924; Paris: Presses Universitaires de France, 1963), p. 108.

in an élan of gratitude and love. In one case, it is like the jealous and fearful god, the severe legislator, who does not permit his orders to be transgressed; in the other, it is the divinity who cares for us and for whom the believer sacrifices himself with joy.

What constitutes the authority which colors so readily the word of the priest is the elevated idea he has of his mission; for he speaks in the name of a god in which he believes and toward which he feels closer than the crowd of the profane. The lay teacher can and must have something of this sentiment. He too is the organ of a great moral person which transcends him; this is society. Just as the priest is the interpreter of his god, so the teacher is the interpreter of the great moral ideas of his time and country.[43]

In short, society has "all that it takes [*tout ce qu'il faut*]" to inspire the idea of the sacred, "because it is to its members what a god is to believers." [44] Durkheim perceived social metaphysics as the symbolic groundwork for a conception of social ethics which allowed for sentiment and emotion.

One will notice the analogy between this line of reasoning and that by which Kant demonstrates God. Kant postulates God because, without this hypothesis, morality is unintelligible. We postulate a society specifically distinct from individuals because otherwise morality is without an object and duty without an anchor point. . . . Between God and society one must choose. . . . I may add that, from my point of view, this choice leaves me indifferent, because I see in divinity only society transfigured and conceived symbolically.[45]

Thus, from beginning to end, morality constituted the center of Durkheim's thought. And he believed that his substantively rational conception of morality was not undermined but fortified and completed by his social philosophy. Some quasi-religious basis was necessary for all morality and social solidarity. But the beliefs that justified religion had increasingly lost credibility in

[43] *L'Education morale* (first pub. 1934; Paris: Presses Universitaires de France, 1963), pp. 78, 72–73.
[44] *Formes élémentaires de la vie religieuse,* p. 245.
[45] *Sociologie et philosophie,* pp. 74–75.

the modern world. For Durkheim, sociology itself had the task of providing a theoretical foundation for religion. Thus Durkheim made the almost Thomistic effort to reconcile reason and faith, but in a secularized fashion adapted to the needs of modern society.

The vision of a society based upon truth and justice and able to reconcile reason and the ritual attitude of sacred respect was vital to Durkheim's idea of structural reform in modern society. It was also important for his idea of the special mission of sociology in his own France. Social mystique was intended as a means of strengthening resolve and inspiring action for the achievement and maintenance of the normal society. In *The Elementary Forms,* Durkheim's concluding call for a revival of the spirit and a renewal of the work of the French Revolution gave vibrant proof that his last major work was conceived against the background of the need for social action to effect a passage from pathology to normality in modern society.

If we find it difficult to imagine what the feasts and ceremonies of the future could consist in, this is because we are going through a stage of transition and moral mediocrity. The great things of the past which filled our fathers with enthusiasm do not excite the same ardor in us, either because they have passed into common usage to such an extent that we are unconscious of them, or else because they no longer answer our present aspirations. . . . In a word, the old gods are growing old or are already dead, and others are not yet born. This is what made vain the attempt of Comte to organize a religion with old historical memories artificially revived. It is from life itself and not from the dead past that a living cult can emerge. But this state of incertitude and confused agitation cannot last forever. A day will come when our societies will know again those hours of creative effervescence in which new ideals will surge up and new formulas will crystallize to serve for a while as a guide to humanity. Once these hours have been experienced, men will spontaneously feel the need to keep their memory alive through feasts which periodically reproduce their creations. We have already seen how the French Revolution established a whole cycle of holidays to keep the principles with which it was inspired in a state of perpetual youth. If this institution quickly fell away, it was because the revolutionary faith lasted but a moment, and disappointment and discouragement rapidly succeeded the first moments of enthusiasm. Although the work miscarried, it enables us to imagine what might have happened in other conditions; and everything leads us to believe that it will be taken up again sooner or later.[46]

Since Durkheim's death, quasi-religious ideologies have become social and political in nature. But little in modern history has realized his generous hope for a solidaristic society based on reason and justice. Durkheim died before his optimism could be severely tested by major contemporary events. On a more theoretical level, however, he at times seemed to sense the tenuous basis of a social metaphysic which accepted the breakdown of comprehensive normative and cognitive paradigms as the *ne plus ultra* of modern experience. At these times, he offered intimations of an integration of the natural sciences, technology, and social structure into grippingly inclusive structures which extended the gift of solidarity to all of existence. Before his neo-Kantian colleagues at the Société Française de Philosophie, he observed: "Nothing tells us that nature will not take up in the future, in a new form, the moral quality which it has lost. Perhaps a time will come when we will find it morally blameworthy to perform any unnecessary destruction." [47]

The one basic aspect of symbolic systems in archaic societies which *The Elementary Forms* placed in sharp relief was the importance of the microcosm-macrocosm schema in the "totalization" of shared experience. Social metaphysic induced Durkheim to perceive the cosmic archetype as a generalized projection of the specifically social institution. But a minor theme of *The Elementary Forms* was the manner in which the social microcosm might be integrated into cosmic paradigms which allowed for

[46] *Formes élémentaires de la vie religieuse*, p. 611.
[47] *Bulletin de la Société Française de Philosophie*, sessions of Feb. 11, March 22, 1906 (Paris: Alcan, p. 170).

an intelligible articulation of other aspects of both literal and metaphoric perspectives on reality. Whether one reads *The Elementary Forms* as the narrow and somewhat mystified basis for an ideology of the specifically social and the exclusively moral or as an intimation of some broader vision of culture in the most comprehensive sense, one may conclude that in it Durkheim became the Plato of the Australian blackfellows in order to emerge as the Angelic Doctor of consensual society.

Epilogue

This book focuses on the workings of Durkheim's thought because I believe that a thinker of Durkheim's stature deserves the type of intellectual portrait which he has never fully received. My treatment of Durkheim's life can make no pretense to "psychobiographical" status. Moreover, I treat Durkheim's relation to his own historical context largely as a background factor. In one important sense, Durkheim's thought was a response to the problems confronting the Third Republic in France. But his ideas were not merely symptomatic of his milieu. His reaction to prior thinkers and intellectual traditions was most often selective and discriminating, as it tends to be in all major thinkers. In general, I have subordinated the problem of intellectual influences on Durkheim to that of the structure of Durkheim's thought.

As for Durkheim's influence on others, there are notable omissions in this book. The thought of Talcott Parsons does not receive the explicit attention it deserves, because Parsons' ideas have implicitly conditioned much of what I have written, and because the emphasis of the present work is primarily on social thought in France. I refer only scantily to the work of the *Année* school: I devote some attention to Marcel Mauss. And I try to indicate the ways in which Claude Lévi-Strauss, the "inconstant disciple," built, often in highly critical or problematic ways, upon the Durkheimian heritage. But important thinkers like Maurice

Halbwachs, Marcel Granet, and Georges Davy are shortchanged, because I believe that the work of the *Année* school can be better treated in a broader, more synthetic study of modern French social thought.

This book, then, concentrates on the thought of Durkheim and attempts to reconstitute his ideas in a way that is faithful to his presentation of them and that indicates his concern for important problems in social life. What may one conclude about Durkheim's thought itself?

On a practical level, Durkheim attempted a reconciliation of liberal, conservative, and radical traditions. The dominant force in his thought was what I have termed his philosophical conservatism, and this served as the capstone of his attempted dialectical synthesis. Above all, Durkheim wanted the emergence of a society that reconciled legitimate order and progress, reason and sentiment, structure and creativity. With increasing insistence, he saw modern society as passing through a transitional period which confronted men with the problem of anomie. Anomie was especially pronounced in the economy. And the corporative group was Durkheim's specific means of overcoming social pathology and instituting normality in modern life. In general, he tried to work out a selective and discriminating critical perspective on modern society. With this view of social normality, he asked what deserved to be preserved and what ought to be changed in modern social life. But often Durkheim was not penetrating enough in his investigation of existing social realities and not thoroughgoing enough in his conception of needed reforms. His tendency to avoid the hard problem of specific processes and agents of change was abetted by his inclination to envision ideals abstractly and to project their approximate realization into an indeterminate future.

Durkheim's thought vacillated between an analytic dissociation of reality and a dialectical vision. At times there surfaced between these two types of thought a more tragic sense of life. But the tragic sense was the most muted element of Durkheim's thought. History, for Durkheim, was often the anomically up-rooting, tragic process of social pathology. But his insight into the tragic elements of history, as well as the forcefulness of his dialectical vision of their transcendence, was impaired by the nature of his reckoning with Marx. A more direct confrontation with Marx would at least have sharpened Durkheim's ideas. And it might have provided him with a conception of "praxis" which revealed how men in concrete situations experienced social pathology and how they attempted to overcome it. As it was, Durkheim remained largely caught up between a Carte-sianized neo-Kantianism and a Hegelian notion of dialectics. This bind facilitated his ultimate turn toward social metaphysic as the instrument of logical closure for his thought. Society itself be-came the surrogate for God in modern life.

The most interesting aspect of Durkheim's thought was the dialectical dimension and its relation to his philosophical con-servatism. The concepts of the tree of social life and of social normality and pathology provided a "holistic" perspective which need not have ended in a social metaphysic. Durkheim did see history in dialectical terms as a struggle between anomic forces and meaningful order. But absent was a concrete notion of the role of men in this process. Like Hegel, Durkheim leaves us with a vision of history in terms of processes abstracted from human agents.

Although Durkheim failed to develop a concrete notion of men as agents in history, he did intend his ideas to serve as guides to social action. Especially important in this respect were his concepts of the tree of social life and of social normality and pathology. These ideas furnished a way of synthesizing a con-ception of universal values and a critical theory of moral rela-tivism. There were certain universal values—autonomy, rec-iprocity, community, and the sacred. But their manifestations depended on specific historical and social circumstances. To the extent that moral relativism led to their realization in the normal state of a given type of society, it was justified. To the extent that it conferred legitimacy on pathological states of society, it was a form of "false consciousness."

The goal of social life was the creation and maintenance of a state of society that was both rationally justified and symbolically legitimated. This was not a static state. It included and required a significant measure of change which corresponded to the destructive and creative margin of anomie in life. Yet, once the normal state had been achieved, man's fundamental commitment was to its maintenance and to the use of his freedom in evaluating alternatives and warding off unwanted change. Anomie, in this state of commitment, would be restricted to a marginal aspect of the ordinary personality and to a marginal group of extraordinary individuals in society. This notion of social normality was essential to Durkheim's philosophical conservatism.

Durkheim's fatal flaw was an inability to extend his own commitment to the point of thinking and working more completely for the realization of his vision. But one may derive from Durkheim an appreciation of the rare combination of intellectual rigor and moral fervor which respects careful, discriminating thought and avoids self-righteous dogmatism. If anything, the questions of explanation, understanding, prescription, and action which Durkheim raised were more complex and problematic than he admitted. Durkheim came to believe that ultimately one needs myths to make sense of things. His merit was in seeking myths which complemented reason instead of contradicting it. But an existentially gripping myth must do much more than Durkheim's social metaphysic was able to do.

Selected Bibliography

Works in Chronological Order

"Albert Schaeffle," *Revue philosophique*, I (1885), 84–101.

"La Philosophie dans les universités allemandes," *Revue internationale de l'enseignement*, XIII (1887), 313–338, 423–440.

"La Science positive de la morale en Allemagne," *Revue philosophique*, XXIV (1887), 33–58, 113–142, 275–284.

"Cours de science sociale: Leçon d'ouverture," *Revue internationale de l'enseignement*, XV (1888), 23–48.

"Introduction à la sociologie de la famille," *Annales de la Faculté des Lettres de Bordeaux*, 1888, pp. 257–281.

De La Division du travail social. 7th ed. Paris: Presses Universitaires de France, 1960. First pub. 1893.

"Crime et santé sociale," *Revue philosophique*, XXXIX (1895), 518–523.

Les Règles de la méthode sociologique. 15th ed. Paris: Presses Universitaires de France, 1963. First pub. 1895.

"La Prohibition de l'inceste et ses origines," *Année sociologique*, I (1896–1897), 1–70.

Le Suicide. Paris: Presses Universitaires de France, 1960. First pub. 1897.

"L'Individualisme et les intellectuels," *Revue bleue*, 4th series, X (1898), 7–13.

"Deux Lois de l'évolution pénale," *Année sociologique*, IV (1899–1900), 65–95.

"La Sociologie en France au XIXe siècle," *Revue bleue*, 4th series, XIII (1900), 609–613, 647–652.

"La Sociologie et son domaine scientifique." In Armand Cuvillier, *Où va la sociologie française?* pp. 177–208. Paris: Librairie Marcel Rivière, 1953. Article first pub. 1900.

"Sur le totémisme," *Année sociologique,* V (1900–1901), 82–121.

"De quelques formes primitives de classification." With M. Mauss. *Année sociologique,* VI (1901–1902), 1–72.

"Sociologie et sciences sociales." With P. Fauconnet. *Revue philosophique,* LV (1903), 465–497.

"Sur l'organisation des sociétés australiennes," *Année sociologique,* VIII (1903–1904), 118–147.

"Sociologie et sciences sociales." In *De la méthode dans les sciences,* pp. 259–285. Paris: Alcan, 1909.

"Sociologie religieuse et théorie de la connaissance," *Revue de métaphysique et de morale,* XVII (1909), 733–758. Except for Section III (pp. 754–758), which treats the problem of the relation of sociology to psychology and philosophy, is incorporated in the Introduction to *Les Formes élémentaires.*

Les Formes élémentaires de la vie religieuse. 4th ed. Paris: Presses Universitaires de France, 1960. First pub. 1912.

"Le Dualisme le la nature humaine et ses conditions sociales," *Scientia,* XV (1914), 206–221.

L'Allemagne au-dessus de tout. Paris: Colin, 1915.

Qui a voulu la guerre? With E. Denis. Paris: Colin, 1915.

"Introduction à la morale," *Revue philosophique,* LXXXIX (1920), 79–97.

"La Famille conjugale," *Revue Philosophique,* XCI (1921), 1–14.

Education et sociologie. Introd. by Paul Fauconnet. Paris: Alcan, 1922.

Sociologie et philosophie. Preface by C. Bouglé. Paris: Presses Universitaires de France, 1963. First pub. Paris: Alcan, 1924. Contains "Représentations individuelles et représentations collectives," 1898; "Détermination du fait moral," 1906; and "Jugements de valeur et jugements de réalité," 1911.

L'Education morale. Paris: Presses Universitaires de France, 1963. First pub. 1925.

Le Socialisme. Ed. with Introd. by Marcel Mauss. Paris: Alcan, 1928.

L'Evolution pédagogique en France. 2 vols. Ed. with Introd. by Maurice Halbwachs. Paris: Alcan, 1938.

Leçons de sociologie. Foreword by Hüseyin Nail Kubali. Introd. by Georges Davy. Paris: Presses Universitaires de France, 1950.

Montesquieu et Rousseau: Précurseurs de la sociologie. Foreword by Armand Cuvillier. Introductory note by Georges Davy. Paris: Marcel Rivière, 1953.

Pragmatisme et sociologie. Ed. with Introd. by Armand Cuvillier. Paris: Librairie Philosophique J. Vrin, 1955. Reconstructed from students' notes for a course given in 1913–1914.

English Translations in Chronological Order

The Elementary Forms of the Religious Life. Trans. Joseph Ward Swain. London: Allen & Unwin; New York: Macmillan, 1915.

Germany above All. Trans. J. S. Paris: Armand Colin, 1915.

Who Wanted War? With E. Denis. Trans. A. M. Wilson-Garinei. Paris: Armand Colin, 1915.

The Division of Labor in Society. Trans. with Introd. by George Simpson. New York: Macmillan, 1933.

The Rules of Sociological Method. Trans. Sarah A. Solovay and John H. Mueller. Ed. George E. G. Catlin. New York: Free Press, 1964. First pub. 1938.

Suicide. Trans. John A. Spaulding and George Simpson. Ed. with Introd. by George Simpson. Glencoe, Ill.: Free Press, 1951.

Sociology and Philosophy. Trans. D. F. Pocock. Introd. by J. G. Peristiany. Glencoe, Ill.: Free Press, 1953.

Education and Sociology. Trans. with Introd. by Sherwood D. Fox. Foreword by Talcott Parsons. Glencoe, Ill.: Free Press, 1956.

Professional Ethics and Civic Morals (trans. of *Leçons de sociologie*). Trans. Cornelia Brookfield. Preface by H. Nail Kubali. Introd. by Georges Davy. London: Routledge & Kegan Paul, 1957.

Socialism. Trans. Charlotte Sattler. Ed. with Introd. by Alvin W. Gouldner. New York: Collier Books, 1962. First trans., *Socialism and Saint-Simon,* Yellow Springs, Ohio: Antioch Press, 1958.

Essays on Sociology and Philosophy. Ed. Kurt Wolff. New York: Harper & Row, 1964. First pub. Columbus: Ohio State University Press, 1960. Includes a letter to A. R. Radcliffe-Brown, trans. with commentary by J. G. Peristiany; "The Dualism of Human Nature and Its Social Conditions," trans. Charles Blend; prefaces to *Année sociologique,* I (1896–1897) and II (1897–1898), trans. Kurt

Wolff; "Sociology and Its Scientific Field," trans. Kurt Wolff; "Sociology," trans. Jerome D. Folkman; and the first five and the thirteenth and fourteenth lectures of *Pragmatism and Sociology*, trans. Charles Blend.

Montesquieu and Rousseau: Forerunners of Sociology. Trans. Ralph Manheim. Foreword by Henri Peyre. Ann Arbor: University of Michigan Press, 1960.

Moral Education. Trans. Everett K. Wilson and Herman Schnurer. New York: Free Press of Glencoe, 1961.

Incest: The Nature and Origin of the Taboo. Trans. with Introd. by Edward Sagarin. Pub. with Albert Ellis, *The Origins and the Development of the Incest Taboo*. New York: Lyle Stuart, 1963.

Primitive Classification. With M. Mauss. Trans. with Introd. by Rodney Needham. Chicago: University of Chicago Press, 1963.

Selected Works about Durkheim

Achille-Delmas, F. *Psychologie pathologique du suicide*. Paris: Alcan, 1933.

Adams, George P. "The Interpretation of Religion in Royce and Durkheim," *Philosophical Review*, XXV (1916), 297–304.

Aimard, Guy. *Durkheim et la science économique*. Paris: Presses Universitaires de France, 1962.

Alpert, Harry. "France's First University Course in Sociology," *American Sociological Review*, II (1937), 311–317.

———. "Durkheim's Functional Theory of Ritual," *Sociology and Social Research*, XXIII (1938), 103–108.

———. *Emile Durkheim and His Sociology*. New York: Russell & Russell, 1961. First pub. 1939. Contains the most comprehensive bibliography of Durkheim's works.

———. "Emile Durkheim: Enemy of Fixed Psychological Elements," *American Journal of Sociology*, LXII (1958), 662–664. "Durkheim-Simmel Commemorative Issue."

———. "Emile Durkheim: A Perspective and Appreciation," *American Sociological Review*, XXIV (1959), 462–465.

Apechié, M. "Quelques remarques critiques sur la sociologie d'Emile Durkheim," *Archives de philosophie du droit et de sociologie juridique*, VI (1936), 182–195.

Aron, R. *Les Etapes de la pensée sociologique*, Paris: Gallimard, 1967.

——, A. Demangeon, J. Meuvret, R. Polin, *et al. Les Sciences sociales en France: Enseignement et recherche.* Paris: Hartmann, 1937.

Azevedo, Thales de, Nelson de Sousa Sampaio, and A. L. Machado Neto. *Atualidade de Durkheim.* Bahia, Brazil: University de Bahia, 1959.

Badawi, El Sayed Mohamed. "La Doctrine pédagogique d'Emile Durkheim." Thesis, Sorbonne, 1945.

Barnes, Harry Elmer. "Durkheim's Contribution to the Reconstruction of Political Theory," *Political Science Quarterly*, XXXV (1920), 236–254.

—— and Howard Becker. *Social Thought from Lore to Science.* New York: Heath, 1938. Vol. II, chap. xxii.

Barth, Paul. *Die Philosophie der Geschichte als Soziologie.* 4th ed. Leipzig: Reisland, 1922. I, 628–642.

Bayet, A. *La Science des faits moraux.* Paris: Alcan, 1925.

Bellah, Robert N. "Durkheim and History," *American Sociological Review*, XXIV (1959), 447–461. In Robert A. Nisbet, ed., *Emile Durkheim* (Englewood Cliffs, N.J.: Prentice Hall, 1965), pp. 153–176.

Belot, Gustave. "L'Utilitarisme et ses nouveaux critiques," *Revue de métaphysique et de morale*, II (1894), 404–464.

——. "Emile Durkheim: *L'Année sociologique*," *Revue philosophique*, XLV (1898), 649–657.

Benoit-Smullyan, Emile. "The Sociologism of Emile Durkheim and His School." In *An Introduction to the History of Sociology*, ed. Harry Elmer Barnes, chap. xxvii. Chicago: University of Chicago Press, 1948.

Bentley, A. F. "Simmel, Durkheim, and Ratzenhofer," *American Journal of Sociology*, XXXII (1926), 250–256.

Bierstedt, Robert. *Emile Durkheim.* New York: Dell, 1966.

Blondel, Charles. *Introduction à la psychologie collective.* 6th. ed. Paris: Librairie Armand Colin, 1964. First pub. 1927.

Bouglé, Célestin. *L'Evolution du solidarisme.* Paris: Bureau de *La Revue politique et parlementaire*, 1903. Extract from *Revue politique et parlementaire*, March 1903.

——. *Leçons de sociologie sur l'évolution des valeurs.* Paris: Colin, 1922.

——. *Le Solidarisme.* Paris: Marcel Giard, 1924.

——. "Le Spiritualisme d'Emile Durkheim," *Revue bleue,* LXII (1924), 550–553.

——. "Emile Durkheim." In *Encyclopaedia of the Social Sciences.* New York: Macmillan, 1930–1935.

——. *Qu'est-ce que la sociologie?* 6th ed. Paris: Alcan, 1932.

——. *Bilan de la sociologie française contemporaine.* Paris: Alcan, 1935.

——, G. Davy, M. Granet, R. Lenoir, and R. Maublanc. "L'Oeuvre sociologique d'Emile Durkheim," *Europe,* XXII (1930), 281–304.

—— and M. Déat. *Le Guide de l'étudiant en sociologie.* 3d ed. Paris: Rivière, 1931.

Branford, Victor. "Durkheim: A Brief Memoir," *Sociological Review,* X (1918), 77–82.

Brunschwicg, L., and E. Halévy. "L'Année philosophique, 1893," *Revue de métaphysique et de morale,* II (1894), 564–590.

Bureau, P. *Introduction à la méthode sociologique.* Paris: Bloud et Gay, 1923.

Clark, Terry N. "Emile Durkheim and the Institutionalization of Sociology in the French University System," and "The Structure and Functions of a Research Institute: The *Année Sociologique,*" *Archives européennes de sociologie,* IX (1968), 37–72, 72–92.

Commémoration du centenaire de la naissance d'Emile Durkheim. Annales de l'Université de Paris, No. 1 (Jan.–March 1960). Foreword by Jean Cazeneuve. Speeches by J. Sarrailh, H. H. Janne, G. Davy, A. Lalande, R. Lacroze, R. Aron, G. Gurvitch, and H. Lévy-Bruhl. Articles by G. LeBras, C. Lévi-Strauss, and R. Lenoir. Concludes with a short unpublished writing of Durkheim: "Les Raisons d'être. Morale de la société en général."

Conze, E. "Zur Bibliographie der Durkheim-Schule," *Kölner Vierteljahrshefte für Soziologie,* VI (1927), 279–283.

Cuvillier, Armand. "Durkheim et Marx," *Cahiers internationaux de sociologie,* IV (1948), 75–97.

——. *Où va la sociologie française?* Paris: Librairie Marcel Rivière, 1953.

Davy, Georges. *Emile Durkheim: Choix de textes avec étude du système sociologique.* Paris: Rasmussen, n.d.

————. "La Sociologie de M. Durkheim," *Revue philosophique,* LXXII (1911), 42–71, 160–185.

————. "Emile Durkheim: L'Homme," *Revue de métaphysique et de morale,* XXVI (1919), 181–198; "Emile Durkheim: L'Oeuvre," XXVII (1920), 71–112.

————. *Sociologues d'hier et d'aujourd' hui.* Paris: Alcan, 1931. Especially Part II, "La Famille et la parenté d'après Durkheim," and Part III, "La Psychologie de McDougall et la sociologie durkheimienne."

————. "Sur les conditions de l'explication sociologique et la part qu'elle peut faire à l'individuel," *Année sociologique,* 3d series (1949), pp. 181–196.

————. Introduction to Emile Durkheim, *Leçons de sociologie.* Paris: Presses Universitaires de France, 1950.

————. "Emile Durkheim," *Revue française de sociologie,* I (1960), 3–24.

————. "Durkheim, Montesquieu and Rousseau." In *Montesquieu and Rousseau: Forerunners of Sociology,* pp. 144–154. Ann Arbor: University of Michigan Press, 1965.

DeGré, Gerard L. *Society and Ideology: An Inquiry into the Sociology of Knowledge.* New York: Columbia University Bookstore, 1943. Chap. iii.

Dennes, William Ray. "Durkheim." In *The Method and Presuppositions of Group Psychology.* Berkeley and Los Angeles: University of California Press, 1924.

Deploige, S. *Le Conflit de la morale et de la sociologie.* 3d ed. Paris: Nouvelle Librairie Nationale, 1923.

Dohrenwend, Bruce P. "Egoism, Altruism, Anomie: A Conceptual Analysis of Durkheim's Types," *American Sociological Review,* XXIV (1959), 446–472.

Douglas, Jack D. "The Sociological Analysis of Social Meanings of Suicide," *Archives européennes de sociologie,* VII (1966), 249–276.

Duprat, G. L. "Auguste Comte et Emile Durkheim." In *Gründer der Soziologie.* Jena: Fischer, 1932.

Duvignaud, Jean. *Durkheim: Sa vie, son oeuvre.* Paris: Presses Universitaires de France, 1965.

———. "Anomie et mutations sociales." In Georges Balandier, ed., *Sociologie des mutations*. Paris: Editions Anthropos, 1970.

Elbow, Matthew H. *French Corporative Theory, 1789–1948*. New York: Columbia University Press, 1953.

Essertier, D. *Psychologie et sociologie*. Paris: Alcan, 1927.

———. "Philosophes et savants français du XXe Siècle." In *La Sociologie, extraits et notices*. Paris: Alcan, 1930.

——— and C. Bouglé. "Sociologie et psychologie: Remarques générales," *Annales sociologiques*, series A, I (1934), 121–148.

Faguet, Emile. *Sur le suicide*. Paris: Société française d'Imprimerie, 1907.

Fauconnet, Paul. "The Pedagogical Work of Emile Durkheim," *American Journal of Sociology*, XXVIII (1923), 529–553. In French in *Revue philosophique*, XCIII (1922), 185–209, and as Introd. to Emile Durkheim, *Education et sociologie* (Paris: Alcan, 1922).

———. "The Durkheim School in France," *Sociological Review*, XIX (1927), 15–20.

——— and Marcel Mauss. "Sociologie," *Grande Encyclopédie*, XXX, 165–176.

Friedmann, Georges. "La Thèse de Durkheim et les formes contemporaines de la division du travail," *Cahiers internationaux de sociologie*, XIX (1955), 45–58.

Gehlke, Charles Elmer. *Emile Durkheim's Contributions to Sociological Theory*. New York: Columbia University Press, 1915.

Ginsberg, Morris. "The Place of Sociology." In *The Social Sciences: Their Relations in Theory and in Teaching*, pp. 190–207. London: Le Play House, 1936.

———. "Durkheim's Ethical Theory" and "Durkheim's Theory of Religion." In *On the Diversity of Morals*, chaps. iv, xiv. New York: Macmillan, 1957.

Gold, Martin. "Suicide, Homicide, and the Socialization of Aggression," *American Journal of Sociology*, LXII (1958), 651–661. "Durkheim-Simmel Commemorative Issue."

Goldenweiser, Alexander A. "Religion and Society: A Critique of Emile Durkheim's Theory of the Origin and Nature of Religion." In *History, Psychology, and Culture*, pp. 361–373. New York: Knopf, 1933.

Gunzel, K. *Die gesellschaftliche Wirklichkeit: Eine Studie der Emile Durkheim's Soziologie.* Ohlau: Eschenhagen, 1934.

Gurvitch, Georges. *Essais de sociologie.* Paris: Sirey, n.d.

——. "La Science des faits moraux et la morale théorique chez E. Durkheim," *Archives de philosophie du droit et de sociologie juridique,* VII (1937), 18–44.

——. *La Vocation actuelle de la sociologie: Vers une sociologie différentielle.* Paris: Presses Universitaires de France, 1950. Vol. II, chaps. viii–x.

Halbwachs, Maurice. "La Doctrine d'Emile Durkheim," *Revue philosophique,* LXXXV (1918), 353–411.

——. *Les Origines du sentiment religieux d'après Durkheim.* Paris: Stock, 1925.

——. *Les Causes du suicide.* Paris: Alcan, 1930.

——. *Morphologie sociale.* Paris: Colin, 1938.

Hendin, Herbert. *Suicide and Scandinavia.* New York: Doubleday Anchor, 1965.

Henry, Andrew F., and James F. Short. *Suicide and Homicide.* Glencoe, Ill.: Free Press, 1954.

Hoefnagels, Harry. *La Sociologie face aux "problèmes sociaux."* Bruges: Desclée de Brouwer, 1962.

Hoffding, Harold. "Les Formes élémentaires de la vie religieuse," *Revue de métaphysique et de morale,* XXII (1914), 828–848.

Jyan, Choy. *Etude comparative sur les doctrines pédagogiques de Durkheim et de Dewey.* Lyons: Bosc Frères et Riou, 1926.

Lacombe, Roger. *La Méthode sociologique de Durkheim: Etude critique.* Paris: Alcan, 1926.

LaFontaine, A. P. *La Philosophie d'E. Durkheim,* 4th ed. Paris: J. Vrin, 1926.

Lapie, Paul. "La Définition du socialisme," *Revue de métaphysique et de morale,* II (1894), 199–204.

Leguay, P. "M. Emile Durkheim." In *Universitaires d'aujourd'hui.* Paris: Grasset, 1912.

Lenoir, Raymond. "Emile Durkheim et la conscience moderne," *Mercure de France,* CXXVII (1918), 517–595.

Leuba, James H. "Sociology and Psychology: The Conception of Religion and Magic and the Place of Psychology in Sociological Studies" and "Sociology and Psychology: A Discussion of the Views of Durkheim and of Hubert and Mauss," *American Journal of Sociology*, XIX (1913), 323–342.

Lévi-Strauss, Claude. "French Sociology." In *Twentieth Century Sociology*, ed. Georges Gurvitch and Wilbert E. Moore, chap. xvii. New York: Philosophical Library, 1945.

Lévy-Bruhl, Henri. "Rapports du droit et de la sociologie," *Archives de philosophie du droit et de sociologie juridique*, VII (1937), 21–25.

Lévy-Bruhl, Lucien. *La Morale et la science des moeurs*. 4th ed. Paris: Alcan, 1904.

——. *La Mentalité primitive*. 4th ed. Paris: Alcan, 1925.

Lowie, Robert H. *Primitive Religion*. New York: Universal Library, 1952. First pub. 1924. Chap. vii.

——. *The History of Ethnological Theory*. New York: Farrar and Rinehart, 1937. Chap. xii, especially pp. 196–212.

Marcia, George M. *Emile Durkheim: Soziologie und Soziologismus*. Jena: Gustav Fischer, 1932.

Marjolin, Robert. "French Sociology: Comte and Durkheim," *American Journal of Sociology*, XLII (1937), 693–704, 901–902.

Masson-Oursel, Paul. "La Sociologie de Durkheim et la psychanalyse," *Psyché*, II (1947), 1439–1442.

Mauss, Marcel. "In Memoriam: L'Oeuvre inédite de Durkheim et de ses collaborateurs," *Année sociologique*, n.s., I (1923), 7–29.

——. "Rapports réels et pratiques de la psychologie et de la sociologie," *Journal de psychologie*, XXI (1924), 892–922.

——. "Division et proportions des divisions de la sociologie," *Année sociologique*, n.s., II (1924–1925), 98–176.

McGovern, William Montgomery. *From Luther to Hitler: The History of Fascist-Nazi Political Philosophy*. Boston: Houghton Mifflin, 1941. Chap. ix.

Merton, Robert K. "Durkheim's Division of Labor in Society," *American Journal of Sociology*, XL (1934), 319–328.

Mitchell, Marion M. "Emile Durkheim and the Philosophy of Nationalism," *Political Science Quarterly*, XLVI (1931), 87–106.

Mousâ, Munîr Mushâbik. "Théorie de l'origine de la religion chez Durkheim." Thesis, Sorbonne, 1958.

Naegele, Kaspar D. "Attachment and Alienation: Complementary Aspects of the Work of Durkheim and Simmel," *American Journal of Sociology,* LXII (1958), 580–589. "Durkheim-Simmel Commemorative Issue."

Neyer, Joseph. "Ethics and Sociology: *A Study in Durkheim and French Neo-Positivism.*" Ph.D. dissertation, Harvard, 1942.

Nisbet, Robert. "Conservatism and Sociology," *American Journal of Sociology,* LVIII (1952), 165–175.

——, ed. *Emile Durkheim.* Essays by Harry Alpert, Robert N. Bellah, Morris Ginsberg, Robert K. Merton, and Hanan C. Selvin. Englewood Cliffs, N.J.: Prentice-Hall, 1965.

——. *The Sociological Tradition.* New York: Basic Books, 1966.

Nizan, Paul. *Les Chiens de garde.* Paris: Maspero, 1965. First pub. 1932.

Ottaway, A. K. C. "The Educational Sociology of Emile Durkheim," *British Journal of Sociology,* VI (1955), 213–227.

Ouy, Achille. "La Méthode sociologique de Durkheim," *Revue internationale de sociologie,* XXXV (1927), 371–383.

——. "Les Sociologies et la sociologie: Deuxième partie, le sociologisme, Emile Durkheim," *Revue internationale de sociologie,* XLVII (1939), 245–275.

Parodi, Dominique. *La Philosophie contemporaine en France.* 2d ed. Paris: Alcan, 1920. Chap. v.

Parsons, Talcott. *The Structure of Social Action: A Study in Social Theory, with Special Reference to a Group of Recent European Writers.* Glencoe, Ill.: Free Press, 1949. First pub. 1937. Chaps. viii–xii.

Pécaut, Félix. "Emile Durkheim," *Revue pédagogique,* n.s., LXXII (1918), 1–20.

——. "Auguste Comte et Durkheim," *Revue de métaphysique et de morale,* XXVIII (1921), 639–655.

Perry, Ralph Barton. "Des Formes de l'unité." In *Congrès des sociétés philosophiques americaine, anglaise, belge, italienne, et française: Communications et discussions,* pp. 445–470. Paris: Colin, 1921.

——. *General Theory of Value: Its Meaning and Basic Principles Construed in Terms of Interest.* New York: Longmans, Green, 1926. Chaps. xiv–xvii.

Piaget, J. "Logique génétique et sociologie," *Revue philosophique,* CV (1928), 167–205.

Pizzorno, Alessandro. "Lecture actuelle de Durkheim," *Archives européennes de sociologie*, IV (1963), 1–36.

Radcliffe-Brown, A. R. "On the Concept of Function in Social Science," *American Anthropologist*, n.s., XXXVII (1935), 394–402.

Richard, Gaston. *L'Athéisme dogmatique en sociologie religieuse*. Strasbourg: Istra, 1923.

——. "La Pathologie sociale d'Emile Durkheim," *Revue internationale de sociologie*, XXXVIII (1930), 113–126.

Rossi, Peter H. "Emile Durkheim and Georg Simmel," *American Journal of Sociology*, LXII (1958), 579. "Durkheim-Simmel Commemorative Issue."

Schaub, Edward. "A Sociological Theory of Knowledge," *Philosophical Review*, XXIX (1920), 319–339.

Schnore, Leo F. "Social Morphology and Human Ecology," *American Journal of Sociology*, LXII (1958), 620–634. "Durkheim-Simmel Commemorative Issue."

Seeger, Imogen. *Durkheim and His Critics on the Sociology of Religion*. "Columbia University Monograph Series," 1957.

Selvin, Hanan C. "Durkheim's *Suicide* and Problems of Empirical Research," *American Journal of Sociology*, LXII (1958), 609–619. "Durkheim-Simmel Commemorative Issue."

Simiand, F. *Le Salaire, l'évolution sociale et la monnaie*. Paris: Alcan, 1932.

Simpson, George. "Emile Durkheim's Social Realism," *Sociology and Social Research*, XVIII (1933), 3–11.

——. "An Estimate of Durkheim's Work." In *Emile Durkheim on the Division of Labor in Society*, pp. xxv–xliv. New York: Macmillan, 1933.

——. "Methodological Problems in Determining the Aetiology of Suicide," *American Sociological Review*, XVI (1950), 658–663.

——. *Emile Durkheim*. New York: Crowell, 1963.

Sorel, Georges, "Les Théories de M. Durkheim," *Le Devenir social*, I (1895), 1–26, 148–180.

Sorokin, Pitirim. *Contemporary Sociological Theories*. New York: Harper, 1928. Pp. 463–480.

Spencer, Robert F. "Culture Process and Intellectual Current: Durkheim and Atatürk," *American Anthropologist*, LX (1958), 640–657.

Starcke, C. N. *Laws of Social Evolution and Social Ideals.* Copenhagen: Levin and Munksgaard, 1932. Pp. 294–315.

Tarde, G. *Les Lois sociales.* Paris: Alcan, 1898.

Tiryakian, Edward. *Sociologism and Existentialism.* Englewood Cliffs, N. J.: Prentice-Hall, 1962.

———. "Durkheim's 'Two Laws of Penal Evolution,'" *Journal for the Scientific Study of Religion,* III (1964), 262–266.

———. "Introduction to a Bibliographical Focus on Emile Durkheim," *Journal for the Scientific Study of Religion,* III (1964), 248–254.

———. "A Problem for the Sociology of Knowledge: The Mutual Unawareness of Emile Durkheim and Max Weber," *Archives européennes de sociologie,* VII (1966), 330–336.

———. "Le Premier Message d'Emile Durkheim," *Cahiers internationaux de sociologie,* XLIII (1967), 21–23. Followed by an 1883 speech of Durkheim at the Lycée of Sens.

Tosti, Gustavo, "The Delusions of Durkheim's Sociological Objectivism," *American Journal of Sociology,* IV (1898), 171–177.

———. "Suicide in the Light of Recent Studies," *American Journal of Sociology* III (1898), 464–478.

Tufts, James H. "Recent Sociological Tendencies in France," *American Journal of Sociology,* I (1896), 446–457.

Wallis, Wilson D. "Durkheim's View of Religion," *Journal of Religious Psychology,* VII (1914), 252–267.

Webb, C. C. J. *Group Theories of Religion and the Individual.* London: Allen and Unwin, 1916.

Wilson, Ethel M. "Emile Durkheim's Sociological Method," *Sociology and Social Research,* XVIII (1934), 511–518.

Wolff, Kurt H. "The Challenge of Durkheim and Simmel," *American Journal of Sociology* LXII (1958), 590–596. "Durkheim-Simmel Commemorative Issue."

———, ed. *Essays on Sociology and Philosophy.* Essays by Henri Peyre, Joseph Neyer, Paul Bohannan, Hugh Dalziel Duncan, Talcott Parsons, Albert Pierce, Melvin Richter, Lewis A. Coser, Paul Honigsheim, Albert Salomon, Roscoe C. Hinkle, Jr., and Kazuta Kurauchi. New York: Harper & Row, 1964. First pub. 1960.

Worms, René. "Emile Durkheim," *Revue internationale de sociologie,* XXV (1917), 561–568.

Worsley, P. M. "Emile Durkheim's Theory of Knowledge," *Sociological Review,* n.s., IV (1956), 47–62.

Additional Bibliography, 1985

Recent Translations of Durkheim's Works

The Evolution of Educational Thought: Lectures on the Formation and Development of Secondary Education in France (trans. of *L'Evolution pédagogique en France*). Trans. Peter Collins, London and Boston: Routledge & Kegan Paul, 1977.

The Rules of Sociological Method. Ed. with Introd. by Steven Lukes; trans. W. D. Halls. New York: Free Press, 1982.

Pragmatism and Sociology. Ed. with Introd. by John B. Allcock; preface by Armand Cuvillier; trans. J. C. Whitehouse. New York: Cambridge University Press, 1983.

Durkheim: Essays on Morals and Education. Ed. with Introd. by W. S. F. Pickering; trans. H. L. Sutcliffe. London and Boston: Routledge & Kegan Paul, 1979.

Durkheim and the Law. Ed. by Steven Lukes and Andrew Scull. New York: St. Martin's Press, 1983.

Emile Durkheim on Institutional Analysis. Ed., trans., with Introd. by Mark Traugott. Chicago: University of Chicago Press, 1978.

Emile Durkheim on Morality and Society. Ed. with Introd. by Robert N. Bellah. Chicago: University of Chicago Press, 1973.

Durkheim on Religion: A Selection of Readings with Bibliographies. Compiled by W. S. F. Pickering; trans. Jacqueline Redding and W. S. F. Pickering. London and Boston: Routlege & Kegan Paul, 1975.

Selected Writings. Ed., transl., and with Introd. by Anthony Giddens. Cambridge: Cambridge University Press, 1972.

Recent Works about Durkheim

Alexander, Jeffrey. *The Antinomies of Classical Thought: Marx and Durkheim. (Theoretical Logic and Sociology,* vol. 2). Berkeley: University of California Press, 1982.

Chazel, François. *Durkheim: Les règles de la méthode sociologique.* Paris: Hatier, 1975.

Clark, Terry N. *Prophets and Patrons: The French University and the Emergence of the Social Sciences.* Cambridge, Mass.: Harvard University Press, 1973.

Davy, Georges. *L'homme: le fait social et le fait politique.* Paris: Mouton, 1973.

Ene, Maurice Okpo. *Emile Durkheim's Sociological Theory of Religion and of Knowledge: A Critical Analysis.* Heidelberg: Ene, 1973.

Filloux, Jean-Claude. *Durkheim et le socialisme.* Geneva and Paris: Librarie Droz, 1977.

Gasché, Rudolphe. *Die hybride Wissenschaft; zur Mutation des Wissenschaftsbegriffs bei Emile Durkheim und im Strukturalismus von Claude Lévi-Strauss.* Stuttgart: J. B. Metzler, 1973.

Giddens, Anthony. *Capitalism and Modern Social Theory: An Analysis of the Writings of Marx, Durkheim, and Max Weber.* Cambridge: Cambridge University Press, 1971.

———. *Emile Durkheim.* New York: Penguin Books, 1979.

Haselauer, Elisabeth. *Musiksoziologische Studie nach Emile Durkheim.* Vienna and Munich: Doblinger, 1977.

Hirst, P. Q. *Durkheim, Bernard and Epistemology.* London and Boston: Routledge & Kegan Paul, 1975.

Hofmann, Inge. *Burgerliches Denken; zur Soziologie Emile Durkheims.* Frankfurt am Main: Athenäum, 1973.

König, René. *Emile Durkheim zur Diskussion: jenseits von Dogmatismus u. Skepsis.* Munich and Vienna: Hanser, 1978.

Lacroix, Bernard. *Durkheim et le politique.* Paris: Presses de l'Université de Montréal, 1981.

Lukes, Steven. *Emile Durkheim, His Life and Work: A Historical and Critical Study.* Harmondsworth: Penguin, 1973.

Nandan, Yash. *The Durkheim School: A Systematic and Compre-*

hensive Bibliography. Westport, Conn.: Greenwood Press, 1977.

Nisbet, Robert A. *The Sociology of Emile Durkheim.* New York: Oxford University Press, 1974.

Poggi, Gianfranco. *Images of Society: Essays on the Sociological Theories of Tocqueville, Marx, and Durkheim.* Stanford, Calif.: Stanford University Press, 1972.

Pope, Whitney. *Durkheim's Suicide: A Classic Analyzed.* Chicago: University of Chicago Press, 1976.

Schoffeleers, Matthew. *Religion, Nationalism and Economic Action: Critical Questions on Durkheim and Weber.* Assen: Van Gorcum, 1978.

Taylor, Steve. *Durkheim and the Study of Suicide.* New York: St. Martin's Press, 1982.

Thompson, Kenneth. *Emile Durkheim.* London and New York: Tavistock, 1982.

Wallwork, Ernest. *Durkheim: Morality and Milieu.* Cambridge, Mass.: Harvard University Press, 1972.

Index

Action Française, 18, 56
Aesthetics, 9, 235
Agathon Report, 61-62
Alain (Emile Chartier), 32, 53, 58
L'Allemagne au-dessus de tout (*Germany above All*), 77
Alpert, Harry, 30, 70-71
Altruism, 171-175
Animism, 257
Année sociologique, 1, 2, 41-42, 44, 96, 102, 142, 145, 187, 200, 237, 259, 292
Anomie, 12, 55, 117, 154, 158-170, 181, 184, 228, 293; and anxiety, 160; and change, 159; and conflict, 135; and creativity, 96, 158, 205, 206, 240, 242, 295; and crime, 95; and crisis, 7, 134; and division of labor, 134-138; and egoism, 165-167; and exploitation, 135, 161-162; and *hybris*, 158, 240; and imperialism, 77-78n; in institutional or ideological form, 77-78n, 162-164; and limits, 19, 136, 140, 156-159, 242-243; and modern society, 159; and Saint-Simon, 193; and scarcity, 167-170; and structural contradictions, 160
Aristotle, 158
Aron, Raymond, 5n, 35n, 53, 221n

Bacon, Sir Francis, 269
Balzac, Honoré de, 167n, 197
Barrès, Maurice, 22
Bastide, Roger, 128-129n

Bayet, Albert, 152
Bellah, Robert N., 201n
Belot, Gustave, 52
Bentham, Jeremy, 122
Bergson, Henri, 53, 205, 271
Bernstein, Eduard, 21
Biology, 15, 133-134, 195, 242-243
Bloch, Marc, 196-197
Blondel, Charles, 54, 55, 241n
Blum, Léon, 36n, 67
Bonald, Louis de, 18, 19, 56
Bordeaux, University of, 33, 37, 44, 47, 49, 69, 81
Bouglé, Célestin, 29, 71-72, 128n, 142
Bourgeois, Léon, 69
Bourget, Paul, 72
Boutroux, Emile, 30, 54, 81
Brunetière, Ferdinand, 73
Buisson, Ferdinand, 34, 43, 45

Camus, Albert, 170-171n
Capitalism, 137, 142, 154, 162-163, 182, 193, 215
Cartesianism, 8-10, 46, 50, 207, 258; *see also* Descartes, René, *and* Neo-Kantianism, Cartesianized
Cassirer, Ernst, 272
Catholicism, 57, 60-61, 179, 254
Change in society, 82, 207-208; in *Division of Labor*, 119-124
Chateaubriand, François Auguste René de, 167
Clapham, John, 38
Clemenceau, Georges, 43